Environmental Strategic Communication

Advocacy, Persuasion, and Public Relations

Derek Moscato
Western Washington University

ROWMAN & LITTLEFIELD
Lanham • Boulder • New York • London

Executive Acquisitions Editor: Natalie Mandziuk
Acquisitions Assistant: Yu Ozaki
Sales and Marketing Inquiries: textbooks@rowman.com

Credits and acknowledgments for material borrowed from other sources, and reproduced
with permission, appear on the appropriate pages within the text.

Published by Rowman & Littlefield
An imprint of The Rowman & Littlefield Publishing Group, Inc.
4501 Forbes Boulevard, Suite 200, Lanham, Maryland 20706
www.rowman.com

86-90 Paul Street, London EC2A 4NE

British Library Cataloguing in Publication Information Available

Library of Congress Cataloging-in-Publication Data

Names: Moscato, Derek, author.
Title: Environmental strategic communication : advocacy, persuasion, and
   public relations / Derek Moscato.
Description: Lanham : Rowman & Littlefield, [2023] | Includes
   bibliographical references and index. | Summary: "This socially
   conscious text gives students a theoretical basis for environmental
   public relations and the tools with which to apply this knowledge. This
   includes hard skills such as green op-ed writing, eco feature writing,
   publicity tactics including news releases, the art of interviewing for
   television and video, and social media acumen"— Provided by publisher.
Identifiers: LCCN 2023033409 (print) | LCCN 2023033410 (ebook) | ISBN
   9781538152287 (cloth) | ISBN 9781538152294 (paperback) | ISBN
   9781538152300 (epub)
Subjects: LCSH: Environmentalism—Public relations. | Publicity.
Classification: LCC GE195 .M676 2023 (print) | LCC GE195 (ebook) | DDC
   659.2/933372—dc23/eng/20231012
LC record available at https://lccn.loc.gov/2023033409
LC ebook record available at https://lccn.loc.gov/2023033410

Contents

Acknowledgments

This book is a testament to the efforts, insights, and innovations from a community of scholars, communication and media practitioners, environmentalists, policymakers, and advocates who prioritize principles of place and planet in their work. While I cannot list every individual who provided inspiration for this book, I would like to offer my gratitude for their commitment to the overarching practice of environmental strategic communication in all its forms.

I also owe a big thanks to the community of students and administrators at Western Washington University who have supported my efforts in the field of environmental media more broadly, and this project specifically. To this end, I would like to make special mention of WWU's Department of Journalism, the College of Humanities and Social Sciences, the Office of Research and Special Programs, and the Honors Program. I'm also grateful for the opportunity to teach in Western's Environmental Journalism program, an important collaboration between WWU's Department of Journalism and the College of the Environment.

Additionally, I owe a big thanks to the support of several scholarly institutes at the Western Washington campus, notably the Salish Sea Institute, the Center for Canadian-American Studies, and the Border Policy Research Institute. These research and teaching hubs have provided ongoing support for many of the examples and cases provided in this book.

Similarly, I would like to thank the many environmental media, communication, and advocacy practitioners regionally and nationally who have provided real-world inputs or insights that are referenced across this book. I also owe a sincere thanks to my colleagues and mentors from the University of Oregon, who continue to provide the sort of collaboration and support that inspires this kind of undertaking.

Many professionals at Rowman & Littlefield contributed to the publication of this endeavor. I am grateful to Natalie Mandziuk and Yu Ozaki for keeping me on track, along with the larger R&L editing and publishing team. I would also like to thank the reviewers of this book, whose constructive feedback in the early stages provided important direction and the encouragement to keep pushing forward.

Introduction

"We are, as a whole, still in that low state of civilization where we do not understand that it is also vandalism wantonly to destroy or to permit the destruction of what is beautiful in nature—whether it be a cliff, a forest, or a species of mammal or bird. Here in the United States we turn our rivers and streams into sewers and dumping-grounds. We pollute the air, we destroy forests and exterminate fishes, birds and mammals—not to speak of vulgarizing charming landscapes with hideous advertisements. But at last it looks as if our people were awakening. Above all we should realize that the effort toward this end is essentially a democratic movement!"

—Theodore Roosevelt

How do we conceptualize the environment as a communicative process in this era of ecological disruptions and hyper-partisanship? Perhaps we can take inspiration from words written for this country over a century ago. U.S. president Theodore Roosevelt, an early champion of wildlife protection in the United States, wrote the above for *The Outlook*, a weekly magazine, in 1913. Roosevelt, still known as the "conservation president" for his timeless championing of America's wild spaces, based his simultaneous lament and optimism on his trips to western Dakota Territory, where he grappled with how an industrializing nation and indeed a planet would continue to interface with the planet's natural order. And yet, Roosevelt's assertion that pro-environmental efforts are perfectly aligned with the goals of democracy continues to resonate in the twenty-first century.

Just as Roosevelt saw over a century ago, we are witnessing the dawn of another "environmental awakening," one that promises to transform our political, economic, and social institutions in ways that can make our planet more livable, more just, and more prosperous as measured by human health and happiness. This growing embrace of a greener planet by organizations from the private, public, and not-for-profit sectors underscores the prominence of environmentalism within strategic environmental communication practice. Breakthroughs in ecological communication are advancing environmentalism and science through advocacy, persuasion, and public engagement. But they are also helping evolve the terminology that we use to understand forms of environmental communication.

For example, since the 1980s, environmentalism has been understood not only in alignment with conservation of the natural world or urban-industrial impacts, but also with related objectives of human quality of life, responsible management of the economy, and sustainability of communities. This transition of environmentalism, from a more fragmented approach to an overarching socioeconomic worldview and political outlook, helps explain the rise of environmental political candidates in our democracy (Slocombe, 1984). This transition also helps explain the increasing emphasis on individual cognition over the past half-decade as a site of interest for environmental advocates and professional communicators. As citizens, we are more than ever bound to think and act with ecological impacts in mind. The term *environmentalism*, according to Zelezny and Schultz (2000), refers to "the processes associated with actions intended to lessen the impact of human behavior on the natural environment." This framework includes psychological criteria such as behaviors, intentions, attitudes, beliefs, and motives. But it also includes the actions that carry forward this psychology into the world, such as individual and community action, public policy impact, and even environmental activism.

The latter term has been the object of intense interest on the part of social scientists, industry professionals, and the media, especially since the advent of organizations that carry out such actions on a regular basis. According to one definition, environmental activism represents the actions and discourses put forth by environmentally focused organizations and units (Seguin, Pelletier, and Hunsley, 1998). The commitment of such activism is to change environmental conditions or policy, and this is reflected in various attempts to influence people's attitudes and behaviors toward the environment. These attempts are realized through persuasion and protest, in alignment with advocacy, fundraising, and other vehicles of strategic communication and promotion.

Global ecological events, such as climate change, degraded air and water sources, and warming oceans, have served as a catalyst for environmental discourses generally, and strategic appeals in particular—especially as organizations consider the ecological impacts of unchecked consumerism, economic growth, and extraction of natural resources. Even as climate change mitigation becomes a growing concern with the global public, other ecological issues of the highest importance—wildlife conservation, urban sustainability, clean energy, and environmental justice for marginalized communities—are also gaining traction in the larger public arena thanks to the work of strategic appeals, organized advocacy, and corporate social responsibility crusades. All of this has led to a wave of strategic environmental communication from both institutions and issue-specific advocates. Sustainability communication, for example, is now firmly entrenched within the domain of corporate social responsibility for many companies. At the same time, green advocates are utilizing new strategies to shift public opinion on key issues and foster policy change.

This book features conceptual foundations, best practices, and real-world cases that provide the would-be advocate, green communicator, or corporate social responsibility (CSR) practitioner with confidence to create, to engage, and to lead the environmental mission on behalf of organizations, mission-defined groups, and individuals. In doing so, this book explores the evolving interplay between strategic communication and environmental action and leadership, as well as between the material realm of ecology and the discursive dimensions of advocacy and communication. Specific areas of focus include public engagement focused on behavior change or public policy, green appeals for environmental protection or conservation, and environmentally geared social marketing/advertising campaigns. It also looks to the future as environmental communication intersects with new developments in digital media, industry adoption, and globalization. These areas include organizational public opinion efforts through traditional or digital media outreach, eco-communication within corporate social responsibility, and international campaigns drawing from public diplomacy and global public relations.

Environmental advocates and public communicators have never played a more important role in our society than they do at this moment in time. As the planet contends with simultaneous environmental challenges—pollution of precious waterways, threats to wildlife, degradation of environmental conditions for at-risk or disenfranchised populations, and concerns for the climate—green communicators are promoting ecologically minded approaches to public policy and the global economy. They do so through lobbying of publics, policymakers, and politicians and by producing press releases, informational reports, white papers, and even documentaries for public consumption on social media and streaming channels. Finally, and perhaps most importantly, they provide key disruptions to the ecological status quo through letter-writing campaigns, strategic alliances, public demonstrations, and educational events.

The environmental public communication practitioner is, therefore, not only a conduit between organizations and publics. They are a producer and distributor of content that provides rhetorical and material meaning to some of our planet's most pressing issues, and they do so in the name of engagement, persuasion, and impact. This book aims to tie together this complex landscape of environmental advocacy concepts, tactics, and context to better equip the would-be green communicator with conceptual insights and practical knowledge. *Environmental Strategic Communication* provides students with theoretical- and professional-level understandings in the arenas of sustainability, ecology, green media, environmental advocacy, and corporate social responsibility. Given this broad reach, this is a focus of study highly relevant for students of public relations, journalism, environmental studies, green marketing, political science, sociology, and related disciplines.

But this book also draws from the author's professional and personal experiences witnessing the rapid evolution of environmental communication and a need for specific strategies and tactics within this arena. Several years ago, the author developed a specialized journalism class at Western Washington University focused on environmental advocacy in order to address changes occurring across geographies, countries, societies, and industries. For example, strategic campaigns were increasingly woven into the toolbox of nonprofit organizations. Simultaneously, public relations offices for major companies and communication agencies were increasingly reshaping the field in terms of corporate social responsibility and impact. And yet, a textbook grounded in strategy and tactics was not available for the would-be advocacy practitioner seeking that foundation in action-oriented professional environmentalism. A text was needed that could not only emphasize the conceptual and contextual underpinnings of green communication, but also address strategic processes, tactics, and outcomes.

This book, therefore, prepares students who are interested in public communication with a focus on best practices in environmental outreach and strategic engagement. As the issues of climate change, sustainability, and ecological protection become paramount in public life, so too practitioners within the PR and advocacy fields are confronting an unprecedented need to position their organizations as champions for environmental thinking and action. Some companies situated within ecological debates—such as resource extraction organizations and transportation companies—are increasingly tasked with establishing accountability to their publics on account of their ecological or carbon emission impacts. Advocacy and activist organizations are increasingly integrating formalized public relations approaches as well, in order to maximize public support and leverage national and international media attention and fundraising.

Environmental public communication is, of course, still a subset of mass and interpersonal communication. Yet there are several ways in which this text differs from other media and communication texts. First, it integrates mass and public communication theory with perspectives from environmental communication and ecological theory (including green persuasion, ecological modernism, environmental justice, and political economy). Second, it allows for extensive focus on environmentally minded organizations, including consumer companies such as Patagonia and REI, activists and NGOs like Greenpeace and the Sierra Club, and ecologically minded government and state interests such as the United Nations Environment Program and the Arctic Council. To this end, this book is driven by specific ecological approaches and debates, but also by organizational-driven communication and concepts. Finally, this book aims to help students understand the principles embedded within corporate social responsibility, a philosophy that underpins the social/ environmental engagement of corporations and firms. The CSR trend, and related developments like the environmental, social, and governance framework and socially responsible investing, represent an important conceptual consideration for students of environmental studies or public relations. CSR in particular also represents a positive driver of industry, jobs, and career growth. Students with an understanding of best practices in CSR and environmental public relations are better equipped to navigate ecological challenges facing industry, government, and NGO jobs.

Ultimately, this book aims to complement interdisciplinary environmental programming that recognizes the fast-evolving role of strategic ecological communication and its critical importance to the future of our planet. More than ever, the ecological debates taking place in our public squares, our civic commons, our community centers, and our government or industry boardrooms dictate not only what kind of action we will take to protect the earth, but also how that action will win hearts and minds to lay down the foundation for long-term solutions. The intention of this book, then, is not the championing of the polished organizational communicator who parrots a set of prescribed talking points from senior management, a board of directors, or rigid political ideology. Rather, it is to provide a foundational reference point for the ecosystem of advocates, public communicators, media professionals, and strategists who work with their respective organizations and their grassroots bases to make the planet a healthier, more resilient, and more sustainable home for humankind.

REFERENCES

Seguin, C., Pelletier, L. G., and Hunsley, J. (1998). Toward a model of environmental activism. *Environment and Behavior*, 30(5), 628–52.

Slocombe, D. S. (1984). Environmentalism: a modern synthesis. *The Environmentalist*, 4(4): 281–85.

Zelezny, L. C., and Schultz, P. W. (2000). Psychology of promoting environmentalism: Promoting environmentalism. *Journal of Social Issues*, 56(3): 365–71.

Chapter One

Historic Milestones and Trailblazers

This chapter focuses on the people, places, and events that helped shape strategic environmentalism as we know it today. Learning objectives of this chapter include the contextualizing of environmental communication within a larger U.S. and international history, and the tracing of key figures who helped shape the trajectory of the modern environmental movement in the twentieth century. The examples provided in this chapter demonstrate the breadth of history's environmental communicators and their diversity of backgrounds and communication approaches.

HOW ANCIENT COMMUNICATION MEDIATED THE PLANET

Human appeals to the protection of nature and the environment go as far back as civilization itself. In 2014, on the Indonesian island of Sulawesi, researchers made a startling discovery of ancient communication: paintings from 35,000 to 40,000 years ago that featured renderings of the human hand and a pig. Not only did these paintings show that cave art emerged independently in different parts of the world, it also showed that human beings were creating informational and abstract expressions focused on their own existence and the state of the natural world much earlier than was previously thought. Furthermore, it showed that the early development of human intelligence was intertwined with communication about nature itself.

Other archaeological finds have demonstrated that ancient human communication was not only historically rooted in environmental messaging, it was also strategic and intended to achieve specific goals. For example, in the early days of 2023, the online travel publication *Atlas Obscura* highlighted an impressive recent archaeological discovery in India: the five thousand-year-old port city of Dholavira, located in the salt marshes of Gujarut's Thar Desert. The ancient urban settlement located by researchers showcased innovations of that era from South Asia, including the development of transportation arterials, water management systems, and the remnants of well-established artisanal and commercial trade. But the ancient settlement also featured what the publication declared to be one of the most noteworthy discoveries from the country's history: "the world's oldest billboard" (Alagappa, 2023, para. 1). In this sense, the billboard represented one of the longest-standing forms of human strategic communication. Furthermore, as the recent find demonstrates, the sign as an artifact of ancient communication endures over time and space. Harish Alagappa, an author with *Atlas Obscura*, even noted how the ancient billboard is now immersed in the contemporary debate over the planet's environmental challenges, owing in part to the settlement of Dholavira's demise at the hands of natural disaster: "While we cannot decipher what was written on the sign that the people of Dholavira left forgotten in a storeroom before leaving their city for good, its message about the dangers of climate change is clear."

Similarly, faith-based texts from previous millennia have conveyed messages about civilization, wildlife, and the natural world in order to make sense of the human and planetary experience. The Bible provides several important cases in point. Take this passage from Jeremiah 2:7: "I brought you into a fertile land to eat its fruit and rich produce. But you came and defiled my land and made my inheritance detestable." Indeed, the Bible and other spiritual texts are rife with passages devoted to respecting or conserving nature, and to warning readers of the perils of plundering the earth's natural assets. However, some environmental thinkers have disagreed with this assessment. In 1967, Lynn White authored an essay for the journal *Science* called "The Historical Roots of our Ecological Crisis," which connected Christianity to anthropocentrism, or a belief that human beings were the most important entities on the planet.

A RESPONSE TO THE INDUSTRIAL AGE

In many ways, the advent of environmental public relations as we know it today was a reaction to, and inevitable outgrowth of, the industrial age. During the 1800s, as North America's populated areas transitioned from rural living to urbanization, and as the economy moved from agricultural to industrial, issues such as air and water pollution became life-and-death matters. Advances in transportation also played an outsized role in this environmental consciousness. Movement by steamship and train meant that people could move into

Figure 1.1. The cover of the monthly magazine The Masses *showed the massacre during the Colorado Coal Strike at Ludlow, Colorado. (John Sloan/Library of Congress.)*

remote areas that were previously the domain of nature or of America's Native American tribes. These same transportation routes opened up areas like the North and the West to the industrial economy, with commodities such as lumber and wheat transported across the Great Plains and Upper Midwest to trading hubs such as Chicago and New York City.

One of the key moments for the advancement of environmental communication comes from Ivy Lee, who is considered one of the earliest proponents of traditional public relations. A former journalist, Lee served as a consultant for the Rockefeller family in the wake of the Colorado coal strike of 1913–1914. The bloody strike was a dark moment for labor relations in the United States, as three strikers and one militiaman were killed during the standoff. Kirk Hallahan, a professor of public relations at Colorado State University, examined original manuscripts to understand Lee's work as a consultant and staff member for John D. Rockefeller Jr. He found that Lee's work was instrumental in establishing improved government relations, media relations, and labor relations (Hallahan, 2002). Lee's communication work at the mine helped position public relations as a management function to navigate the complexity facing business-labor relations.

WOMEN LEAD THE CHARGE

Throughout the twentieth century, a number of key women were transforming the practice of ecological conservation and environmental protection through their writing and advocacy. They not only sought to protect the environment in isolation from the human condition, but in most cases, they saw an intertwining of the human condition with ecosystems and environmental processes. Some of these women drew from their experience as civic leaders or community advocates to parse out environmental injustices and social ills. One early ecofeminist, Caroline Bartlett Crane, raised awareness of environmental degradation during a time when the industrial growth in the United States was ravaging land and water. In the early decades of the twentieth

Figure 1.2.   Press correspondents with Jane Addams, 1916. (Harris & Ewing/Library of Congress.)

century, she found significant ecological challenges in cities, including urban sanitation and unhygienic living conditions.

During this era of conflict between industrialization and human rights, another reformer and activist, Jane Addams, similarly fought against environmental injustices in the inner city. She challenged the civic establishment of her time to implement social and environmental reforms and improve everyday living conditions. This included new ways of helping the urban poor through improved housing and working conditions, and the upgrading of sanitary standards, such as garbage collection.

In their wake, another early trailblazer, Margaret "Mardy" Murie, came to be known as "the grandmother of the conservation movement" because of her tireless work promoting environmental protection causes in the 1950s, and for helping establish the Arctic National Wildlife Refuge in 1960 (Tietjen, 2022). Murie was invited to the White House in 1964 to witness the passing of the Wilderness Act, which was signed into law by President Lyndon B. Johnson. The act not only directed federal land agencies to manage wilderness areas, but it also established a preservation system intended for the long-term good of American citizens. The legacy of the Wilderness Act is the National Wilderness Preservation System, which comprises a network of over eight hundred wilderness areas. These areas are managed by different agencies of the federal government: the National Park Service, the Bureau of Land Management, the U.S. Fish and Wildlife Service, and the U.S.D.A. Forest Service.

KLONDIKE GOLD

The resurgence of interest in the 1890s Klondike Gold Rush, buoyed in part by movies, documentaries, and streaming television programs, raises new opportunities for assessing the environmental impact of this seminal moment. Many of the locations central to the Yukon's gold rush story are now ghost towns, or have been preserved to some degree in their historic form for the benefit of tourists. The discovery of gold in the Klondike region of Canada's Yukon Territory in 1896 set off a historic stampede of mining prospectors looking to make their own personal fortune in the region. Between 1896 and 1899, an estimated 100,000 miners headed north to the area. The area's gold rush represents a fascinating story about prospecting, far-north precious metals exploration, and turn-of-the-century mining towns. But it also represents a story about environmental communication. The stories of the Klondike are relatively well-known, in part because of the hardships facing prospectors. But these stories also resonate because of the skilled writers—including Rex Beach, Robert Service, and Jack London—who relayed the saga of

Figure 1.3.   Packers ascending the summit of Chilkoot Pass in 1898 during the height of the Klondike gold rush. (Library of Congress.)

adventure, ecology, and exploitation to audiences across the world (Morse, 2010). Woven into accounts of the gold rush are mainstream themes and appeals of the great outdoors and the rush of adventure. Such stories have captured the imaginations of popular audiences because they are narrative constructions dealing with dramatic human challenges.

The gold rush was not only recorded through texts, however. It was also image-driven. In short, photographs were the medium that conveyed the fascinating and dangerous world of the Klondike Gold Rush. In his account of the gold rush, author Pierre Berton (2011) described the importance of one image—of miners ascending Alaska's Chilkoot Pass on their way to the Klondike—to forming a public understanding of the entire event. Even today, the idea of a "gold rush" can shape the way we think about a topic. Media stories surrounding carbon trading and offsetting schemes, for example, sometimes use gold rush imagery to simplify how they are understood to the public (Nerlich and Koteyko, 2010). The gold rush also revealed elements of a broader industrial culture, which gave corporations an outsized influence over gold miners' labor practices and daily lives. According to historian

Kathryn Morse, "Gold mining thus brought miners not only to nature, but to the heart of certain aspects of industrial culture." Morse argues that the work performed during Klondike mining was infused with a "culture of gold" that gave it a holy aura—positioning the precious metal as a "divinely ordained source of wealth" (Morse, 2010, 116).

CASE STUDY: JOHN MUIR KEEPS THE FAITH

Contemporary environmental communication on the part of issue advocates or deep ecologists harkens back to the legacy of one of the foremost historical figures in environmental public relations: John Muir. An early advocate of wilderness preservation in the United States, Muir is considered "one of the patron saints of twentieth-century American environmental activity" for his prolific, poetic writings about wild landscapes, which helped ordinary Americans rethink their relationship with nature (Holmes, 1999). Such preservation efforts led to the establishment of Yosemite National Park, among other nationally protected geographies. Muir also co-founded in 1892 an environmental group known today for its wide-ranging green advocacy across the United States: the Sierra Club.

Even as Muir is widely recognized as the father of the environmental movement in the United States—particularly in light of his integral role in the establishment of national parks and the founding of the Sierra Club—his legacy as a writer and strategic communicator of science and the environment is sometimes overlooked. Over the course of his decades-long fight to save America's wild spaces and ecologically threatened landscapes—including forests, mountainscapes, watersheds, and canyons—Muir proved to be as prolific as he was influential. Muir wrote extensively for leading national magazines, including *Harper's Magazine* and *The Atlantic*, in extending his ecological worldview and pushing back against the interests of America's industrial and capital sector, which included not only lumbermen, gold miners, and land squatters, but also Wall Street, federal politicians, and government stewards of American forests. He did so with appeals rooted in his own Christianity and faith that conflated naturally with an environmental ethic he single-handedly developed and articulated.

This intersection of faith and advocacy is rooted in civic discourse and persuasion for social change. Religious and faith-based communicators have historically leveraged media channels to fulfill missions of persuasion and outreach for their audiences. At the same time, religion as a communication vehicle has been utilized in public relations and advocacy campaigns to enhance social justice, environmental protection, and health promotion.

Figure 1.4.   Theodore Roosevelt and John Muir set up camp at Glacier Point in Yosemite Valley, California, in 1903. (Library of Congress.)

The environmental activism of Muir provides a foundational milestone for green communication, allowing practitioners and advocates to contemplate the role of rhetorical appeals that drive environmental change. Muir's legacy also helps show how contemporary environmental communicators might fuse green appeals with faith-based messages in order to further their ecological objectives while aligning practical and spiritual narratives.

The legacy of John Muir remains embraced in the realms of deep ecology and environmental conservation, and his enormous impact on the evolution of the green movement is well established in environmental scholarship. Muir's long-standing public debates with Gifford Pinchot over the management of natural resources—including the construction of the Hetch-Hetchy Valley dam—have served as an important contemporary focus because they juxtapose Muir's embrace of comprehensive wilderness protection with Pinchot's nuanced view that natural resources management aligns with longer-term economic benefits (Smith, 1998). These two different conceptions, articulated as "conservationism" and "preservationism," highlight not only differing ecological worldviews but also a difference between public and private perspectives even as historians point to the commonalities established between the two (Meyer, 1997).

Furthermore, Muir's various modes of outreach during the late nineteenth century and into the twentieth—including his array of books, poems, speeches, publicity events, newspaper articles and op-eds—ultimately positioned the ecologist, explorer, and writer as a literal and metaphorical trailblazer in the fields of environmental communication and public relations. While Muir's legacy is well considered by the ranks of deep ecologists and environmental historians, his contribution to media and communication is unique for its rhetorical style, its faith-based invocations, and its real-world underpinnings.

It is within this national arena in which Muir's editorial output thrived. His magazine writing was prolific, and in addition to *The Atlantic* and *Harper's* included features for *Appleton's* and *The Century*. Much of the legacy of this magazine opinion leadership is focused on Muir's advocacy for Yosemite. Yet in many ways it also represents an important turn in the production of environmental media. Muir's turn-of-the-twentieth-century literary work was defined by integrating a "sublime response" of rhetoric and aesthetics with a literary persona that worked to move the reader beyond a passive reading experience into an active mode of first-person outdoors experience and social engagement (Oravec, 1981). Muir therefore not only whisked the reader to the grandeur of the soaring mountaintop, endless forest, or roaring river, he also encouraged their contemplation of life and mortality within this natural order. Muir's magazine advocacy regularly juxtaposed the natural splendor of America's wild spaces with a reader's own mortality and belief in a higher power.

ORGANIZATIONAL PROFILE: THE ADVENT OF EARTH DAY

The 1960s and 1970s in the United States provided an ideal set of circumstances for further growth of environmental public communication. At university campuses across the country, anti-war activists fumed about the U.S. government's military interests abroad. Meanwhile, newspaper and broadcast news reports of environmental conflicts and protests over issues like nuclear development, toxic waste, and air pollution were raising awareness of the environment in ordinary households. All of this created ideal conditions for what is now one of the most influential environmental days on the annual calendar: Earth Day.

Every April, millions of people around the world pause to consider their relationship to the planet. They might ponder the world they are leaving for their children, their individual impact on the earth, or their relationship to the globe's ecology. The spirit of Earth Day provides opportunities for reflection but also action. Today it is one of the signature environmental events, and its growing popularity is a reflection of the growing global interest in protecting the planet.

The idea for the first Earth Day came from a junior U.S. senator in Wisconsin, Gaylord Nelson. After witnessing an oil spill off the coast of California, Nelson wanted to tap into an emerging public awareness of environmental

*Figure 1.5. Earth Day in New York City in 1980.
(Bernard Gotfryd/Library of Congress.)*

problems. In 1969, he announced the idea for a college teach-in aimed at the national media, and in the spirit of bipartisanship, he invited a conservative congressman, Pete McCloskey, to co-chair. Another young activist, Denis Hayes, was also invited to lead the teach-in. The group chose April 22, 1969, for the event, in part because it fell between university students' final exams and spring break. Soon after that, the event was expanded to include not only university campuses but also churches, civic groups, and other organizations. According to EarthDay.org, it was then that the event was renamed as "Earth Day." The renaming provided instant media attention, and twenty million Americans participated in the day's theme of environmental protection (EarthDay.org, 2022).

Perhaps the greatest legacy of Earth Day is how it continues to attract citizens from different walks of life and across the political spectrum. According to the Earth Day organization, "groups that had been fighting individually against oil spills, polluting factories and power plants, raw sewage, toxic dumps, pesticides, freeways, the loss of wilderness and the extinction of wildlife united on Earth Day around these shared common values." The following year, Earth Day 1970 achieved what the organization dubbed "a rare political alignment, enlisting support from Republicans and Democrats, rich and poor, urban dwellers and farmers, business and labor leaders."

Earth Day not only brought on a new spirit in environmental advocacy, it also led to the creation of the U.S. Environmental Protection Agency and the passage of like-minded laws including the National Environmental Education Act, the Occupational Safety and Health Act, and the Clean Air Act. According to Adam Rome, an environmental historian at the University of Buffalo, Earth Day has shifted its focus over the years. In its early years, organizers focused on a larger overhaul of society and collective action, whereas the modern version is more focused on individual or community action, whether that takes the form of planting trees or buying ecologically friendly products. Earth Day reached its fiftieth anniversary in 2020, and the annual event has continued to raise awareness among millions. But it has also adapted to changes in the way the global public consumes media. In the contemporary media and public life environment, it is just as commonplace to participate in Earth Day via a Zoom conference or a Twitter hashtag as at a live event. Yet even as digital initiatives, annual Earth Day events still serve as a crucial generator of public attention for the green movement, and as an important news peg for media outlets looking to provide greater coverage on these issues.

CASE STUDY: LOVE CANAL PRESENTS A TURNING POINT FOR THE ENVIRONMENTAL MOVEMENT

Love Canal is recognized as one of the greatest environmental disasters of the modern era in the United States. Its legacy of runaway toxic dumping by chemical companies in a western New York State community and the tragic health outcomes for thousands of local residents have provided a cautionary tale for American citizens and industries. The Love Canal tragedy took place in the eastern section of Niagara Falls, New York. Over a century ago, the neighborhood was established by visionary William T. Love as a model community, with a canal connecting the upper and lower sections of the Niagara River in order to afford local residents with economic opportunity and cheap energy. The plan, however, did not work out as envisioned, and what was left of the partially completed canal was eventually turned into an industrial chemical dumpsite. In the 1950s, the dumpsite was covered up and a residential community of working-class homes was built over it. Devastating health impacts would soon emerge.

Writing for the U.S. Environmental Protection Agency's *EPA Journal*, Eckardt C. Beck (1979) noted that Love Canal was just the tip of the iceberg for this type of environmental disaster. "We suspect that there are hundreds of such chemical dumpsites across this Nation," he noted. "Unlike Love Canal, few are situated so close to human settlements. But without a doubt, many of these old dumpsites are time bombs with burning fuses—their contents slowly leaching out. And the next victim cold be a water supply, or a sensitive wetland."

The historian Elizabeth Blum, in her book *Love Canal Revisited: Race, Class, and Gender in Environmental Activism* (2008), has found that various forms of community activism, environmentalism, and ecofeminism emerged from the movement to stop the Love Canal disaster. Blum noted that some activists ignored the concerns of lower-income residents and those who lived in government housing. However, compensating for this disparity of voice, another activist group drew from alliances with the environmental movement and the National Association for the Advancement of Colored Peoples (NAACP) to provide a more representative approach to the mainstream and primarily white, middle-class activists.

DISCUSSION QUESTIONS

1. How do contemporary civic transportation issues such as air travel and public transit advance dialogue about the environment in the way that rail and steamships did over a century ago?
2. Why did women play such an outsized role in environmental protection throughout the twentieth century, particularly in community contexts?
3. What does Earth Day mean to the public today, and how might this differ from its original objectives?

KEYWORDS

Conservationism
Conservation movement
Environmental injustice
Preservationism
Urbanization

KEY EVENTS, LOCATIONS, AND ORGANIZATIONS

Bureau of Land Management
Colorado coal strike
Earth Day
Love Canal
National Park Service
National Wilderness Preservation System
Occupational Safety and Health Act
U.S. Fish and Wildlife Service
U.S. Forest Service
Wilderness Act

REFERENCES

Alagappa, H. (2023). The mystery of the world's oldest billboard. *Atlas Obscura*. Retrieved from: https://www.atlasobscura.com/articles/oldest-billboard-in-world.

Beck, E. C. (1979). The Love Canal tragedy. *EPA J.* 5: 17.

Blum, E. D. (2008). *Love Canal Revisited: Race, Class, and Gender in Environmental Activism*. University Press of Kansas.

EarthDay.org. (2022). History of Earth Day. Retrieved from: https://www.earthday.org/history/.

Hallahan, K. (2002). Ivy Lee and the Rockefellers' response to the 1913–1914 Colorado coal strike. *Journal of Public Relations Research*, 14(4): 265–315.

Holmes, S. J. (1999). *The Young John Muir: An Environmental Biography*. Madison: University of Wisconsin Press.

Meyer, J. M. (1997). Gifford Pinchot, John Muir, and the boundaries of politics in American thought. *Polity*, 30(2): 267–84.

Morse, K. T. (2010). *The Nature of Gold: An Environmental History of the Klondike Gold Rush*. Seattle: University of Washington Press.

Nerlich, B., and Koteyko, N. (2010). Carbon gold rush and carbon cowboys: A new chapter in green mythology? *Environmental Communication*, 4(1): 37–53.

Oravec, C. (1981). John Muir, Yosemite, and the sublime response: A study in the rhetoric of preservationism. *Quarterly Journal of Speech*, 67(3): 245–58.

Rome, A. (2021). The genius of Earth Day. *Environmental History*.

Smith, M. B. (1998). The value of a tree: Public debates of John Muir and Gifford Pinchot. *The Historian*, 60(4): 757–78.

Tietjen, J. S. (2022). Infrastructure Pioneers. In *Women in Infrastructure*. Edinburgh: Springer, Cham, 23–71.

Chapter Two

Opinion Leadership

This chapter focuses on the interplay of environmentalism, social influence, and human cognition—and in particular how communicators successfully relay green ideas to the public and policymakers. Learning objectives of this chapter include understanding communication strategies such as the diffusion and adoption of green ideas and the role of opinion leaders and celebrities in ecological appeals. The examples provided in this chapter demonstrate the important role of these influencers in helping organizations and issues gain traction with the media and the public.

AQUAMAN SOUNDS THE ALARM ON MARINE PLASTICS

When Hollywood actor and green entrepreneur Jason Momoa took to Instagram in 2022 to shave his head to protest plastic pollution, the world took notice. After all, Momoa's long hair was a defining part of the actor's public image. Shaving it off would inevitably draw attention to Momoa the celebrity but also to the movie star's concern for the health of the planet's oceans. "I'm shaving off the hair. Doing it for single-use plastics," said Momoa, who in 2022 was named as a U.N. Environment Program Advocate for Life Below Water (Contino, 2022). "I'm tired of these plastic bottles, we gotta stop, plastic forks, all that shit, it just goes into our land, goes into our ocean." With his public action, the star of *Aquaman* and *Game of Thrones* made the issue of plastics top-of-mind on the social media platform, gaining one million likes on Instagram plus a flurry of stories from publications like *Parade* and *Page Six*. In one swoop (or shave, in this case), Momoa made his millions of fans think about the degradation of our oceans, the problems inherent with single-use plastics, and the power of individuals and communities to hasten this environmental threat.

I'm tired of these plastic bottles.

Settings

0:15 / 0:38

Jason Momoa Shaves His Head to Protest Single-Use Plastics

NowThis News
2.36M subscribers

Subscribe

👍 13K   👎   ↗ Share   ···

Figure 2.1. Aquaman *actor Jason Momoa, the U.N. Environment Program Advocate for Life BelowWater, shaved his famous long hair to protest single-use plastics. (Still from YouTube.)*

This interplay of individual psychology, group dynamics, and ecological phenomena lie at the heart of successful environmental public relations. The processes that encourage individuals or organizations to behavioral change or action are rooted in how we think, how we connect to our family members and friends, and how we interact with the natural world. In environmental public relations, specific strategic tactics can help make particular topics more prominent, sway public policy decisions, or bolster the social messaging of governments or corporations. The bottom line is that the strategic mediation of green messages is more prominent and more important than ever before.

Just have a look around your own neighborhood, workplace, or college campus. You might find signs imploring you to recycle, compost, use clean energy, or reduce your carbon footprint. You might be exposed to the green appeals of a local politician or company trying to secure your vote or customer loyalty. Or you might see nearby posters and billboards, or hear public service announcements on the radio, that raise awareness of environmental health threats such as exposure to toxins and air pollution. All of these communication forms are part of a larger process that helps individuals and groups think, act, and engage in the name of nature.

And these messages are on the rise in public life and in politics. According to an analysis by Kantar Media/CMAG, advertisements mentioning the environment, energy, or climate change surged to over 125,000 during the 2014 midterm election cycle, establishing a new record according to the *New York Times*. Furthermore, environmental advertising continued to be a vehicle for environmental and climate change dialogue during the 2016 and 2020 U.S. presidential election campaigns, with topics such as climate change and energy extraction taking center stage.

Green-themed stories, public service announcements, advertisements, and social marketing appeals exist wherever you go. And they are often championed by expert voices. It's not uncommon to encounter leading sustainability advocates and spokespersons who come from industry or government, such as Catherine Caruana-McManus, who is responsible for advising organizations on IBM's Smarter Cities Initiative for sustainable and intelligent urban ecosystems across water, education, infrastructure, transport, health, and energy use in the built environment; or Anna Jones-Crabtree, the U.S. Forest Service's first Sustainable Operations coordinator, who works to reduce the agency's environmental footprint alongside a mission of land management. There are thousands of like-minded sustainability communicators who carry out similar work across the country and the world.

The output of environmental communicators in swaying audiences to ecologically friendly perspectives would therefore appear to be a permanent fixture. But go back to your own neighborhood or day-to-day work or school environment for a second. You probably tune into some messages while ignoring others, and some might have even caused you to change your behavior or think differently about an important issue. Successful communicators employ techniques such as opinion leadership, ideas adoption, and calls to mobilization to make sure that the messages you receive make a real difference and don't just contribute to media clutter.

RISE OF THE ECOLOGICAL CELEBRITY

On the eve of the 2019 United Nations Climate Action Summit, scientists and media professionals changed the tenor of global warming debates by adopting the expression of "climate change emergency" in engaging with media audiences and the public (Hertsgaard, 2019, para. 1). Soon this language moved from university classrooms and lofty news publications like the *New York Times* to speeches and interviews from popular performing artists and Hollywood celebrities. For example, in the run-up to the U.N. Conference on Climate Change (COP26), high-profile individuals such as *The Office* star Rainn Wilson, author Levison Wood, and English actor Cel Spellman lent their names to a video message about the climate movement that was produced by the University of Exeter in conjunction with Green Futures and Arctic Basecamp. They were joined by award-winning American musician Billie Eilish,

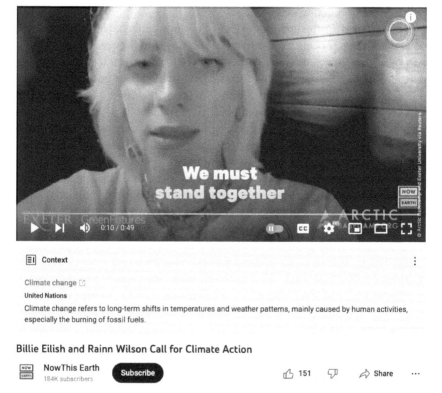

Figure 2.2. Musician Billie Eilish was among a group of celebrities who called on world leaders to take action on climate change ahead of the COP26 conference in Glasgow, Scotland. (Still from YouTube.)

who called for greater attention to "the climate emergency in a critical decade for our planet." Her appeal stood not only for the present moment, but also for the planet's long-term health. "We must stand together and speak up to save our planet, not just for us but for our future generations," she said.

Eilish's call to action serves as another good example of how celebrities shape contemporary environmental discussions. As the environment becomes a central concern for the public and politicians, organizations have turned to the media—including branding, social marketing, and advocacy endeavors—to deploy persuasive messages about specific green actions that can have a positive societal and ecological impact.

The integration of celebrities into environmental appeals is effective because of their existing standing with publics, their ability to convey messages across a wide swath of media and communication platforms, and their ability to rhetorically situate environmental issues as topically relevant and intensely personal. In our own way we "know" these celebrities, and so we are more inclined to trust them. As high-profile entertainers, artists, athletes, and politicians embrace issues such as climate change, wildlife conservation, animal ethics, and responsible consumption of products, they simultaneously raise the profile and the attention given to these critical topics. They also raise the stakes when opposition to environmental initiatives intensifies as a result of growing public awareness and increased media attention.

This value of celebrities in traditional brand messages is well documented. Beyond the realm of consumer goods and services, they are increasingly engaged by NGOs, advocacy groups, and companies to persuade publics on a wide range of issues. In some cases, they serve as organizational ambassadors, lending their star power to raise awareness and attract audiences. In others, they serve more specific roles, including the narration of public service announcements and advertisements that appear on television, radio, YouTube, or organizational websites. In this sense, they play the role of both organizational advocate and opinion leader. They might lend their high profile to the nonprofit or NGO they represent, but they also have the ability to change the way the public thinks about a pressing topic.

For example, in 2021 a number of social and environmental organizations—including the Indigenous Environmental Network, Natural Resources Defense Council, and IllumiNative—called on President Biden to shut down the Dakota Access pipeline in a letter released to the public. But it was the co-signing celebrities, such as New York Jets football quarterback Aaron Rodgers, actor Don Cheadle, and musician Dave Matthews, who helped the story gain extra traction in the media. The letter was even signed by several actors from the movie *The Avengers*. The impact of celebrity involvement therefore provides environmental topics and initiatives with greater credibility for audiences versus traditional policy experts or issue activists. It is one thing to hear about alarming climate volatility from an obscure scientist or an environmental journalist. It's quite another to hear from a favorite musician, actor, or athlete, who might even integrate the emotionality of an issue like climate change into their art, their performance, or their competition.

STAR POWER FOR ECOLOGICAL CHANGE

Many well-known figures from public life have immersed themselves heavily into environmental or climate issues including former U.S. vice president Al Gore (winner of the Nobel Peace Prize for his 2007 documentary *An Inconvenient Truth*), Leonardo DiCaprio (whose foundation lobbies for forest conservation, healthy oceans, and renewable energy), musician Neil Young (an opponent of oil and gas pipelines and an advocate of hybrid electric cars), the supermodel Gisele Bundchen (founder of the Clean Water Project), and Montreal-based rock band Arcade Fire (whose members advocated for the Leap Manifesto focusing on climate activism and action).

Some organizations have included celebrity messengers in their communication repertoire to attract greater attention or adjoin a message to a larger societal narrative. For example, when DiCaprio decided to become an official investor in Beyond Meat, the plant-based meat firm in 2017, it would have made perfect sense for his fans but also for customers of the company. That's because DiCaprio had long been an outspoken advocate of sustainable food practices as well as climate issues. Having a random celebrity take on this role of investor and advocate, particularly if they weren't concerned with the company's mission, might not have been nearly as effective.

For advertisers, celebrity endorsements can play a significant role in consumer awareness, image-shaping, and decision-making, according to a study by Petra Glover (2009), a senior lecturer at the University of West London. Furthermore, the perceived expertise of celebrity spokespersons drives the willingness of audiences to buy a product (Ohanian, 1991). Returning to the example of DiCaprio and his relationship to Beyond Meat, this suggests a necessary alignment between the celebrity's personal experience or reputation and the issue or product being supported.

Yet the role of celebrities as conduits for social change has seen mixed results. The usage of a national celebrity in the wrong context can actually reduce the effectiveness of a public service announcement (Toncar, Reid, and Anderson, 2007). Nor does the inclusion of celebrities into social and environmental disputes ensure victorious outcomes for one side, as key issues can be eclipsed by the entry of such star power into a conflict, especially because of celebrities' existing and unique relationships to audiences (Meyer, 1995). These preexisting relationships can overshadow the effectiveness or outcomes of social campaigns, and they underscore the complexities of celebrity engagement in environmental and social issues. Their ability to foster opinion or attitudinal change relies upon the agency of audiences. One such explanation of this interaction between targeted audiences and celebrity spokespersons comes from a fascinating concept known as parasocial interaction.

AUDIENCE TIES THROUGH PARASOCIALIZATION

Have you ever found yourself relating to a famous musician or star athlete as if they were a personal acquaintance? If you can relate to them as a friend or family member, your relationship might qualify as parasocial interaction. Although its origins lie in the field of psychology, parasocial interaction as a communication process did not receive much attention until the 1970s when scholars looked to the influential role of television (Giles, 2002).

Parasocial interaction suggests that media users develop relationships with figures in the media based on some form of identification. Consider your parasocial relationship with a television news anchor or weatherperson appearing on your favorite local newscast. You might have an affinity for such a person based on their cheerful disposition or expert insights. For news audiences, the parasocial relationship with the TV anchorperson is based on an affective tie that creates an illusion of being genuine and reciprocating (Levy, 1979). But parasocial interaction exists in all media forms where personalities are present. We interact with these people because we know their values and morals, and their inevitable decisions. For TV and streaming programs, higher levels of parasocial interaction exist when characters break the so-called fourth wall by speaking directly to the audience by looking at the camera (Auter, 1992). That helps explain audience affinity for the character of Jim on the hit series *The Office*, or the entire assemblage of characters on *The Trailer Park Boys*. Another measure by which some researchers point to the relatability of media stars is the degree to which you might choose to have a beer or coffee with them. A study using a "drinking-buddy" scale as a proxy for parasocial interaction showed that the metric could be a predictor of attraction to political candidates (Powell, Richmond, and Cantrell-Williams, 2012).

So how does this extend into the realm of green persuasion and public relations? Within environmental communication, parasocial interaction can influence audience beliefs and behavior. Celebrities with a higher "parasociability rating" (and yes, such a thing exists) are more likely to induce voters to select an endorsed candidate (Centeno, 2015). This raises the ability of celebrities

WORLD • DAVOS

Pharrell Williams and Al Gore Announce 'Live Earth' Concert in June

Figure 2.3.   Time Magazine *highlighted the announcement by Pharrell Williams and former U.S. Vice President Al Gore to host the Live Earth Concert to raise awareness on environmental issues. (Naina Bajekal/*Time Magazine.*)*

to influence individuals' attitudes, much like a family member can. Pharrell Williams, who participated in the Climate Reality Project in 2016, provides a helpful case in point. Williams appeared on programs like *Live Earth: The World Is Watching* to raise awareness of climate issues and at the same time engaged in the Rock the Vote program to encourage voters to show up at the polls on Election Day.

DIFFUSION AND ADOPTION OF GREEN IDEAS

The impact of celebrities in green public relations has been confirmed by social scientists, who have assessed audience engagement and attitudinal change based on who is delivering the environmental message. But contrary to what you might think, this opinion leadership isn't the exclusive domain of celebrities. You may recognize opinion leaders in your own life: family members, classmates, coworkers, and community members. The digital media landscape has reenergized examinations of opinion leadership in public life, particularly around how modern audiences engage with an unprecedented array of news and media outlets (Mangold and Bachl, 2018).

Opinion leaders are fascinating because of their fluid, informal nature. They can be encountered in institutional settings such as classrooms or news media outlets. But they can also be found holding court at dinner tables, community centers, and Facebook discussions. To this end, opinion leaders are not "leaders" in a traditionally defined sense. Unlike politicians, government bureaucrats, or corporate executives, they do not enjoy formal authority over organizations, institutions, or individuals. Rather, their influence is derived from their informal status as respected, connected, and well informed (Watts and Dodds, 2007).

We listen to opinion leaders because, in general, we respect them. The late communication theorist Elihu Katz (1957) helped establish the three criteria used to differentiate this group from everyone else: Who they are, what they know, and whom they know. These factors can be critical when decision-makers integrate a new idea or innovation into environmental planning or thought leadership. For example, a regional plan to eradicate the spread of invasive plant species that adversely impact habitats sounds great on paper, but the plan might not gain traction unless the right people in the community are empowered to share and promote this information to their own networks of friends, neighbors, and coworkers.

Drivers of electric vehicles provide another case in point. Does ownership of an electric car imply opinion leadership? The answer is contingent upon whether the owner tells others about their experience driving one. Opinion leaders use interpersonal communication to share their opinions, as opposed to "early adopters" who merely influence others through nonverbal means, such as being seen using a product (Nisbet and Kotcher, 2009). Unlike early adopters, opinion leaders tend to communicate both the pros *and* cons of a product, and become more involved in a product category than other adopter groups (Weimann et al., 2007). Thus, your neighbor driving the latest Tesla model is sending a message of adoption by merely driving the vehicle, but the opinion leadership happens when they tell you how eco-friendly it is or how much they enjoy driving it.

In environmentalism as in other areas of society, people who are perceived as leaders tend to be natural communicators: They tend to do a lot of talking (Bavelas et al., 1965). This helps explain why the most extroverted of actors, musicians, and athletes also tend to be more vocal on social and environmental topics. It also suggests the possibility of identifying "consumer opinion leaders" by their ability to communicate extensively and with substance about a product. Marketing research by Charles King and John Summers established the importance of these group leaders in helping consumers declutter a convoluted media landscape. Consumers gather information from a wide spectrum of media channels and outlets, and this acquisition helps them develop attitudes and make decisions (King and Summers, 1970). Within this process, interpersonal communication on the part of opinion leaders helps these consumers refine and finalize these attitudes and decisions.

WHEN GOOD IDEAS TURN BAD

The act of speaking out and telling others what they think, however, does not mean that opinion leaders are necessarily right or wrong, or that they embrace every new idea. So-called discontinuers have been found to seek information more actively and influence groups about why they shouldn't try out a new technology or innovation (Leonard-Barton, 1985). Similarly, technically or ecologically inefficient technologies can cause some to reject an innovation or idea. For example, media stories about a wind turbine that has ceased to function properly might send a signal to a local community that the overarching wind energy system is not meeting clean energy expectations. Or the wind turbine could be blamed for killing local bird species. An earlier example of this challenge is the mediation of former U.S. president George W. Bush riding a Segway, which is a zero-emission personal transporter. Bush famously fell from the two-wheeled device, which raised doubts in the media and with the public about the viability of the Segway as a safe and ecologically friendly mode of commuting. In some ways, the former president's infamous encounter with the Segway was detrimental to not only his reputation but also that of the Segway. After many years of languishing popularity, the stand-up personal transporter was finally retired in 2020.

Still, opinion leadership is surprisingly overlooked as a complement to traditional grassroots or media strategies in climate change–related campaigns (Nisbet and Kotcher, 2009). Thus, successful campaigns might integrate several approaches. Meera Venkatraman (1989), a professor of marketing at Suffolk University, has distinguished between opinion leadership and early adoption of green technology products, and stresses the importance of individuals who embrace both activities. Opinion leaders are those who are most concerned, knowledgeable, and articulate about green issues. Yet people prefer gathering information from people who are both familiar with specific issues or ideas and also more involved in their own social networks.

Therefore, you might even run into green opinion leadership at your local grocery store, bike shop, or fashion retailer. Individuals who make a special effort to buy green think of themselves as opinion leaders, and are especially engaged in consumer activities like gathering product information and the act of shopping itself (Shrum, McCarty, and Lowrey, 1995). Given the challenges facing the planet today, it is more important than ever to understand the role of communication in shifting our beliefs and attitudes, which in turn can lead to more successful advocacy and public interest campaigns.

DISCUSSION QUESTIONS

1. What are some recent examples of music, film, and sporting celebrities contributing to the promotion of environmental ideas?
2. How do regular citizens engage with issues such as land planning, air quality, and conservation in their own communities?
3. What is the role of parasocial interaction in the age of YouTube and Instagram?

KEYWORDS

Attitudinal change
Diffusion of innovation
Early adopters
Interpersonal communication
Interpersonal influence
Opinion leadership
Parasocial interaction
Persuasion

REFERENCES

Auter, P. J. (1992). Psychometric: TV that talks back: An experimental validation of a parasocial interaction scale. *Journal of Broadcasting & Electronic Media*, 36(2): 173–81.

Bavelas, A., Hastorf, A. H., Gross, A. E., and Kite, W. R. (1965). Experiments on the alteration of group structure. *Journal of Experimental Social Psychology*.

Centeno, Dave De Guzman. (2015). Constructing celebrities as political endorsers: Parasocial acts, cultural power, and cultural capital. *Philippine Political Science Journal*, 36(2): 209–32.

Contino, K. (2022). Jason Momoa shaves off his signature long hair. *Page Six*. Retrieved from: https://pagesix.com/2022/09/06/jason-momoa-shaves-off-his-long -hair-see-his-new-look/.

Dalrymple, K. E., Shaw, B. R., and Brossard, D. (2013). "Following the leader: Using opinion leaders in environmental strategic communication." *Society & Natural Resources* 26(12): 1438–53.

Giles, D. C. (2002). Parasocial interaction: A review of the literature and a model for future research. *Media Psychology*, 4(3): 279–305.

Glover, P. (2009). "Celebrity endorsement in tourism advertising: Effects on destination image." *Journal of Hospitality and Tourism Management*, 16(1): 16–23.

Hertsgaard, M. (2019). "We're losing the race": UN secretary general calls climate change an "emergency." *The Guardian*.

Katz, E. (1957). The two-step flow of communication: An up-to-date report on an hypothesis. *Public Opinion Quarterly*, 21(1): 61–78.

King, C. W., and Summers, J. O. (1970). Overlap of opinion leadership across consumer product categories. *Journal of Marketing Research*, 7(1): 43–50.

Leonard-Barton, D. (1985). Experts as negative opinion leaders in the diffusion of a technological innovation. *Journal of Consumer Research*, 11(4): 914–26.

Levy, M. R. (1979). Watching TV news as para-social interaction. *Journal of Broadcasting & Electronic Media*, 23(1): 69–80.

Mangold, F., and Bachl, M. (2018). New news media, new opinion leaders? How political opinion leaders navigate the modern high-choice media environment. *Journal of Communication*, 68(5): 896–919.

Meyer, D. S. (1995). The challenge of cultural elites: Celebrities and social movements. *Sociological Inquiry*, 65(2): 181–206.

Nisbet, M. C., and Kotcher, J. E. (2009). A two-step flow of influence? Opinion-leader campaigns on climate change. *Science Communication*, 30(3): 328–54.

Ohanian, R. (1991). The impact of celebrity spokespersons' perceived image on consumers' intention to purchase. *Journal of Advertising Research*.

Powell, L., Richmond, V. P., and Cantrell-Williams, G. (2012). The "Drinking-Buddy" scale as a measure of para-social behavior. *Psychological Reports* 110(3): 1029–37.

Shrum, L. J., McCarty, J. A., and Lowrey, T. M. (1995). Buyer characteristics of the green consumer and their implications for advertising strategy. *Journal of Advertising*, 24(2): 71–82.

Toncar, M., Reid, J. S., and Anderson, C. E. (2007). Effective spokespersons in a public service announcement: National celebrities, local celebrities and victims. *Journal of Communication Management*.

Venkatraman, M. P. (1989). Opinion leaders, adopters, and communicative adopters: A role analysis. *Psychology & Marketing*, 6(1): 51–68.

Watts, D. J., and Dodds, P. S. (2007). Influentials, networks, and public opinion formation. *Journal of Consumer Research*, 34(4): 441–58.

Weimann, G., Tustin, D. H., Van Vuuren, D., and Joubert, J. P. R. (2007). Looking for opinion leaders: Traditional vs. modern measures in traditional societies. *International Journal of Public Opinion Research*, 19(2): 173–90.

Chapter Three

Public Relations, Advocacy, and Activism

This chapter focuses on the interplay of public relations and advocacy strategies with environmental communication. Learning objectives of the chapter include the contextualizing of environmental public relations and advocacy through U.S. and international examples, and the tracing of key concepts from the field of public relations that helped shape the trajectory of modern strategic environmentalism. The examples provided in this chapter demonstrate the conceptual underpinnings of environmental public relations and advocacy, and how such communication shapes successful public communication campaigns.

THE SIERRA CLUB BUILDS ON TRADITION OF DIALOGUE AND ENGAGEMENT

The Sierra Club is one of America's oldest, largest, and most influential environmental groups. As a grassroots environmental organization, it strives to promote public health, sustainability, and natural conservation through a prolific communication mix of activism, education, political lobbying, and legal action. Every day, strategic communication practice drives this advocacy. The Sierra Club's national and regional offices regularly issue press releases, media advisories, organizational statements, and environmental studies. The organization also engages stakeholders, members, and the general public through engagement opportunities and action items. In recent years, the Sierra Club's press room issued applause for the creation of an Office of Environmental Justice and External Civil Rights; broke news that Shell had canceled its investment in a fracked gas export terminal proposed for southwest Louisiana; and issued a statement lamenting coal plant expenditures by the state of Virginia. Its employment of public and media relations allows the Sierra Club to amplify its reach, influence key decision-makers across the country, and build trust and rapport with stakeholders and the public.

The Sierra Club isn't alone in its usage of extensive public relations to bolster its green mission. The roles of strategic communication and public dialogue in impacting environmental and social change have enjoyed a dynamic trajectory over the past century, coinciding with social and environmental shifts in our society. Going back a century ago, the profession of public relations was based on the primarily company-sanctioned perspectives of practitioners like Edward Bernays, Ivy Lee, and Arthur Page. Bernays drew from the traditions of psychology and persuasion to situate public relations as a powerful force for influence in modern society. Lee and Page helped foster a concept of public relations as a management function that optimized relations between an organization and the public.

In turn, the public relations industry they helped foster during the first half of the twentieth century became the platform for a growing field over the coming decades, and a mode of communication practice that was embraced not only by companies, but also nonprofits, community organizations, and environmental advocates. James Grunig, a mass communications theorist from the University of Maryland, drew from thinkers such as John Dewey and Jürgen Habermas in developing a framework that would explain public relations' role in society. Dewey and the Chicago School of Philosophy envisioned an instrumental role for communication in civil society, and its role in facilitating democratic citizenship. Habermas, a German philosopher whose work addresses the intersection of communication, ethics, and democracy, offered a theory of the *public sphere* that recognized the importance of including all voices in societal argumentation for the optimization of public life and society.

PUBLIC RELATIONS' FOCUS ON PUBLICS

Based on these perspectives, Grunig proposed a model of public relations that established two-way, *symmetrical* communication as the aspirational outcome of public relations. This model moved the field away from the tradition established by Edward Bernays, who often employed psychological tactics to sway audiences for company or government causes. Instead, Grunig connected the concept of public relations to an ongoing, two-way dialogue between an organization and its stakeholders or publics. Furthermore, this dialogue existed on a level playing field. Grunig's definition of public relations as a function that mediates between organizations and publics is one that is championed by professional bodies such as the International Association of Business Communicators (IABC) and the Public Relations Society of America (PRSA).

The idea of symmetry or equal-footing dialogue has compelled organizations to create avenues for hearing their constituents and to reach consensus for organizational goals (Grunig and Grunig, 2013). Grunig's theory also argues that it effectively deals with organizational relationships, including interfacing productively with environmental activists, and the rise of interactive public relations activities, such as social media. The remarkable uptake of two-way digital platforms such as Twitter, Instagram, and TikTok—where audiences and constituents have the opportunity to "talk back" to professional communicators on the same technology platform and engage with organizations—holds strong potential for the practice of symmetry. However, this is contingent upon organizations listening to their publics online and responding to them, especially as they look for mutual areas of benefit (Grunig and Kim, 2021).

Publics are defined by their levels of problem recognition, constraint recognition, and involvement for the same issues or problems. Grunig's situational theory (2005) differentiates between active and passive or latent publics, and categorizes these publics based on their behavior toward specific social or political issues. Specific environmental issues can divide publics into high- or low-involvement tendencies, and these categorizations intertwine with four behavioral approaches: problem-facing, constrained, routine, and fatalistic. In addition, an overlooked group that strategic communicators need to be

	High Involvement	Low Involvement
Problem-Facing Behavior High Problem Recognition Low Constraint Recognition	*Active Public*	*Active/Aware Public*
Constrained Behavior High Problem Recognition HighConstraint Recognition	*Aware/Active Public*	*Latent/Aware Public*
Routine Behavior LowProblem Recognition Low Constraint Recognition	*Active (Reinforcing) Public*	*None/Latent Public*
Fatalistic Behavior LowProblem Recognition High Constraint Recognition	*Latent Public*	*Non Public*

Figure 3.1.   Prioritizing stakeholders for public relations (Rawlins, 2006). Adapted from Grunig's Situational Theory of Publics.

mindful of is inactive publics, who typically have low levels of knowledge of, or involvement with, a political or environmental issue (Hallahan, 2000).

One of the practical takeaways from this breakdown of different stakeholders is that strategic communicators will spend more time focusing on active publics, because by their very nature they are engaged with the organization, they are more aware of ecological issues, and they tend to be more motivated to act on various social challenges and opportunities. Building on the situational theory of publics, public relations scholar Brad Rawlins takes this evolving breakdown of stakeholders one step further, dividing stakeholders into four distinct groups: advocate (active and supportive), dormant (inactive but supportive), adversarial (non-supportive but active), and apathetic (inactive and non-supportive or adversarial) (Rawlins, 2006). The first two groups might provide the environmental communicator with favorable interpersonal communication to groups and networks along with message amplification and live-time engagement such as volunteering. The latter two categories, however, might result in campaign failure or even organizational crisis if they are not afforded their due attention.

Other public relations theories developed for social, environmental, or risk communication issues have emerged to make sense of how organizations utilize specific strategic communication tactics to meet communication objectives or ward off crisis. For example, a collaborative effort between Ketchum Public Relations in Atlanta, the University of Georgia, and the University of Alabama developed a concept known as *contingency theory*, which puts forth eighty-six variables that organizations need to be cognizant of in developing communication programs and responses, particularly during times of organizational emergency (Cancel et al., 1997).

GREENPEACE CHANGES THE PR EQUATION

When facing environmental problems or opportunities, organizations must decide to what degree they will choose to self-advocate or accommodate a disgruntled or oppositional group. In the case of environmental advocacy, some corporations choose to accommodate or work with adversarial groups, while others are inclined to advocate for themselves or downplay any conflict for fear of damage to their organizational reputation (Cancel, Mitrook, and Cameron, 1999). The flip side of this scenario emphasizes the role of environmental activists as strategic and often necessary disrupters. Since the 1990s, some scholars and activists have challenged the prevailing view of public relations as a two-way, symmetrical enterprise. In part this arose from contested issues that emerged in the 1960s and 1970s—including anti-war activism, civil rights, and the rise of modern environmentalism. In many ways, activism has changed traditional public relations equations and forced practitioners to reconsider their approaches (Derville, 2005). Another scholar studying the phenomenon of environmental activists and their relationship with companies was Larissa Grunig (1989), who noticed the success of informational but also rhetorical tactics within environmental debates, many of which were polarizing and confrontational. In many cases, the two-way communication ideal, while useful for organizations, was not always the goal for green activists or the optimal mode for publics within larger environmental disputes.

The early legacy of Greenpeace provides a case in point. For example, Greenpeace had a number of encounters with multinational company DuPont, which for much of the twentieth century was one of the worst corporate polluters in the United States. In exploring the conflict between Greenpeace and DuPont, researchers Murphy and Dee (1992) noted that the two organizations had different motivations that precluded any kind of consensus. Especially important is that Greenpeace's motives and extreme actions were rooted in a win-at-all-costs mindset. Because of Greenpeace's organizational structure and the different objectives of the movement, it was impossible for Greenpeace to meet DuPont halfway—what green supporters might have dubbed as "compromise" or even "co-optation." A similar observation was made by Michael Karlberg (1996), who applied the public relations lens to the well-publicized fights over clear-cut logging in British Columbia during the 1990s. Karlberg argued that the public relations field, including researchers, had not kept up with changes brought about by environmental activists, and that the profession was remiss in not elevating communities and publics to a greater extent. In Karlberg's view, the field needed to move from theoretical symmetry to symmetry in practice.

Public relations is also closely connected to cultural practices. Addressing the public relations outcomes gap identified by Karlberg and others, Caroline Hodges of the Media School at Bournemouth University in the United Kingdom has situated the public relations role as one of *cultural intermediation*. This includes the role of strategic communication within the urban landscape, which comprises everything from public speeches and protests to outdoor signage and retail messaging. Given the relationship between citizens of a metropolitan region and their urban environment, such an approach is particularly useful in studying how social movement or advocacy organizations utilize their civic outdoor spaces as a means of engaging publics. Environmental public communication, like the physical setting in which it can be embedded, continues to evolve, and environmentalism is helping drive this process. Fortunately, these shifts have increasingly moved the concept of public relations to a better alignment with the public and publics.

ACTIVISM AND ADVOCACY BY NGOS AND NONPROFITS

To properly understand the role of public discourse in impacting environmental and social change, one must go beyond traditional mass media disciplines such as public relations, political communication, and journalism and engage with the dynamic communication realms of advocacy and activism. Grassroots campaigns and activist movements have been among the most significant factors in determining contemporary forms of environmentalism.

Along with communication scholars, sociologists and political scientists have long sought to understand the processes that make activists and social movements successful. Social psychology plays a major role, especially in terms of how activist organizations recruit, retain, and engage their memberships. A theoretical framework of note comes from sociologist Douglas McAdam, whose study of the Civil Rights Movement gave rise to his political process model. This model shows that successful social movements draw from and take advantage of current and historical circumstances. The trajectory of such movements, hinged upon such an "aligning of stars," should then follow the pathway that is articulated in the diffusion of innovation model. In other words, the social movement and its ideas spread from core members or activists to larger audiences, thus paving the way for more support, more sympathy, and more impact. In the case of civil rights, McAdam noted that influential and well-placed Black churches were critical for the transmission of ideas during the Civil Rights Movement, as political ideas spread from church leadership to the congregation and then outward to social clubs, businesses, and other networks.

Another activism expert, Clifford Bob, provides a more pragmatic view of the role of strategic communication in environmental social movements. His study of the Ogoni people's movement in Nigeria, which focused on both human rights and environmental issues, highlights the advantages of infusing activism with strategy. Comparing the concurrent Ogoni movements within the country, he noted that the more successful environmental movement (the Movement for the Survival of the Ogoni People) had established strong media contacts with journalists from the BBC, acquired funding from Greenpeace, and positioned itself toward a more strident environmental position as a result of Greenpeace's involvement (Bob, 2005). This shows the critical role of mediated and strategic activism. Environmental activists who are savvy with media publications and have extensive journalist contacts have an advantage over other groups, and are more likely to grow their membership and gain a foothold with publics and the media.

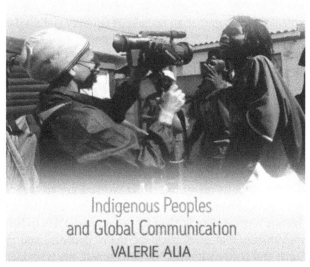

Figure 3.2. The late Valerie Alia's book The New Media Nation *shows how Indigenous communities globally increasingly use digital and independent media technologies to overcome barriers in the corporate media to communicate traditional and local cultures but also pressing human rights and environmental issues. (Berghahn Books)*

Globalization has created new publics and constituencies within environmental and social activism that are not always readily apparent at the country or organization level. An example comes from North America's Indigenous nations, whose tribal communities sometimes emphasize sovereignty and deemphasize traditional nation-state citizenship. As issues like climate change and oil extraction impact such groups, new approaches will be needed to assess their communication in light of competing interests, national objectives, and even interpretations of history and the environment. The late Valerie Alia, an expert in Indigenous mass media and communication, referred to the convergence of Indigenous media voices from around the world as a "New Media Nation." Within such an international media configuration, tribal and Indigenous communities can bypass traditional or corporate media institutions and communicate with each other and their stakeholders directly via independent modes of communication such as digital, satellite, and broadcasting.

The existence of public communication for social change at different levels—grassroots, local, state, national, global—is necessary to incorporate the complexity of today's social and ecological issues. The spiral of advocacy model (Mundy, 2013) shows how civil rights organizations in seven U.S. states used a ground-up approach, as opposed to the more predominant top-down explanations, to garner an agenda of equality and civil rights at the national level. Understanding the existing and emerging forms and trajectories of grassroots advocacy and activism is helpful not only for understanding social change movements, but also the institutions that such movements interface with.

WOMEN TAKE THE LEAD IN GREEN
ADVOCACY AND PUBLIC RELATIONS

Perhaps it should come as no surprise that women are so well represented in the realms of environmental advocacy and leadership. After all, there is a tradition of female engagement in shaping environmental activism, ideology, and social movements that goes back for many decades, and includes the marine biologist and conservationist Rachel Carson, the prominent ecofeminist and philosopher Carolyn Merchant, and the social activist and filmmaker Naomi Klein.

They are joined by dozens of other leading intellectuals, scholars, and activists. And they have led some of the most prominent green movements, including the uprising of citizens in western New York State in the wake of the Love Canal disaster. It's not just that individual women have historically taken on bold intellectual and leadership positions in the arena of environmentalism. Previous research has shown that women collectively are more inclined to oppose global warming and climate change than men are (Joireman, 2014; McCright, 2010).

Women continue to take up leadership roles with international and national organizations. For example, by 2018, North America's three national Greenpeace organizations (Canada, Mexico, and the United States) all had women situated in executive director roles. Greenpeace USA most recently featured two women—Annie Leonard and Ebony Martin—as co–executive directors. This leadership is helping green organizations like Greenpeace not only serve women effectively, but also to consider differences in gender when trying to persuade publics with communication campaigns or even paid advertising.

This strong representation in environmentalism is not without its own challenges. According to a 2018 research report from Mintel, a UK-based market intelligence firm, there is an emergent "eco gender gap" showing that men are less likely to pursue environmentally friendly behaviors than women, and this phenomenon has real-world implications for green communicators. Part of this disconnect might be attributed to green marketing that reinforces gender stereotypes of both men and women. According to Mintel, "At a time where so many advertisers are exploring what it means to be a man, there are opportunities for brands to create campaigns that will reposition environmentally friendly behaviors as part of modern masculinity."

In the future, women are expected to play an even larger role in dealing with planetary climate change. In particular, women in the Global South will be at the forefront of the issue because of their proximity to the most significant environmental impacts in developing countries and their ability to personally establish on-the-ground solutions. One of these leaders already making an enormous difference is Vanessa Nakate, the founder of the Rise Up Climate Movement. Nakate, who is from Uganda, established the campaign to stop

Figure 3.3.   Vanessa Nakate, the founder of the Rise Up Climate Movement, established the advocacy effort to stop the deforestation of the Congo rainforest. Her environmental campaign was later adopted by other countries in Africa and Europe. (SaveCongoRainforest.wixsite.com.)

the deforestation of the Congo rainforest. Her communication and lobbying campaign was later adopted by other countries in Europe and Africa.

Nakate has been a leading voice for young people in global climate change discussions, and has used her own life experiences to connect ecological disasters to weather volatility and disruptive ecological events. "The climate issue is a life issue," she told EarthDay.org. "We have to keep fighting until we see the action that we are demanding. Above all, I want people to stop dying as a result of climate change."

TACTITIAN'S TOOLBOX: CALLS TO ACTION FOSTER AUDIENCE ACTION

Creating a cohesive message that aligns members of an environmental or social movement organization remains a constant challenge. How do members of a group connect a specific problem to an overarching social or ecological issue? For example, members of an organization concerned with reducing automobile emissions in their community might come to the cause, and to the organization, for a multitude of reasons. Some individuals might have human health concerns, while others are concerned with regional climate issues, while others yet are concerned with larger matters of environmental justice.

Social movement collective action frames provide one opportunity for groups to better understand their mission. In short, these collective action frames offer a means to simultaneously understand an issue and contextualize it in the bigger picture. The sociologists Richard Snow and John Benford (2000) described collective action frames as imparting a shared understanding of multiple scenarios: a situation in need of change, an attribution of blame, an articulation of a different course of action, or a call to action for interested parties. This builds upon an earlier focus on frame alignment processes, such as the alignment of different frames within a movement, and the amplification of frames to larger audiences through public events and media outreach (Snow et al., 1986). These are known as *micromobilization* processes, and they are used to align a social movement organization's goals and ideology with the values and beliefs of targeted individuals.

Related to this is what is often referred to in public communication and marketing as a *call to action*. For the green communicator looking to mobilize an organization's members as well as members of the public or the media, this mode of outreach provides a means of activating members and stakeholders and extending the power of communication beyond persuasion and cognitive shift.

Tell Congress: Support the Green New Deal

PETITION

(Ron and Jeanne Crumly on their land on the proposed Keystone XL pipeline route in Nebraska. (Photo: Mary Anne Andrei) Add your name: Support the Green New Deal Today, Rep. Alexandria Ocasio-Cortez and Sen. Ed Markey are introducing the Green New Deal resolution in Congress. [1] The Green New Deal seeks to protect farmers and [...]

Figure 3.4.   Bold Nebraska, an affiliate of the national advocacy organziation Bold Alliance, worked with an alliance of farmers, ranchers, and tribal communities to protest the contentious Keystone XL petroleum pipeline project. The organization used calls to action to activate its base of supporters to engage state-based and national politicians, and to raise money for the organization. (BoldNebraska.org.)

This public communication tactic typically takes the form of a targeted phrase that implores the audience of a text or message to some kind of direct action (Deshpande, 2013; Luttrell and Capizzo, 2021). It is intended to provoke an immediate response or engagement by urging audiences to make contact with the organization, learn more about a product or issue, or even make a physical visit to a location or event (Guillory, 2015). At the heart of the call to action, therefore, is a two-way communication that emphasizes active public engagement with an organization. These calls are used by public relations practitioners in tandem with specific public relations or branding channels, such as blogs, to allow audiences to deepen their engagement with organizations (Luttrell and Capizzo, 2021).

CASE STUDY: HASHTAG ACTIVISM AND #IDLENOMORE

The digital and social media revolution of the past two decades has had profound implications for business and politics. But it has also transformed the way marginalized communities engage with the public to tell their story and shift public policy in their quest for social and environmental justice. One such means is through hashtag activism.

The term *hashtag activism* entered the public consciousness by way of *New York Times* media columnist David Carr (2012), who described the extension of social movements into the mainstream through social networks. The social media hashtag is a communication organizing tool for digital platforms. It allows activists (and indeed any social media users invested in any issue or event) to aggregate and streamline messages for social networks such as Twitter and Instagram. By allowing users to cluster their social media messages, such as tweets, around a single issue, they are able to maximize their communication potential through more powerful networks, wider message distribution, and sometimes even message virality.

In the last decade, there has been growing public interest in hashtag activism in the wake of the digital efforts of the Arab Spring and Occupy movements and, more recently, the social justice campaigns for #BlackLivesMatter and #MeToo. Another movement that leveraged the hashtag's potential is that of #IdleNoMore. The movement became a digital rallying cry for Canada's

Coast Protectors @CoastProtectors · Sep 25, 2019   ...
"There is no justice for #IndigenousPeoples without **climate** justice." -- Grand Chief Stewart Phillip

#StrikeforClimateJustice #GlobalClimateStrike #cdnpoli #StopTMX #bcpoli #TransMountain #NoTankers #NYCClimateStrike #NativeTwitter #IdleNoMore #ClimateWeekNYC #ClimateWeek2019

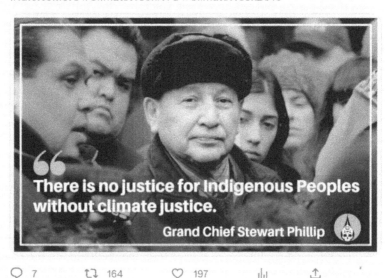

○ 7   ↻ 164   ♡ 197   ılıl   ⬆

Figure 3.5.   This 2019 Twitter post, quoting Grand Chief Steward Phillip of the Union of British Columbia Indian Chiefs, shows the staying power of the #IdleNoMorehashtag as a means to aggregating messages about Indigenous communities and climate change. (@CoastProtectors/Twitter.)

Indigenous nations that were adversely impacted by the country's social and environmental policies. One of the takeaways from the #IdleNoMore movement in Canada was that tribal nations can use social media to not only amplify messages of their own, but also provide counterpoints to reports in the mainstream, traditional press. In other words, the hashtag allows activists to push back against traditional media narratives that are cloaked in outdated or biased views from journalists who aren't well versed in a specific topic or willing to engage fairly with participants in a public controversy.

In the case of #IdleNoMore, Canada's national daily newspapers, like the *Globe and Mail*, eventually began sourcing stories from the hashtag itself, which ushered in a new wave of media coverage of Canada's First Nations and Aboriginal communities, and the opportunity for activists to shift the narratives in the press. The #IdleNoMore movement was not only reaching millions of Canadians; the hashtag then became the foundation for a larger Indigenous peoples movement in the United States and around the world.

CASE STUDY: TRANSBOUNDARY ADVOCACY HIGHLIGHTS CONCERNS FOR WATER AND WILDLIFE

In 2022, communities in the Pacific Northwest received some promising news about the future of the ecologically important Skagit River, and specifically the long-term health of the river's headwaters just north of the Canadian border, about three hours east of Vancouver, British Columbia. As a result of a public relations effort driven by environmental stakeholders from the United States and Canada, the B.C. government entered into an agreement with an entity called the Skagit Environmental Endowment Commission (SEEC) to have all mining rights at the headwaters site—also known as the Donut Hole—purchased from a Canadian gold mining company and turned over to provincial oversight. In other words, the gold exploration program slated for the upper reaches of this river, which travels through the heart of the North Cascades National Park Complex, had been effectively quashed.

The campaign was notable for its dramatic flavor, as the cross-border collective of advocacy groups situated themselves as the protagonists in a moral showdown with a company called Imperial Metals. The gold mining outfit, of course, shared a name with the antagonistic Imperial Army in the *Star Wars* film franchise. "There is no doubt that Imperial Metals is aptly named," noted Washington Wild's Tom Uniack, referring to the company's scope of operations across British Columbia. "We felt like Rebel Fighters on the hot planet," he said, referring to a popular scene from the movie *Star Wars: The Empire Strikes Back*. But the coalition of advocates also used a more grounded advocacy, where conservationists spent time guiding members of the media and key decision-makers around the headwaters area. "One of the things we do is 'on the ground,'" said Joe Foy of the Wilderness Committee in British Columbia. "I went up there multiple times in all of the seasons; we took multiple videos, including drone videos, made available to all of our allies including our Washington State allies and also the media." Foy's guided trips for reporters, along with his production of videography showcasing the ecological value of the area, paid major dividends in subsequent media coverage.

There were many good reasons for protecting the 5,800-hectare (14,330-acre) section of mountain peaks, lush valleys, and rushing creeks in this north-of-the-border stretch of the Cascades ecosystem, surrounded by western Canada's E.C. Manning and Skagit Valley Provincial Parks. They included impacts on outdoor recreation but also the ongoing health of the larger Skagit watershed, which helps define significant parts of the Pacific Northwest's geography and cultural heritage. The Skagit River's long-standing tribal history was also a significant factor. Several tribes located in the Skagit basin—including the Swinomish, Upper Skagit, and Sauk-Suiattle—voiced formal opposition to the mining project due to worries for established treaty rights for fishing and hunting in the larger watershed. The Samish Tribe also highlighted the toxic threat to the large number of bald eagles that converge on the river during the winter months to feed on salmon.

These concerns for wildlife habitat loom especially large, including the plight of northern spotted owls, which have been decimated over the years by logging and other industrial encroachments. The larger headwaters area is also prime habitat for mule deer and black bears, and it could play a central role in the proposed reintroduction of grizzly bears to the North Cascades ecosystem south of the border. The Skagit River also provides an important barometer for the health of migratory fish. In a 2022 press release issued by the B.C. government, Skagit endowment co-chair Leo Bodensteiner noted that the upper Skagit River "transcends geographical boundaries as this watershed provides a critical corridor for salmon, steelhead and bull trout, which have protected status on both sides of the border."

To their credit, and in the spirit of an emergent ecological diplomacy, governments in Canada and the United States are increasingly vocal about the health of their countries' shared rivers, lakes, and oceans. Canadian politician John Horgan noted that the Skagit public relations effort could be a precursor to productive cross-border deliberations about other transboundary watersheds in the region, including the Columbia, Nooksack, and Fraser Rivers, along with the Salish Sea. The cross-border movement formed to oppose the Donut Hole mining project was therefore historically significant.

The coalition of environmental advocates deployed a prolific operation of media relations, government lobbying, and public engagements to facilitate a larger, regional dialogue about the importance of the transboundary Skagit watershed across multiple jurisdictions in Cascadia. But there is more to the Donut Hole saga than a vocal alliance of conservation groups, tribal leaders, politicians, and small businesses stopping a lucrative precious metals project in its track. The untold story was the establishment of an effective cross-border advocacy infrastructure that can foster collaborative dialogue and policy action in the borderlands and beyond—without getting hung up on national interests or differences.

The U.S./Canada Skagit River ordeal has sounded the alarm on other threats to shared transboundary watersheds—including extraction projects that loom over Cascadia's watersheds—and underscores the critical role of environmental diplomacy in the years ahead. Public relations efforts like #SavetheSkagit show that a combination of communication acumen and cross-border diplomacy goes a long way in preserving North America's shared ecosystems for future generations.

DISCUSSION QUESTIONS

1. What are the advantages of symmetric public relations for environmentalists? Are there cases where it is disadvantageous?
2. How should environmental activists interface with organizations, and vice versa?
3. What factors have contributed to women playing an outsized role in global leadership for environmental protection and the climate movement?
4. How does diffusion work? Why is it important in the work of activism and advocacy?
5. Describe a "call to action" that you are familiar with. Were you moved to act by an appeal or request?
6. How does the spiral of advocacy work? How might it bring positive change to a community or region?

KEYWORDS

Activism
Advocacy
Call to action
Collective action frame

Cultural intermediation
Diffusion
Eco gender gap
Hashtag activism
Micromobilization
Nongovernmental organization (NGO)
Nonprofit
Political process model
Public relations
Publics
Social movement
Spiral of advocacy
Stakeholders
Symmetry

KEY EVENTS, LOCATIONS, AND ORGANIZATIONS

Greenpeace
#IdleNoMore
Love Canal
Movement for the Survival of the Ogoni People
Rise Up Climate Movement
Sierra Club

REFERENCES

Alia, V. (2022). *The New Media Nation: Indigenous Peoples and Global Communication.* New York: Berghahn Books.

Benford, R. D., and Snow, D. A. (2000). Framing processes and social movements: An overview and assessment. *Annual Review of Sociology*, 611–39.

Bob, C. (2005). *The Marketing of Rebellion: Insurgents, Media, and International Activism.* Cambridge, UK: Cambridge University Press.

Cancel, A. E., Cameron, G. T., Sallot, L. M., and Mitrook, M. A. (1997). It depends: A contingency theory of accommodation in public relations. *Journal of Public Relations Research*, 9(1): 31–63.

Cancel, A. E., Mitrook, M. A., and Cameron, G. T. (1999). Testing the contingency theory of accommodation in public relations. *Public Relations Review*, 25(2): 171–97.

Carr, D. (2012). Hashtag activism, and its limits. *New York Times*, March 25.

Derville, T. (2005). Radical activist tactics: Overturning public relations conceptualizations. *Public Relations Review*, 31(4): 527–33.

Deshpande, P. (2013). 5 tips every content curator needs to write better calls to action. *Content Marketing Institute*. Retrieved from: https://contentmarketinginstitute .com/articles/tips-content-curator-write-better-calls-to-action/.

Grunig, J. E. (1989). A situational theory of environmental issues, publics, and activists. In Grunig, L. A. (ed.), *Environmental Activism Revisited: The Changing Nature of Communication through Public Relations, Special Interest Groups, and the Mass Media*, 50–82.

Grunig, J. E. (2005). Situational theory of publics. *Encyclopedia of Public Relations*. Thousand Oaks, CA: Sage, 778–80.

Grunig, J. E., and Grunig, L. A. (2013). Models of public relations and communication. *Excellence in Public Relations and Communication Management*, 285–325.

Grunig, J. E., and Kim, J. N. (2021). 15 The four models of public relations and their research legacy. In Valentini, C. (ed.), *Public Relations*, Vol. 27, 277.

Grunig, L. A. (1989). Environmental activism revisited: The changing nature of communication through organizational public relations, special interest groups and the mass media. *Monographs in Environmental Education and Environmental Studies*, Vol. V.

Guillory, S. (2015). How's your press release call to action? *Cision*. Retrieved from: https://web.archive.org/web/20150803072457/http://www.cision.com/us/2015/05/ hows-your-press-release-call-to-action/.

Hallahan, K. (2000). Inactive publics: The forgotten publics in public relations. *Public Relations Review* 26(4): 499–515.

Joireman, J., and Liu, R. L. (2014). Future-oriented women will pay to reduce global warming: Mediation via political orientation, environmental values, and belief in global warming. *Journal of Environmental Psychology* 40: 391–400.

Karlberg, M. (1996). Remembering the public in public relations research: From theoretical to operational symmetry. *Journal of Public Relations Research*, 8(4): 263–78.

Luttrell, R. M., and Capizzo, L. W. (2021). *Public Relations Campaigns: An Integrated Approach*. Thousand Oaks, CA: Sage.

McCright, A. M. (2010). The effects of gender on climate change knowledge and concern in the American public. *Population and Environment*, 32(1): 66–87.

Mintel.com. (2018). The eco gender gap. Retrieved from: https://www.mintel.com/ press-centre/social-and-lifestyle/the-eco-gender-gap-71-of-women-try-to-live -more-ethically-compared-to-59-of-men.

Mundy, D. E. (2013). The spiral of advocacy: How state-based LGBT advocacy organizations use ground-up public communication strategies in their campaigns for the "Equality Agenda." *Public Relations Review*, 39(4): 387–90.

Murphy, P., and Dee, J. (1992). Du Pont and Greenpeace: The dynamics of conflict between corporations and activist groups. *Journal of Public Relations Research*, 4(1), 3–20.

Rawlins, B. L. (2006). Prioritizing stakeholders for public relations. *Institute for Public Relations*, 1: 14.

Snow, D. A., Rochford Jr., E. B., Worden, S. K., and Benford, R. D. (1986). Frame alignment processes, micromobilization, and movement participation. *American Sociological Review*, 464–81.

Chapter Four

Persuasion and Visual Rhetoric

This chapter focuses on the outsized role of persuasion and rhetoric in shaping contemporary strategic environmentalism. Learning objectives of the chapter include the contextualizing of discursive and visual rhetoric in the identification and branding of protected ecologies, and the role of prominent communicators from the past and present in rhetorically configuring environmental appeals. The examples provided in this chapter help demonstrate different approaches of persuasion and rhetoric, and help signify how they can mobilize publics and policymakers to action through the strategic construction of communicative appeals.

A SPEECH TO REMEMBER

During the fall of 2019, the high-profile climate activist Greta Thunberg left a lasting impact on a United Nations audience during her address at the U.N.'s Climate Action Summit in New York City. Thunberg's speech resonated far and wide not only for its informational value, but also for the way it emotionally implored politicians and global leaders to take immediate action on climate change. "You have stolen my dreams and my childhood with your empty words. And yet I'm one of the lucky ones," she exclaimed to the summit. "People are suffering. People are dying. Entire ecosystems are collapsing. We are in the beginning of a mass extinction, and all you can talk about is money and fairy tales of eternal economic growth. How dare you!"

Thunberg's declaration was a way of shaming political inaction. Yet her words not only reverberated throughout the U.N.'s Climate Action Summit. Her speech was watched by millions of people across the world, and was rebroadcast by international media outlets. The now-famous (or infamous)

Figure 4.1. Greta Thunberg's address at the United Nation's Climate Action Summit resonated far and wide. Thunberg, seen here at the 2019 Climate March in Montreal, emotionally implored politicians and global leaders to take immediate action on climate change. (Lëa-Kim Châteauneuf/Wikimedia Commons.)

"how dare you" speech is the perfect example of how communication infused with rhetorical appeals can shift public awareness and opinion surrounding a public interest issue like climate change. Thunberg's address is one of the more recent examples of a long-standing tradition of persuasion and rhetoric in environmental public relations.

CHANGING HEARTS TO SAVE AMERICA'S WILD SPACES

At the heart of John Muir's legacy of environmental advocacy was the expert usage of rhetorically constructed persuasion. Muir sought to change hearts and minds for the conservation of forests and wild spaces; for preserving the ecological sanctity of a rapidly industrializing country at the turn of the twentieth century; and for pushing back against the worst excesses of the resource extraction economy, including forestry and mining but also runaway agriculture and urban development. He did this by grounding his rhetorical appeals—articulated in speeches, stories, poems, and reports—with a moral authority derived from his faith and his vision of nature as the perfect creation of a higher power. Muir's long-standing green advocacy presents a compelling focal point for understanding the confluence of persuasion and media because his appeals to nature established green advocacy as the precursor to transformations in American life.

Over the course of several decades of publishing his feature articles for the press along with poems, books, and speeches, Muir didn't just advocate for immediate or local policy changes. His persuasion represented a larger call to the shifting political, economic, and spiritual paradigms in the country. Muir's environmental advocacy channeled a higher power to connect America's forests, plains, and mountainscapes to notions of the afterlife and supernatural creation. Historians know this persuasion to be part of the fabric of many institutions at the turn of the twentieth century. Yet there has been a return to this tradition of rhetorically constructed environmental persuasion. The rhetorical turn for many of these social institutions, which thrived during the nineteenth century before giving way to other styles, is again enjoying popularity in the twenty-first century.

Over the course of his decades-long fight to save America's natural spaces—including forests, mountain ranges, and watersheds—Muir proved to be a prolific strategic communicator. He wrote extensively for leading national magazines, including *Harper's* and *The Atlantic*, in extending his ecological worldview and pushing back against the interests of lumbermen, gold miners, and land squatters, but also federal politicians and forest managers. In the August 1897 issue of *The Atlantic*, for example, in his essay "The American Forests," Muir established North America's wild spaces as a direct creation of a higher power, in direct contrast to the reckless exploitation of nature during his time: "The forests of America, however slighted by man, must have been a great delight to God," he wrote. Yet, he continued, "The outcries we hear against forest reservations come mostly from thieves who are wealthy and steal timber by wholesale. They have so long been allowed to steal and destroy in peace that any impediment to forest robbery is denounced as a cruel and irreligious interference with 'vested rights,' likely to endanger the repose of all ungodly welfare."

Here, Muir drew from a strong basis of Christian faith to immerse his appeals to conservation in the kind of environmental idealism that was prevalent during the turn of the twentieth century. Yet Muir's advocacy was unique in that his rhetoric was laden with populist appeals that simultaneously attacked the federal government, big banks, and forestry companies. Today, Muir's written construction of nature serves as a medium through which humanity can learn or recalibrate not only the sense of higher purpose, but the configuration of a moral order. We might consider his advocacy in relation to theology more broadly, particularly in the embrace of an ecological spirituality (Shore-Goss, 2016).

THE

ATLANTIC MONTHLY:

A Magazine of Literature, Science, Art, and Politics.

Vol. LXXX. — AUGUST, 1897. — No. CCCCLXXVIII.

THE AMERICAN FORESTS.

THE forests of America, however slighted by man, must have been a great delight to God; for they were the best he ever planted. The whole continent was a garden, and from the beginning it seemed to be favored above all the other wild parks and gardens of the globe. To prepare the ground, it was rolled and sifted in seas with infinite loving deliberation and forethought, lifted into the light, submerged and warmed over and over again, pressed and crumpled into folds and ridges, mountains and hills, subsoiled with heaving volcanic fires, ploughed and ground and sculptured into scenery and soil with glaciers and rivers, — every feature growing and changing from beauty to beauty, higher and higher. And in the fullness of time it was planted in groves, and belts, and broad, exuberant, mantling forests, with the largest, most varied, most fruitful, and most beautiful trees in the world. Bright seas made its border with wave embroidery and icebergs; gray deserts were outspread in the middle of it, mossy tundras on the north, savannas on the south, and blooming prairies and plains; while lakes and rivers shone through all the vast forests and openings, and happy birds and beasts gave delightful animation. Everywhere, everywhere over all the blessed continent, there were beauty, and melody, and kindly, wholesome, foodful abundance.

These forests were composed of about five hundred species of trees, all of them in some way useful to man, ranging in size from twenty-five feet in height and less than one foot in diameter at the ground to four hundred feet in height and more than twenty feet in diameter, — lordly monarchs proclaiming the gospel of beauty like apostles. For many a century after the ice-ploughs were melted, nature fed them and dressed them every day; working like a man, a loving, devoted, painstaking gardener; fingering every leaf and flower and mossy furrowed bole; bending, trimming, modeling, balancing, painting them with the loveliest colors; bringing over them now clouds with cooling shadows and showers, now sunshine; fanning them with gentle winds and rustling their leaves; exercising them in every fibre with storms, and pruning them; loading them with flowers and fruit, loading them with snow, and ever making them more beautiful as the years rolled by. Wide-branching oak and elm in endless variety, walnut and maple, chestnut and beech, ilex and locust, touching limb to limb, spread a leafy translucent canopy along the coast of the Atlantic over the wrinkled folds and ridges of the Alleghanies, — a green billowy sea in summer, golden and purple in autumn, pearly gray like a steadfast frozen mist of interlacing branches and sprays in leafless, restful winter.

To the southward stretched dark, level-topped cypresses in knobby, tangled swamps, grassy savannas in the midst of them like lakes of light, groves of gay sparkling spice-trees, magnolias and palms, glossy-leaved and blooming and

Figure 4.2. In his essay "The American Forests," environmentalist John Muir established North America's wild spaces as a direct creation of a higher power. Muir wrote extensively for leading national magazines, including Harper's *and* The Atlantic, *to convey a message of conservation. (Public domain.)*

One of the important takeaways from Muir's magazine advocacy, including his work with *The Atlantic*, is how environmentalism was uniquely embedded in his articles. Muir's arguments were rhetorical and practical at the same time. They communicated the essence of the soil, the mountaintops, and the alpine rivers, and made them simultaneously real *and* supernatural. How did Muir thread this needle? He invoked his own religious faith to connect humankind's destiny to immediate practices, policies, and problems in the ecological space. This totality of advocacy for nature lies at the heart of Muir's environmental rhetoric.

NAMING THE SALISH SEA AND GREAT BEAR RAINFOREST

When visitors to Seattle's iconic waterfront look out onto picturesque Elliott Bay, they may not realize that they are also catching a glimpse of a much larger ecosystem that transcends regional waters and international borders. The bay, along with Puget Sound's many inlets, straits, and basins, exists as part of the much larger Salish Sea.

The name "Salish Sea" was adopted as a name for the coastal waters off southwestern British Columbia and western Washington in 2009. As a relatively recent geographic phenomenon that sprawls across two nation-states and numerous tribal nations, the rhetorically constructed identity of the Salish Sea presents a compelling case. It represents the renaming of both Puget Sound in Washington State, the Georgia Strait in neighboring British Columbia, and the cross-border Strait of Juan de Fuca that funnels the inland waters into the open Pacific.

For outsiders, and even for local citizens, the mishmash of names previous to the Salish Sea naming provided a barrier to holistic discussion about what is really a cohesive ecosystem. Long-standing environmental concerns in the area related to oil tanker traffic, protection of orcas, and the health of salmon populations made getting this geographic identity right especially important.

In 1988, Bert Webber, a marine biologist at Western Washington University, called for a geographic moniker that would capture the entire ecosystem sprawling across the U.S./Canada border. To make this "branding" of the Northwest's inland marine waters happen, Webber went to politicians and the public via lectures, meetings, and media relations. The idea was that having a name to identify an entire area would call special attention to the trans-border interests of not only water and wildlife, but also culture and history. It would pay special recognition to a critical stakeholder: the region's tribal nations. "If you see something, a place that doesn't have a name, there's that old kind of rule of thumb that you can't know something that doesn't have a name," said

Massive phytoplankton bloom
Salish Sea, Aug. 19, 2016

Landsat 8 data courtesy of U.S. Geological Survey
Processed by Pierre Markuse

Figure 4.3. This aerial image of the Salish Sea is typical of the photographs and maps that have helped to grow broad public awareness of this cross-border system that connects British Columbia and Washington state. Global satellite images such as this one help to foster understanding of marine ecosystems, but also specific maritime phenomena such as the massive phytoplankton bloom shown here. (Pierre Markuse/ Wikimedia Commons.)

Webber in a 2017 interview with KNKX Public Radio. "So this ecosystem needed a name." After decades of hearings, consultations, and presentations, the maritime brand finally received a green light. The term Salish Sea was officially designated by the State of Washington and the province of British Columbia in 2009.

The amalgamation of these bodies of waters through a formal naming process served as recognition of the transboundary nature of ecology and wildlife, as well as the region's alliance of Coast Salish tribal and First Nations communities and their long-standing history in this eco-region. According to Webber, the naming of the Salish Sea has come full circle:

> The path to the name started with the concern over crude oil being transported through Washington State waters of the Salish Sea. This new concern of the local (Salish Sea) governments . . . is also about the risks of oil transportation. The Salish Sea name has its roots in the science of the ecology of the inland sea and the importance of a name for the management of the sea's natural resources. That the name is being used to focus attention on management of the Salish Sea indicates to me that the formal adoption of the name by Tribes, First Nations, and the governments of the United States and Canada was meant to be.

The Salish Sea provides an important example of how narrative building through texts and visuals can support the work of ecological science and policy. The naming of marine channels, inlets, and seas within an overarching strategic umbrella provides an example of spatially oriented rhetoric. In this mode, rhetorical appeals through media, including journalism, public relations, and popular culture, can establish a stronger sense of place, a healthier connection to other species, and the opportunity to envision a more sustainable and ecologically healthier world.

BUILDING AWARENESS AND SHAPING VALUES

John Parham, a media and cultural studies scholar at the U.K.'s University of Worcester, situates this kind of rhetoric focused on the language we use to describe geographic and ecological phenomena as formative or constructive in nature. This *constitutive* language binds us to each other but also to the planet. As a persuasive approach, such language not only establishes an initial awareness among publics and policymakers, but it also shapes or reshapes perceptions and cultivates environmental values. Another environmental communication expert, Robert Cox, places this approach, which emphasizes language and other forms of symbolic communication to change the way we see the world, alongside more pragmatic or practical modes of communication where the goal is to foster awareness but also education, persuasion, and even mobilization. Both constitutive and pragmatic modes of rhetoric help inform how strategic communicators might approach ecological problems and opportunities. But the latter is where public communicators need to fine-tune their understanding of issues, audiences, and public sentiment in order to find short- and long-term success.

Rhetorical approaches to persuasion therefore play a significant role within larger public deliberations about the environment. For example, the concept of dialogism—a perspective that emphasizes two-way communication in the service of public issues—should embrace rhetorical appeals in order to achieve social change (Ganesh and Zoller, 2012). Some scholars have chimed in that the perfectly placed sign, slogan, or photograph can ignite a movement or move the needle in press coverage. Another expert in environmental visual rhetoric, Kevin DeLuca, describes this process for environmentalism as *image politics*—the usage and recognition of environmental skirmishes as a potent and particular means for social activists to communicate on a level playing field against companies and governments (2005).

Figure 4.4. Greenpeace members embark on an environmental project on the Elbe River in Hamburg, Germany, during the summer of 2007. In the past, the organization has emphasized attention-catching publicity opportunities such as conflicts with industrial fishing boats on oceans and rivers in order to heighten public awareness of their mission. (Jan Michael Ihl/Wikimedia Commons.)

These ideographic or image-driven moments help organizations like Greenpeace carve out a major role among environmental movements and other political actors. Greenpeace often leads the way in media and communication innovation through attention-catching publicity tactics. But there is a drawback to this approach. Drawing from the case of environmental protests against Russian whaling ships, Deluca argues that eye-catching visuals such as fleeting television images can flatten an issue, sacrificing granularity for media accessibility: "There are no verbal explanations as to why Greenpeace is trying to save the whales, why the whales need to be saved, why Greenpeace has targeted the Russians, which whales are endangered, and what are Greenpeace's critiques of industrialism, anthropocentrism, and progress" (100). This means that environmental advocates should be aware of the appropriate time and place for playing up an issue for media attention, or for deliberating it more thoroughly for the benefit of publics and policymakers. In other words, Greenpeace's heavy emphasis on visuals can forgo granularity for strategic impact if and when it is necessary, especially when sympathetic media coverage is on the line.

SUBVERSION, PRANKS, AND CULTURE JAMMING

During the fall of 2019, international artists converged upon some of the U.K.'s largest cities to take over outdoor advertising space in order to raise awareness of climate change. The artists' "brandalism" program co-opted one hundred commercial billboards and bus shelters to overlay these advertising platforms with green counter-messages of their own. This guerrilla collective of street artists, designers, and satirists ultimately produced over forty-five works of art in order to relay a message of climate change mitigation to the British public. Even as these environmentalists took aim at global automakers like Volkswagen, Ford, and BMW, they were also changing the rules for how organizations communicate about ecological issues. By hijacking these billboards, they transformed marketing and outdoor advertising into a stage for green persuasion.

This is a perfect example of the tradition of subversive rhetoric in environmental advocacy. Green persuasion is not the sole domain of traditional thought leaders, op-ed writers, and crafters of media campaigns. Rather, creative advocates can successfully alter public attention through head-turning tactics in live-time, catching the attention of media to generate publicity, and ultimately making enough noise to foster real-world social impact. In their 2017 book *Culture Jamming: Activism and the Art of Cultural Resistance*, communication scholars Marilyn DeLaure and Moritz Fink examine how

Figure 4.5.   *A coordinated "brandalism" action across Europe in 2022 saw crews take over five hundred corporate advertising messages with satirical artworks conveying messages denouncing the aviation industry's role in climate change. According to the Brandalism organization, "the allure and glamour of high carbon lifestyles such as frequent flying has been purposefully crafted by the advertising industry and shows no signs of relenting." (Brandalism.)*

tactics like street art, parodies, and media hoaxes are providing an interruption to runaway capitalism and consumerism. Drawing from the term *culture jam*, which describes the media tactics that appropriate the language of capitalism and consumer culture, they show how social and environmental activists "jam" or distort the traditional tools of commercialism to amplify social and environmental movements.

Christine Harold, a professor of communication at the University of Washington, argues that culture jamming can provide an effective, attention-worthy form of activism. The strategy is effective because the rhetorical "sabotaging" of status quo messages can offset the effects of industry marketing. However, environmentalists should be wary about how some companies are picking up on this subversive approach. Harold points to recent product advertisements for consumer goods or corporations that offer "revolution" even as they in reality serve the interests of product sales, shareholder returns, or the corporate bottom line.

One effective path forward for grassroots activists seeking to reclaim culture jamming processes might be realized through play and provocation. Harold invokes another related term—*pranking rhetoric*—to describe a process that similarly mixes innovation, political art, and mass media. The upside of this approach is that it moves discourse away from conflict toward humor and entertainment. In this mode of rhetoric, culture and commerce are turned upside down to confront a changing world.

CASE STUDY: PORTLAND'S BILLBOARD BROUHAHA

If you've seen the Academy Award–nominated film *Three Billboards Outside Ebbing, Missouri*, you're well aware that there is a persuasive power embedded in outdoor communication. While *Three Billboards* is a Hollywood creation, there are plenty of examples of how billboard persuasion can be a catalyst for real-world dialogue and change. One such billboard campaign—featuring contentious environmental appeals from the conservation group Oregon Wild—points to how environmentalists are activating nontraditional media to reach out to new audiences and make a splash with the media. In August 2013, the group, along with its environmental partners, launched a campaign called Clearcut Oregon. Highway and airport billboards in the state of Oregon were purchased, not for cautious appeals, but rather some edgier messaging. Oregon Wild's ads riffed on the U.S. state's iconic postcards of appealing mountain-and-forest scenery. Road-trippers, morning commuters, and airline travelers would have embarked on their journeys by seeing the tongue-in-cheek headline reading "Welcome to Oregon: Home of the Clearcut."

The roadside and airport advertisements were not all for laughs, however. They very seriously depicted a close-up visual of a tract of logged timberland amid pristine Pacific Northwest forest. The goal here was to draw attention to clear-cutting proposals by state legislators and existing logging rules in the state. At one point, the campaign was deemed controversial enough that it was actually banned from Portland International Airport, the state's largest airport, by the managing Port of Portland authority. This irked civil liberties advocates and members of the media. An editorial in Portland's *Oregonian* newspaper referred to the saga as the "Port of Portland's billboard brouhaha." After much legal and media debate, the advertisements were eventually allowed to return to the airport along with the other locations across the state.

But this environmental media "brouhaha" created enough waves in the media to make it an ongoing point of public deliberation. On the one hand, the anti-clear-cut logging message was well received by conservationists, outdoor recreation enthusiasts, and the larger environmental community. However, the message was also seen as adversarial by those who viewed

Figure 4.6.   *"Welcome to Oregon, Home of the Clearcut" billboard advertisement produced by Oregon Wild and its partners. The ad campaign satirized the U.S. state's iconic postcards of appealing mountains-and-forests scenery in order to raise awareness of clearcut logging practices in the state. (ClearcutOregon.com.)*

the timber industry as a critical component of the state's economic and jobs picture.

All of this debate begs the question: Did the controversy created by the billboards' messaging win over more Oregonians to the anti-logging position? Or were audiences left unmoved by the edgy billboards and ensuing media coverage? A research study of the Oregon Wild saga using media artifacts from the Clearcut Oregon campaign found that individuals who were exposed to media coverage of the campaign did feel more knowledgeable about this important ecological issue. However, the media coverage did not create greater affinity for Oregon Wild, the sponsor organization.

While the combination of provocative environmental advertising and subsequent media coverage builds greater attention (and insight) of an issue, it doesn't necessarily impart a greater degree of goodwill for the original messenger. This could be attributed to the differences of controlled versus uncontrolled media, such as the difference between paid advertising and news reporting. Once it became a topic of interest to journalists, the Clearcut Oregon campaign became much more politicized and also more complex, in part because the media coverage featured a wide range of voices and stakeholders.

While it's true that media coverage can reinforce a message and amplify it to a much larger audience, it can also muddy the waters by fostering competing arguments or confusing narratives. Still, in the wake of *Three Billboards Outside Ebbing, Missouri*'s popularity and message about the value of outdoor media, it's hard to see social and environmental advocates resisting the allure of these impactful yet unconventional modes of persuasion in the future.

ORGANIZATIONAL PROFILE: GREENPEACE

Since its inception in the 1970s, Greenpeace has earned a reputation for being among the most successful environmental organizations in the world. The organization has its roots in Vancouver, British Columbia, where it launched a well-publicized protest to raise awareness about nuclear weapons testing off the shore of Alaska.

Media and communication have always been a key part of Greenpeace's strategy, and this goes back to its earliest days. During the 1970s, founding member Robert Hunter wrote a daily column for the *Vancouver Sun* during the group's Amchitka mission to interfere with U.S. nuclear testing by sailing a boat out to the scene. Fellow founding member Terry Simmons argued prophetically for the role of media in advocacy. In his study of Washington State's High Ross Dam controversy, he showed how a public environmental controversy could also serve as a media campaign. Then a graduate student at Simon Fraser University in nearby Burnaby, British Columbia, he argued that the decades-long controversy over the raising of the High Ross Dam on the Canada/U.S. international border would not have been possible without media interest: "A public controversy is in large part a media campaign" (Simmons, 1974). He and his media-savvy Greenpeace colleagues, many of whom were journalists and considered themselves hardwired to the theories of famous communication theorist Marshall McLuhan (Dale, 1996), were onto something early on that countless others from the environmental community would eventually emulate.

Today, Greenpeace has established an unwavering presence in the global community by constantly delivering appeals and advocacies that break through to a wide swath of regional and global media. All of this communication savvy builds upon the organization's legacy as a sophisticated producer of green media. During the 1990s, the organization was even given the moniker of "McLuhan's children" (Dale, 1996, 1) as a result of its members' attention to not only the content of their communication but also the media forms in which this information is transmitted. It also underscored Greenpeace's reliance on actions that must resonate with mass audiences and not just political or social elites. The term "McLuhan's children" pays homage to the media theorist's obsession with media technologies and audience psychology, and to the Greenpeace founders who found a way to activate these media capabilities to transform audiences at home. Their advocacy efforts from a half-century ago continue to resonate with modern environmentalists.

TACTICIAN'S TOOLBOX: THE ORGANIZATIONAL SPEECH

Greta Thunberg's now-famous "how dare you" speech at the U.N.'s Climate Action Summit reminds us that a public presentation delivered with the right words and a good knack for timing and delivery can be as powerful as any form of persuasion. Words delivered in live-time are a powerful tonic that can indeed change hearts and minds and drive individuals and nations to action. There really isn't a purer form of persuasion than the issue-based or organizational speech. As Thunberg has shown repeatedly, the art of public speaking—and writing for public speaking—in many ways has risen to an art form. That's because while it requires technical competence and savvy wordsmithing, it also invites creativity, innovation, charisma, and a presence of emotion and physicality.

Thomas Bivins, a media ethicist and public relations scholar at the University of Oregon, notes in his book *Public Relations Writing* that speeches typically fall into three categories: informational, persuasive, and entertaining. In the realm of environmentalism, most public speaking engagements will fall into the first two areas. Informational speeches are often given by government representatives or company leaders to explain the nuts and bolts of a new project or perhaps to highlight the rationale for a special campaign or product innovation. Persuasive speeches, on the other hand, aren't just delivered to hand over facts and data. Rather, they construct a narrative using rhetorical devices to sway the audience to a point of view, a behavioral change, or even

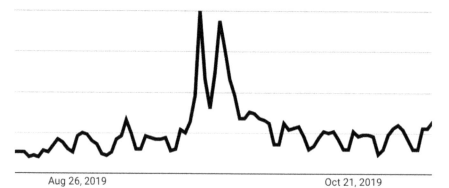

Aug 26, 2019   Oct 21, 2019

Figure 4.7. Public interest in the term "climate change", as measured by Google searches, spiked during the fall of 2019 as a result of the September climate strikes as well as Greta Thunberg's provocative "How dare you" speech given at the United Nations Climate Action Summit on September 23. (Google Trends.)

immediate action. That was the impact of Thunberg's 2019 Climate Action Summit speech, as her words gave significant momentum to the international movement to address greenhouse gas emissions.

As a communication professional, you are just as likely to write a speech for someone else in your organization as you are to deliver it yourself. As Thomas Bivins notes, this is no easy task: "It requires that you know intimately the person for whom you are writing. You need to know his or her style of speaking, body language, tone of voice, speech patterns, and, most important, personality." That's one of the reasons why you will want to meet with the person giving the speech and learn more about their motives, their ideas, and what exactly they are trying to articulate.

Whether you are writing for someone else or yourself, it is important that you divide the speech up into three major sections: the introduction, the main section, and the conclusion. This ensures that your speech is logically coherent and meets the expectations of your audience. An introduction allows you as a speaker to find ways to engage your audience at the beginning of your presentation through friendly banter, a powerful anecdote, or even some humor. This provides a foundation for the kind of engagement that will allow you, in the speech's main section, to walk your audience through the arguments to support your worldview or organizational mission. Finally, the conclusion not only provides an off-ramp for your audience as they transition from your key arguments to the end of your communication, but also gives you the opportunity to summarize your arguments, emphasize your core points, and perhaps leave a call to action such as a fundraising appeal or an opportunity to learn or engage more.

DISCUSSION QUESTIONS

1. Does the naming of ecological spaces like the Great Bear Rainforest or Salish Sea make a difference in terms of how the public relates to them?
2. Why are pranks, subversions, and other media stunts often a popular approach for environmental activists? What examples have you personally encountered or heard about?
3. Can you think of a successful deliverer of speeches in politics or the environment? What makes their oration or speechwriting stand out?
4. Greta Thunberg's speech to the U.N.'s Climate Action Summit served as a rallying point for the global environmental community, but it also irked some people for its adversarial tone. Was Thunberg successful in getting her point across, or was the message's content drowned out by its rhetorical form?

KEYWORDS

Constitutive rhetoric
Culture jamming
Green persuasion
Guerrilla marketing
Ideograph
Image politics
Rhetoric
Subversion

KEY EVENTS, LOCATIONS, AND ORGANIZATIONS

Coast Salish
Great Bear Rainforest
Salish Sea
U.N.'s Climate Action Summit

REFERENCES

Dale, S. (1996). *McLuhan's Children: The Greenpeace Message and the Media.* Toronto: Between the Lines.

DeLaure, M., and Fink, M. (2017). *Culture Jamming: Activism and the Art of Cultural Resistance.* New York: New York University Press.

DeLuca, K. M. (2005). *Image Politics: The New Rhetoric of Environmental Activism.* London: Psychology Press.

Ganesh, S., and Zoller, H. M. (2012). Dialogue, activism, and democratic social change. *Communication Theory*, 22(1): 66–91.

Shore-Goss, B. (2016). *God is Green: An Eco-Spirituality of Incarnate Compassion.* Eugene, OR: Wipf and Stock Publishers.

Simmons, T. A. (1974). The Damnation of a Dam: The High Ross Dam Controversy. MA thesis, University of California.

Chapter Five

Ethics

This chapter focuses on the important role of ethics as a driver of environmental communication and advocacy. Learning objectives of the chapter include understanding ethical positioning for environmental communicators, and the role of ethics in configuring appropriate collaboration and civic action. The chapter also explores concepts describing unethical approaches in environmental communication or advocacy, including greenwashing and astroturfing. The examples provided in this chapter demonstrate the prominence of ethics as a foundation for environmental communication.

THINKING THROUGH FIRE

As the summer of 2022 drew to a close, the Pacific Northwest found itself in straits remarkably similar to years previous. Wildfires burned on both sides of the Cascade Range, derailing the best-laid plans of vacationers and creating a blanket of smoke that sprawled across much of Idaho, Oregon, and Washington State. That noxious mix of particle and gaseous pollutants, a gray haze that turned the sky eerily apocalyptic, also saw residents of major cities such as Portland and Seattle holed up in their homes and offices with windows closed and air purifiers set to max.

For two-plus decades, the West has been experiencing its driest period during the past thousand years, thus rendering much of the region's forestland a tinderbox on an annual basis. Not surprisingly, the new regularity of wildfire season has ushered in unprecedented government attention. With thirty-two active wildfires resulting in the evacuation of thousands of citizens in her state, Oregon's Governor Kate Brown declared a state of emergency and implored President Joe Biden to do the same.

The same scene of panic, public health threat, and ecological devastation has played out far too often across North America. And in some cases, the situation has turned truly catastrophic. In summer 2021, the Canadian village of Lytton in British Columbia burned to the ground during that wildfire season. Along with the disastrous environmental-social impacts of fires have emerged a series of questionable policy positions and partisan media debates pertaining not only to wildfire response and mitigation, but also to the root causes of this ecological challenge.

The cantankerous dialogue surrounding wildfires serves as a metaphor for the disruptive information wars undermining the potential for more productive action on what should be a bipartisan issue. In her book *Global Burning: Rising Antidemocracy and the Climate Crisis*, author Eve Darian-Smith (2022) implores the environmental community to start thinking about wildfires beyond their immediate ramifications as they relate to natural disasters. Darian-Smith, a professor of international studies at the University of California Irvine, reminds us that the years between 2018 and 2021 were especially bad for fires not only in the United States but also in Brazil and Australia. Wildfires are thus a global phenomenon, and they are increasingly linked to larger challenges facing the planet.

Drawing from environmental justice and ecological philosophy, Darian-Smith offers a helpful concept of "thinking through fire" (2022, 28) that moves beyond the existing frames of politics and business. She critiques the growing sentiment for an environmental future that seeks out easy technological answers to ecological and climate challenges such as forest fires without addressing the underpinning economic, political, and social systems that gave rise to this problem in the first place.

Wildfires, as a prominent form of environmental catastrophe, are described by Darian-Smith as the inevitable outgrowth of our breakdown in liberal democratic principles and the corresponding erosion of our natural world. Yet, as technological modernization marches on in the names of climate change mitigation, clean energy, and sustainability, the same mistakes that fuel wildfires globally seem sadly inevitable. Wildfires are indeed natural but also social phenomena that are linked to environmental practice, economic activity, and resource policy across the globe. Yet their near-certain regularity in the coming years reminds us that environmental and crisis communicators must rise above the fray to not only serve in a reactive role for media, but also address publics about underlying causes for wildfire disasters, appropriate responses to fire crises, and potential solutions moving forward. In too many of these cases, government agencies and journalists take part in a form of blame game that undermines the public's trust in institutions and distracts from productive responses to wildfires (Nilsson and Enander, 2020). To undo this spiral of inaction and negativity, organizations need to embrace an ethos of environmental collaboration and civic action.

THE TRUST PROBLEM

The global public looks to the government and business institutions to tackle an array of environmental problems and issues. But their expectations for forward-thinking and ethical action are not always met. That much was made clear in 2021 when public relations firm Edelman released its annual Trust Report. Edelman's survey, which featured over 33,000 respondents from twenty-eight countries, found very high levels of concern for issues like the environment and human rights. Over 70 percent of respondents counted themselves as concerned about climate change. And 40 percent of respondents were actually fearful of the impacts of climate volatility.

And yet, the public has major concerns about the leadership of the social institutions that tend to social and environmental issues, including the climate. According to the same report, 57 percent of respondents maintained that their government leaders are "purposely trying to mislead people by saying things they know are false or gross exaggerations." A further 56 percent of respondents felt the same way about business leaders. As for journalists? In addition to not being trusted to do what is right, media professionals were ranked dead last in terms of spokesperson credibility. In countries around the world, media organizations are in increasing disrepute. A majority of Edelman's respondents (61 percent) agreed with the statement that "the media is not doing well at being objective and non-partisan."

ETHICAL POSITIONING FOR THE PLANET

What happened here? How did media professionals fall to such a low standing in the view of the general public—and how can they restore their credibility? In order to navigate these concerns in communication and journalism, it is useful to address them through ethical frameworks and models developed for business, media, and the environment itself. Journalists are acknowledged as being unique from one another in how they approach complex reporting or communication endeavors. That differentiation is marked in part by their preexisting ethics. Some media professionals might trample over specific individuals in order to publish a story that provides a larger societal benefit, while others might stop short of writing a story if it violates a source's individual rights.

In 1980, the social psychologist Donelson Forsyth (1980) developed an ethical positioning model in which two basic dimensions—relativism and idealism—helped establish individual variations in moral behavior. Forsyth's classification is made more granular by establishing the degree to which an individual exhibits the traits of *situationism*, which calls for careful analysis of morally questionable actions; *absolutism*, which adheres more closely to universal moral principles in ethical thinking; and *subjectivism*, which emphasizes personal values.

For observers of political and environmental media and communication, tensions exist within these ethical frameworks. Personal moral codes that emphasize the importance of universal ethical rules are markedly different than those directed by moral relativism. At the same time, some individuals prioritize a fundamental concern for the welfare of other humans or wildlife, while others accept some harm as a means to achieving a greater good. Given its emphasis on moral posturing, Forsyth's model situates morally rigid interpretations of media issues such as environmentalism as potentially removed from ethical situationism.

Take an example like #ClimateChangeisReal or #ClimateEmergency, both of which were popular hashtags on Twitter during the winter of 2022, when the planet endured large-scale weather events such as typhoons, blizzards, and volcano eruptions. Critics of these hashtags might point to their avoidance of contextually deep evaluations of various news stories about weather events and related geographic phenomena. They are more like a blunt instrument than a fine-toothed comb in providing in-depth analysis. But they do raise attention and concern. That leaves these hashtags potentially closer in spirit to moral absolutism. According to Forsyth (1980), "Absolutists, like situationists, are also idealistic; they approve of actions that yield many positive, desirable consequences. However . . . absolutists are not relativistic. They feel that some ethical absolutes are so important that they must be included in any code of ethics."

For the student of environmental public relations, it is worth locating the ethical motivations that underpin green strategy and appeals. Is a specific eco-movement or campaign driven by a tension between moral absolutism among news audiences and a shifting political/media landscape? The political posturing on environmental issues like climate change or sustainable food production often draws from ethical language to mobilize citizen support, yet audiences are also aware that many environmental problems are connected to meeting basic human necessities, including food, shelter, and mobility. Furthermore, does a strategic campaign or movement place a moral expectation on news outlets that mirrors their individual or group-level ethical beliefs? Environmental media professionals must be reflective and flexible in the face of a shifting landscape of environmental topics and public viewpoints about them. Some issues, particularly those where human life is imperiled, might require a high ground arising from moral absolutism. Others, particularly those tangled up in cultural politics, might require a more accommodating approach.

For example, a forestry or mining community reeling from changes in economic activity or environmental policy deserves to have a wide range of stakeholder voices heard, from civic leaders to local workers to disenfranchised citizens. The German philosopher Jürgen Habermas provides another foundation for communication ethics in environmental debates and dialogue. Habermas's discourse ethics provides an idealized conceptualization of communication—especially for social change scenarios—that prioritizes marginalized voices and outcomes of justice (Habermas, 1990; Habermas, 1993). Habermas's discourse ethics provide an important platform from which to conduct communication forms such as social responsibility, activism, international communication, organizational relationships, and stakeholder engagement. That's because one of the aspirational outcomes of discourse ethics is an "ideal speech situation" in which the peripheral voices of society hold the same weight as more powerful institutional entities from government and business.

THE DECEPTION OF GREENWASHING

The focus on ethics in environmentalism is not the exclusive domain of soul-searching media professionals or aggrieved publics. In the lead-up to the U.N. climate talks in Glasgow in 2021, the head of Greenpeace warned against efforts by nations and corporations to "greenwash" their ecological actions. It was a serious accusation leveled at some of the foremost business and government leaders in the world. What was Greenpeace referring to with the word *greenwash*?

The organization had taken issue with a wave of announcements earlier by countries, companies, and industry groups claiming to aim for net-zero emissions status. Those public proclamations, according to Greenpeace, were part of a larger wave of statements and messages that put positive environmental messaging over real action. Greenwashing can take many forms, but at the heart of the term is some degree of deception through the use of appeals, monikers, images, or marketing slogans. While nations may greenwash their polluting industries through the placement of positive green messaging in press releases and media stories, consumer retail companies might greenwash their products through eco-friendly labels and packaging.

According to Stefano Gelmini, head of news for Greenpeace UK, the origins of greenwashing go back to the 1980s. However, the broader societal desire for ecologically driven political and economic policy means that greenwashing is a bigger problem in the contemporary communication environment. Companies and governments might use environmental messages as a means to greater profitability or industrial expansion, or as cover for diminished public policy. According to Gelmini, "The last few years may well go down in history as the golden age of greenwashing." The Greenpeace communication expert argued that the deception embedded in greenwashing is not just a problem for consumers. It impacts the planet, and the damage is already occurring. "Granted, these kinds of shenanigans are as old as advertising itself," he said. "But greenwashing as the deliberate attempt to cover

Greenpeace Canada
@GreenpeaceCA

The Competition Bureau just launched an investigation into the @PathwaysNetZero "Let's clear the air" campaign, following Greenpeace complaint. Net-zero greenwashing is pervasive and there is a distinct need for accountability. #HoldPollutersAccountable

greenpeace.org
Greenpeace Canada complaint spurs formal inquiry into Pathways Alliance a...
The Competition Bureau has announced that it will launch an official investigation into the marketing practices of the Pathways Alliance, a ...

7:04 AM · May 11, 2023 · **3,487** Views

21 Retweets   **6** Quotes   **37** Likes   **1** Bookmark

Figure 5.1.   In recent years Greenpeace Canada has taken issue with petroleum companies' messaging about their own net-zero environmental efforts. The organization's formal complaint in 2022 led to an official investigation of the Pathways Alliance, which represents Canada's six largest oil sands companies. (@GreenpeaceCA/Twitter.)

up or distract from the damage a company is doing to the environment is a more recent phenomenon."

Gelmini compares greenwashing to climate denialism in that both processes delay or avoid appropriate action for dealing with environmental issues such as climate change. But he notes that greenwashing extends this disconnect even further because it creates a false perception that everything is OK with the planet, or that issues can be resolved if they are adjoined to a green-friendly banner. "Under this mass hypnosis, public pressure on polluting companies evaporates and the tough decisions needed to cut carbon emissions are kicked into the long grass," he wrote. "Greenwashing is our Pied Piper to climate doom. So yes, we should worry about it." An example of this disconnect between talk and real action was evidenced at a big box retailer's annual shareholder meeting in 2022. At the meeting, shareholders voted to move the company to a climate emissions reduction commitment. Yet a proposal to improve the company's agricultural practices and supply chain were given the thumbs-down at the same session. In a *Seattle Times* article about the annual meeting, the climate commitment was given top billing, thus providing cover for the company's lack of action on its sustainable sourcing of poultry and other meats.

Another example of greenwashing comes from the world of fast fashion. According to Greenpeace's 2023 "Greenwash Danger Zone" report, prominent fashion and beauty product retailers use feel-good environmental initiatives to sell their ostensibly green products, though these are often "promotion tools that hide the truth about the destructive fast fashion system, with consumers as the target." According to Greenpeace's report, terms such as *sustainable, green,* and *fair* should be scrutinized by publics and consumers to ensure that they can be supported by company practices, including labor conditions and product supply chain.

It is important to note that concerns over greenwashing aren't just articulated by activists and nongovernmental organizations. Increasingly, industries such as advertising and public relations are concerned about the negative ramifications of dressing up industries or specific consumer products with feel-good environmental fluff that serves to distract, confuse, or deceive the general public. Kim Sheehan, a professor emeritus of journalism and advertising at the University of Oregon, and an expert in greenwashing, points to shifts in American psychographics as one reason why companies have been engaged in this behavior for many years. Sheehan, a past president of the American Advertising Association, highlights the growing consumer preference for products that are ecologically friendly or meet some environmental benchmark. According to a U.S. consumer sentiment survey conducted in 2020 by the consulting firm McKinsey, more than 60 percent of U.S.

Figure 5.2.   An environmental activist at a 2021 climate rally in Glasgow, Scotland marches against corporate greenwashing. (Stay Grounded/Wikimedia Commons.)

consumers indicated they would be willing to pay more for environmentally and ethically sustainable products.

That finding is a big positive. However, some companies have responded cynically by marketing products as green or ethical when in fact they fail to live up to their brand promise. Sheehan co-founded the Greenwashing Index, which tracks companies engaging in this form of unethical marketing. What started as a means for companies to deliver greater profits through deceptive messaging has now extended to the arena of global politics. As Greenpeace has pointed out, nation-states have now adopted this practice to tell a more palatable narrative about their ecological action (or lack thereof) to date.

CASE STUDY: TRANSCANADA AND ASTROTURFING

The Houston Astros of Major League Baseball fame are well known for their multiple trips to the World Series in recent years. But the team's old home stadium, the Astrodome, has in a strange way inspired another form of unethical communication that confuses audiences on significant issues of public interest such as the climate. It is called *astroturfing*. Just as greenwashing seeks to deceive publics in the service of profits or power, astroturfing has emerged as a significant concern in the arena of environmental advocacy and persuasion.

Astroturfing describes the practice of creating front groups to participate in public debates and lobby governments on policy issues. Baseball fans (along with enthusiasts of football and soccer) will of course know AstroTurf as the name of the synthetic playing field surface that emulates real grass. It was made famous at the original Astrodome in Houston, where the Astros used to play. Just as AstroTurf presents as a synthetic or fake grass, astroturfing is akin to a fake or deceptive grassroots action. It produces the perception that an idea or organization has authentic community support when in reality it is a fabrication that delivers an inauthentic message. While the practice would appear to be as flimsy as it is unethical, previous research has revealed that astroturfing can be successful. In issues like climate change, for example, it can create uncertainty among publics in order to elevate corporate interests over the protection of the environment (Cho et al., 2011).

In 2014, the oil and gas company TransCanada was ensnared in an astroturfing scandal that captured global headlines. Its public relations agency (which was Edelman, ironically the same global firm that authors the annual Trust Report) created a *Grassroots Advocacy Vision Document* to help TransCanada generate positive publicity for its Energy East pipeline proposal that would ship oil sands bitumen from the province of Alberta to the Atlantic

Figure 5.3. *The Grassroots Advocacy Vision Document, developed by the global public relations agency Edelman to garner support for the Energy East Pipeline in Canada, was criticized by Greenpeace and other organizations as an example of astroturfing. (Edelman.)*

Coast. The document, which was eventually leaked by Greenpeace to the media, was never intended for public consumption, but it did reveal how some unethical practitioners planned to disrupt the debate about oil sands extractions and climate change in Canada. The document proposed a pipeline supporter progression model where direct appeals "to an individual's trigger points" would create fervent pro-pipeline participants, and in turn the pipeline company would actively manage this emergent movement.

After the documents were leaked, an embarrassed TransCanada parted ways with its public relations agency, and the strategy never came to fruition. But the public relations firm was adamant that its intentions were noble, stating its strategy was "to drive an active public discussion that gives Canadians reason to affirmatively support the project." Greenpeace and some journalists were dismissive of this defense, however, on the grounds that TransCanada and Edelman were working to prop up and mobilize activists behind the scenes with ready-made tactics and media strategies. The controversy not only renewed debate about petroleum pipeline construction in North America, but it also put a focus on astroturfing as a potential vehicle for disrupting public opinion on ecological issues.

ESTABLISHING RELEVANCE IN MEDIA PRODUCTION

The challenges associated with astroturfing and greenwashing are reflective of transformations in the larger media milieu that are leading to a more confused setting for deliberating issues related to the environment. Citizens now consume their news not only from traditional journalism enterprises like newspaper and broadcast companies, but also through entertainment programs, online communities of interest, and organizational news services that serve a public relations function. This erosion of boundaries between journalism, public relations, entertainment, and technology has both pros and cons. This cluttered landscape leads to more confusion, but it also brings more citizens into discussions about civic issues. As a result, according to media ethicists Bruce Williams and Michael Carpini (2020), this new information landscape requires an awareness of the political relevance of a much wider range of communication genres and technologies.

Williams and Carpini suggest four elements of politically relevant media that might make all forms of media more influential in a democratic society. These four qualities capture the previous spirit of the bygone news media era, but also take into consideration the new reality of social media, streaming, and emerging media technologies. The four qualities are:

1. Transparency—the ability of an audience to know who is actually producing or articulating the communication. This requires acknowledging a media enterprise's journalistic sources, but also its economic interests.
2. Pluralism—the degree to which a communication organization embraces and articulates a diverse range of social or political perspectives, and the ease of accessibility for these views to be aired or published. Pluralism is connected to traditional journalistic notions of balance and equal time, but it also fosters richer conversations by bringing more voices to the table.
3. Verisimilitude—the taking of responsibility for truth claims made in the media environment, whether these claims are made in traditional journalism vehicles, public relations materials, Hollywood movies, or popular podcasts. In other words, the producers of these media aspire to, and seek out, truth in the course of their communication work.
4. Practice—the degree to which a communicator prepares for and learns about civic engagement; but also actual engagement with civil society, such as providing forums for wider political deliberation, volunteering with local organizations or causes, or participating in national or global social and environmental movements.

These four qualities of transparency, pluralism, verisimilitude, and practice not only help set overriding and achievable end goals for environmental strategic communication, they also serve to disrupt or alter practices that would otherwise lead to public distrust or disengagement.

CASE STUDY: THE COWBOY POLITICS OF RURAL ENVIRONMENTAL ISSUES

During the winter of 2016, in the high desert of eastern Oregon, an armed standoff once again situated the American West as an arena for frontier politics and environmental conflict. The weeks-long struggle at the Malheur National Wildlife Refuge featured armed ranchers, militants, and self-declared patriots from several western states holed up in federal buildings, citing their long-standing grievances over the U.S. government's management of public land. One iconic media photograph from the standoff showed protester Duane Ehmer—adorned in cowboy hat and displaying an American flag—riding his horse Hellbox during a patrol of the snow-covered sagebrush landscape. The image garnered national attention from media outlets, including the *New York Times'* front page—rattling some readers and fascinating others. Such a moment invoked the cowboy as a symbol for larger hinterland

Los
Angeles
Times **Los Angeles Times**
@latimes

···

Trial begins for militants who occupied Malheur National Wildlife Refuge in Oregon standoff lat.ms/2cGGR2N

11:40 AM · Sep 13, 2016

17 Retweets   **2** Quotes   **11** Likes

Figure 5.4.   The standoff at the Malheur National Wildlife Refuge in Oregon during 2016 saw armed ranchers cite longstanding grievances over the U.S. government's management of public land. The rural standoff and subsequent arrests and trials of the protesters attracted significant attention from news organizations such as the Oregonian and the Los Angeles Times. One of the standoff's leaders, Ammon Bundy, is seen here holding a press conference for local and international media. (@latimes/Twitter.)

disputes as well as the polarization between distinct ideologies and worldviews in civic life. The image of Ehmer and Hellbox provided an opportunity to ponder the rich yet contentious mythology generated by the cowboy—and more broadly, the Western frontier—via national media coverage but also the popular culture genre better known as the Western.

John S. Nelson fully fleshed out this idea of the cowboy as a driver of environmental mythology in his 2017 book *Cowboy Politics: Myths and Discourses in Popular Westerns from* The Virginian *to* Unforgiven *and* Deadwood. Nelson, a political theorist at the University of Iowa, asserts that the tradition of Westerns within popular culture fuels political mythmaking in the United States. These novels, movies, and television dramatizations stand as a metaphor for national struggles and even civilization itself. The mythology produced by the Western, therefore, helps navigate complex social and environmental terrain. Nelson's explanation of "cowboy politics" situates the mediated, dramatized frontier as an arena for considering topics of ecology, rural populism, and nationhood. Cowboys, Nelson argues, are inherently connected to the land by virtue of their work, and seek to ward off the advances of the industrial economy: "The green valleys, golden plains, and steep passes yield to the iron rails and rites of an encroaching civilization" (83).

This civic-environmental interpretation of the Western runs contrary to more established and often bleaker understandings of the frontier and Western histories. Yet Nelson shows that Westerns are rooted in a historical mythology about the West, and therefore provide an emotional bridge between the cowboy and the environment. The frontier's lakes, rivers, grasslands, and mountains represent a landscape to be protected, harkening back to the cowboy mythology but also the environmental land ethic that bind community members together. The Western's land ethic is conveyed by a set of ready-made appeals and myths that communicate the alarming challenges facing the American hinterland. That's where media coverage, visual communication, and civic engagement become so apparent.

Figure 5.5.   Protests against the Keystone XL pipeline included traditional environmental groups but also ranchers, farmers, and tribal communities. In this photo, a 2011 protest against the oilsands pipeline took place just outside the White House. (chesapeakeclimate/Wikimedia Commons.)

The prairie fight over the Keystone XL pipeline offers a contemporary case in point. The pipeline saga has reimbued the Great Plains with larger-than-life protest narratives that draw from a cowboy mythology via news coverage, social media, and even a Woodstock-like rock festival featuring musicians Willie Nelson and Neil Young. Environmental advocates were not only successful in organizing publics to learn more about the challenges of petroleum infrastructure, they also assembled an alliance of stakeholders from ranching, farming, and Indigenous communities to re-create a mythology of the West that confronts the arrival of petroleum technology.

Some critics question this approach, however, pointing to its vulnerability to misinterpretation or the negative legacy of westward expansion and the devastating consequences for America's Indigenous peoples. The Oregon standoff, for example, was divisive across the West and the country. Yet Nelson points to Westerns as a way for contemplating the contributions of cultures across the national fabric: American settlers, Native Americans, Mexicans, and Asian immigrants alike. He also ponders the cowboy's enduring representation as an independent spirit in American life. This autonomy might help the hinterland and rural America ward off the worst excesses of industrial expansion.

DISCUSSION QUESTIONS

1. What is the difference between greenwashing and astroturfing? Can you give examples of one or the other, or both?
2. Recent surveys, such as Edelman's Trust Report, have shown that public trust in the media and other institutions is declining to a worrying extent. What role might personality morality and ethics play in this phenomenon?
3. How does the frontier thesis connect to understandings of the American hinterland, and why is this important for the environment?

KEYWORDS

Absolutism
Astroturfing
Cowboy politics
Discourse ethics
Edelman
Greenwashing

Greenwashing Index
Ideal speech situation
Mythology
Pluralism
Practice
Relativism
Situationism
Transparency
Verisimilitude

REFERENCES

Cho, C. H., Martens, M. L., Kim, H., and Rodrigue, M. (2011). Astroturfing global warming: It isn't always greener on the other side of the fence. *Journal of Business Ethics*, 104: 571–87.

Darian-Smith, E. (2022). *Global Burning: Rising Antidemocracy and the Climate Crisis*. Stanford University Press.

Forsyth, D. R. (1980). A taxonomy of ethical ideologies. *Journal of Personality and Social Psychology*, 39(1): 175.

Habermas, J. (1990). Discourse ethics: Notes on a program of philosophical justification. In J. Habermas (ed.), *Moral Consciousness and Communicative Action*. Cambridge, MA: MIT Press, 43–115.

Habermas, J. (1993). *Justification and Application: Remarks on Discourse Ethics*. Cambridge, MA: MIT Press.

Nelson, J. S. (2017). *Cowboy Politics: Myths and Discourses in Popular Westerns from* The Virginian *to* Unforgiven *and* Deadwood. Lanham, MD: Lexington Books.

Nilsson, S., and Enander, A. (2020). "Damned if you do, damned if you don't": Media frames of responsibility and accountability in handling a wildfire. *Journal of Contingencies and Crisis Management*, 28(1): 69–82.

Sheehan, K. B. (2015). The many shades of greenwashing: Using consumer input for policy decisions regarding green advertisements. *Communicating Sustainability for the Green Economy*, 53–65.

Williams, B. A., and Carpini, M. X. D. (2020). The eroding boundaries between news and entertainment and what they mean for democratic politics. In L. Wilkins and C. G. Christians (eds.), *The Routledge Handbook of Mass Media Ethics*. New York: Routledge, 252–63.

Chapter Six

Public Scoping and Engagement

This chapter focuses on the important role of public engagement and inter-action as a mode of environmental communication and advocacy. Learn-ing objectives of this chapter include the implementation of public scoping projects to assess public attitudes and opinion, the role of social license to operate as a guiding principle for communities, and the impact of citizen science as a force for ecological protection and change. The examples provided in this chapter demonstrate the growing role of the public in directing environmental policy and the critical partnership between com-municators and the larger citizenry in areas of ecological advocacy, con-servation, and natural resources.

REBUILDING PUBLIC TRUST AFTER A PIPELINE TRAGEDY

Short- and long-term environmental crises put policymakers, scientists, and politicians on high alert about what has been dubbed an "ecological rift" to explain the disconnect between our planet's natural state and the impacts of the growing human population (Foster, Clark, and York, 2011). An oil spill represents a worst-case scenario in this regard. It situates our reliance on fos-sil fuels at direct odds with the immediate health of the planet. That is why debates over oil and gas infrastructure are so contentious, as publics worry about short- and long-term problems that might arise, such as the degradation of waterways and impacts to local wildlife and human populations.

Even the smallest of pipeline leaks represent a significant threat to com-munities if and when it is not caught in time. Some citizens of the Pacific Northwest have rightfully been wary of petroleum pipeline developments in the region in recent years. They have watched north of the border as several large pipelines have been proposed in British Columbia to transport Alberta's oil sands to markets in the Asia Pacific through West Coast ports. Residents in the Canada/U.S. borderlands region are concerned about not only impacts on global climate change but also the increased oil tanker traffic—and associated risks—in the Salish Sea that such pipelines might bring.

The city of Bellingham, near the Canada border, provides a useful case for contextualizing the breakdown of civic trust after an environmental disaster—and its subsequent rebuilding. Over two decades ago, the Olympic pipeline explosion devastated the community and eroded faith in pipeline infrastructure. A petroleum pipeline owned by Olympic Pipeline Company ruptured and released more than 230,000 gallons of gasoline into Whatcom Creek—a small but geographically significant urban waterway that connects watersheds in northwestern Washington and provides urban greenspace, wildlife habitat, and salmon spawning grounds.

The environmental damage from the 1999 explosion was unprecedented. When the hundreds of thousands of gallons of spilled gasoline ultimately ignited, a fireball roared down the creek, utterly devastating most of the wildlife habitat in its path. The human toll from the events that transpired, including the deaths of three boys, lingers to this day in the Bellingham community. The young lives lost to the disaster are memorialized in the 2019 song "Kids in '99" by American rock band Death Cab for Cutie.

The explosion also caused millions of dollars of damage to civic and private property. Today, the ecological scars of the accident are still evident along the creek's winding path from lake to sea—even as local officials have done important work to repair and improve the conditions of the creek system and adjoining restoration lands. Meanwhile, improved oversight, maintenance, and governance of pipeline assets—thanks to public pressure and civic leadership—have sought to rebuild trust with community members. But the tragic toll of human life is never forgotten.

That's why establishing the public's trust has to be paramount in virtually any resources infrastructure project—pipelines included. One positive legacy of the 1999 pipeline tragedy is the establishment of the Pipeline Safety Trust, which came into being thanks to a grassroots watchdog group called SAFE Bellingham and the families of the deceased, who demanded improved oversight and accident prevention planning. Inspired by a similar organization set up in the wake of the 1989 *Exxon Valdez* oil spill, the Bellingham-based organization has a mandate to advocate for safer pipelines not only in the Northwest but indeed nationally. According to the Pipeline Safety Trust, when local residents are involved in the policymaking process, a vigilance and trust will emerge that restores public confidence and changes the tone of dialogue from confrontation to consensus.

This is emblematic of the *social license to operate* concept in the realm of natural resources policymaking and public relations. Given that it was developed by scholars and practitioners grappling with the rocky relationships between mining companies and the communities in which they operate, a social license inevitably emphasizes the role of community members and other local stakeholders in incorporating a company's enterprise into their collective identity or, conversely, refusing to accept it based on a misalignment with local values. This is where public communication comes into play. Conservationists, regulators, and citizens all come together to determine how a company's resources or commercial projects align with the needs of a local region or city. Bellingham's community response in the aftermath of this tragedy highlights the critical role of engaged citizenship and civic governance to the ability of resources companies to operate in a democratic jurisdiction. Companies must earn the trust of local constituencies before they turn a profit.

The Olympic pipeline explosion provides a key reminder that the movement of petroleum products—whether by pipeline or rail—presents a particular set of complex risk management issues for communities large and small. In other words, communities often face the brunt of social or ecological crisis events. It is contingent upon local stakeholders to determine the degree to which they are willing to take on risks of harm to people and planet. But while the Olympic pipeline explosion reminds us of the potentially disastrous hazards of energy infrastructure, it also provides an example of how civic engagement and the rebuilding of public trust can prevent future tragedies and provide a sustainable path forward. Significant civic involvement can move the focus from a one-off accident response to an ongoing vigilance dedicated to overall safety and accident prevention.

PUBLIC SCOPING AND CROWDSOURCING

For some observers who scan national media headlines, it might be hard to believe that our democratic institutions are in a healthy state. But what is true at the national or international level about diminished democratic conditions doesn't always hold true at the hyperlocal level. A visit to a local city or regional board meeting devoted to parks, transportation, housing, or recreation might change the minds of many skeptics. Local civic institutions such as municipal governments, park boards, and transportation agencies are increasingly engaging citizens to reach consensus on pressing social and environmental issues. Thanks to citizen input and a broader deliberation of issues afforded by social media, traditionally closed planning processes in activities ranging from health care to urban policy are being opened up for public participation.

This democratization of decision-making is emphasized in the *environmental scoping process*, which seeks broad and granular input from agencies, organizations, and the general public after a proposed course of action has been proposed. For example, how should communities plan for an industrial waterfront clean-up, or the rerouting of a public transit system to better serve the environment? The feedback can take the form of survey work, meetings, focus groups, or more informal exchanges. The stakeholders who participate in this public scoping can include local citizens, public interest groups, tribal communities, industry representatives or businesses, and scientists or other technical experts.

Yet some institutions still shy away from engagement with multiple public stakeholders or groups. Why? Whether it's fair or not, crowds historically have received a bad rap. In 1897, the French sociologist Gustave Le Bon authored a revolutionary book titled *The Crowd: A Study of the Popular Mind*. In it, he warned of crowd psychology characterized by "impulsiveness, irritability, incapacity to reason, the absence of judgment of the critical spirit, and the exaggeration of sentiments." His insights were well received by Edward Bernays, the nephew of Sigmund Freud and a key founder of the public relations profession, who saw crowds as a conduit to influence and power in modern society. Yet a century after Le Bon and others considered the masses as a problem to be dealt with, *crowdsourcing* reverses this sentiment. Instead, it recognizes important crowd traits that were ignored for too long—intelligence, creativity, innovation, and enthusiasm. Most importantly, crowdsourcing emphasizes grassroots participation. For organizations with spatial, geographic, or environmental mandates, crowdsourcing can be particularly useful.

A good example of this comes from Southeast Asia. In late 2014, Typhoon Hagupit devastated the Philippines with an unprecedented ferocity. The disaster was marked by twenty-seven deaths and a further one million residents evacuated from their homes. In the worst-hit areas, over 80 percent of homes in the typhoon's path were destroyed. There was at least one positive development from this horrible scene, however. It came in the form of an innovative emergency response program launched by the United Nations. With the Philippines still emerging from the storm's devastation, the U.N. launched a crowdsourcing platform to deliver humanitarian aid, respond to on-the-ground crises, and quickly assess infrastructure damage and needs. The initiative was undertaken by the U.N.'s Office for the Coordination of Human Affairs (OCHA) in conjunction with the crowdsourcing platform Micro-Mappers. The program asked Twitter users to identify posts

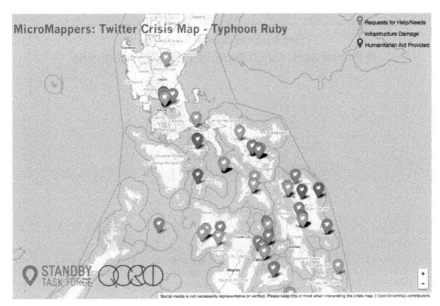

Figure 6.1. To strengthen the humanitarian response to Typhoon Hagupit in 2014, the U.N.'s Office for the Coordination of Human Affairs (OCHA) worked with crowdsourcing platform Micro-Mappers to provide on-the-ground crisis and infrastructure needs in the Philippines. This image from Micro-Mappers shows disaster reports from across the country, crowdsourced by impacted citizens. (Micromappers.)

highlighting damage, emergencies, and individuals in need of help, as well as tweeted photos showing the damage. From this people-sourced information, a crisis map composed of the accumulated information showed where emergency response was needed most.

This is a global example of an organization tapping into the power of the crowd to address an emergent environmental problem. Since then, more companies and government bodies, large and small, have undertaken crowdsourcing initiatives of their own. The premise of crowdsourcing is the combination of crowds and outsourcing. And thanks to the proliferation of the internet, the uptake of mobile technologies, and a steep rise in the use of social networking channels such as Twitter and Instagram, crowdsourcing appears here to stay.

This public input extends into the management of public green spaces as well. An evolving relationship between the public and outdoor spaces, including national parks and wilderness areas, has prompted further deliberation about outdoor recreation. Outdoor recreation experts increasingly are calling for a parks experience that considers the natural and social environments for parks users. Such a multidisciplinary consideration of outdoor recreation tackles issues such as crowding, diversity, and quality of outdoor

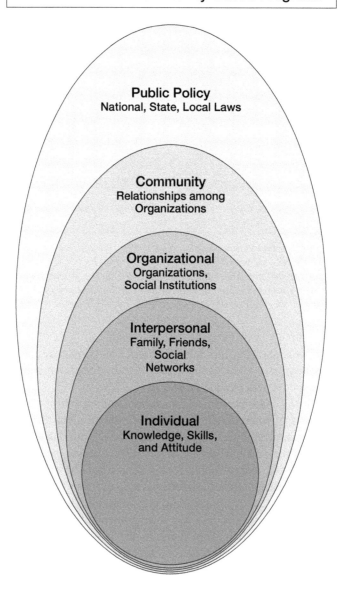

Socio-Ecological Model:
A Framework for Community-Based Programs

Public Policy
National, State, Local Laws

Community
Relationships among
Organizations

Organizational
Organizations,
Social Institutions

Interpersonal
Family, Friends,
Social
Networks

Individual
Knowledge, Skills,
and Attitude

Figure 6.2.   The socio-ecological model developed by Urie Bronfenbrenner during the 1970s provides a framework for community-based programs. The model is based on the organization of a traditional Russian doll set. (Umich hudsonmh/Wikimedia Commons.)

experiences, and managing conflict between parties in such environments (Manning, 2011). Furthermore, wilderness visitors are not a homogeneous population, as they bring a wide range of ideas, life experiences, and value systems to the outdoors. For managers of wilderness and conservation areas, understanding a wide diversity of perspectives is key to facilitating changes and improvements in outdoor spaces, including national and state parks.

TAKING STOCK OF PUBLIC ATTITUDES AND VALUES

One of the challenges for strategic communicators navigating complex environmental topics is understanding the how and why of individual attitudes and beliefs. One means to grappling with this reality is the *socio-ecological model* developed by Urie Bronfenbrenner during the 1970s. The Russian-American psychologist was most interested in how human development occurs within a particular environment, but also the evolving nature of the human-environment relationship and the role of larger contextualizing factors (Bronfenbrenner, 2005).

Bronfenbrenner likened his ecological systems theory to a Russian doll set, with the human experience being contained within a set of increasing larger units. According to Bronfenbrenner, individuals exist within social microsystems featuring close relationships and regular interactions that contain the strongest influences on issues such as human health. Beyond this first and most important system or layer, however, there are other spheres that also play a major role in influencing individual decisions. These include institutions such as churches, schools, workplaces, and neighborhoods; larger social networks and community dynamics; and relevant cultural, social, and religious values. This breadth of elements should therefore be considered when studying the communication or measurement of an environmental issue's prevalence, evaluation, or prevention (Kilanowski, 2017). The larger takeaway is that human beings do not interface with environmental issues in a bubble. Rather, their worldviews and experiences are shaped by various social layers in their lives, including family, friends, faith, and community.

PARADIGM SHIFTS THROUGH CITIZEN SCIENCE

Though he is relatively unknown in the United States, renowned Japanese-Canadian geneticist and media personality David Suzuki is one of Canada's most iconic figures and a leading environmental voice globally. His namesake organization, the David Suzuki Foundation, has weighed in on numerous topics of ecological importance north of the border, from air pollution in big cities to the plight of salmon populations in Canada's most threatened watersheds. Suzuki has been a mainstay of Canadian broadcasting for decades, combining his scientific acumen with a propensity for storytelling and environmental advocacy on programs like CBC's *The Nature of Things*, which has aired on Canada's national network for an astonishing sixty-plus years.

The origins of Suzuki's organization go back to 1989, when Suzuki's radio program *It's a Matter of Survival* warned of an impending planetary crisis because of rampant industrialization, consumerism, and damage to the natural world. What happened next was what the organization rightly called a *paradigm shift*, which describes a massive change in the way a group of people think about or understand a scientific or social issue.

Over seventeen thousand listeners of his radio program wrote to Suzuki looking for ways to follow up on the program in the hopes of avoiding a worst-case scenario for the earth. Based on this feedback, and the meetings that followed with environmental leaders, the David Suzuki Foundation was born. In the beginning, it focused on topics like logging, fishing, pesticides, and at-risk wildlife species. It eventually moved into spaces such as sustainability, climate, and environmental projects in tandem with Canada's First Nations and tribal communities. The foundation has been going strong ever since. The long-term success of the David Suzuki Foundation has shown that citizens aren't just interested in hearing about environmental problems. Rather, they are compelled to engage in ecological action through giving, volunteering, civic engagement, collecting data, and other forms of ecological mobilization.

An example of this kind of action is the Butterflyway Project, a volunteer-led movement that helped bring nature right to people's homes in densely populated neighborhoods across Canada. Launched in 2017, the project initially recruited a team of so-called Butterflyway Rangers to help plant native wildflowers in yards, city parks, streets, and schoolyards to support the hosting of bees and butterflies. By planting pollinator patches in communities and neighborhoods, the program was able to help restore local ecosystems. At the same time, it helped make local areas greener, healthier, and more inviting for neighborhood residents. It's a great example of how volunteer-led engagement, even on a low-key scale, can result in ecological benefits along with an increase in quality of life for those who might not have immediate access to green spaces.

This integration of the public and science is closely related to the concept of *citizen science*, in which members of the public help contribute to scientific studies and outcomes in areas such as public health, environmental governance, and biodiversity monitoring. A key tenet of citizen science is

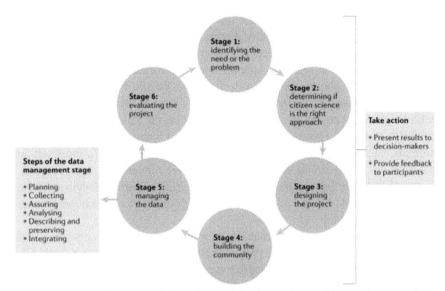

Figure 6.3. The six stages of designing and implementing a citizen science project. (Adapted from Nature.com.)

that it helps fill in knowledge gaps across time and space, with contributions coming from people with local knowledge as well as Indigenous communities (Fraisl et al., 2022). As described in the journal *Nature Sustainability*, citizen science efforts organized by researchers Dilek Fraisl and Omar Seidu have helped the West African nation of Ghana secure crucial data in monitoring the marine problem of plastic debris. Their project has also been integrated into the U.N.'s Sustainable Development Goals, thus allowing the project to build broader public awareness of the issue and establish long-term goals (Olen, 2022).

CASE STUDY: PUBLIC SCOPING RESTORES GRIZZLY BEAR HABITAT

In 2022, the U.S. National Park Service (NPS) restarted a 2017 plan to reintroduce grizzly bears to 9,800 square miles of public land surrounding North Cascades National Park in north-central Washington State. While thousands of the bears once roamed the larger North Cascades ecosystem, which extends to the Canada border, their numbers have dwindled to virtually zero in the region as a result of decades of hunting, habitat intrusion, and ecological degradation.

At the heart of the Parks Service plan was an effort to engage the public through mediation, engagement, and consultation. In turn, feedback through an earlier public scoping process—which collected information from in-person meetings and internet submissions—informed not only the direction of dialogue about wildlife impacts in the Pacific Northwest, but also the agency's specific wilderness directives. Even as the species' potential return signified a return to environmental values, the initiative also received criticism from those who viewed the species as a threat to humans and other animals, including livestock. Not surprisingly, this process found itself in the political crosshairs at various stages. Despite numerous delays, the U.S. Fish and Wildlife Service announced plans in 2023 to draft an Environmental Impact Statement to help foster a grizzly bear population of two hundred over the next half-century.

The debate over the reintroduction of grizzly bears to the ecosystem has become a talking point with the public on the grounds that it mirrors national-level debates about how humankind contends with animal species facing population decline. The high level of political and media interest reflects the degree to which the grizzly bear stands in for a much larger debate about the health of our planet and the relationship between humankind and wildlife. This public deliberation surrounding the introduction of grizzly bears to the North Cascades ecosystem has drawn citizens from across the Pacific Northwest who are keen to share their stories. That's in part because the national park's forests, lakes, and other conservation areas comprise one of the wildest spaces in the continental United States—one that is connected to a much larger wildlife corridor extending eastward to the Okanogon and Kettle mountain ranges of Washington and northward to the Coast and Coquihalla mountain ranges of British Columbia.

The range of handwritten comments and digital submissions received during the public scoping process reveals a wide range of insights from across the political spectrum. For example, one citizen attuned to the plight of grizzlies described them as an extension of ecological life in the region: "I would love to see grizzly bears and all native wildlife thriving in our wilderness." A like-minded comment echoed this sentiment while noting that bears are part of the region's ecological history: "An extraordinary piece of our shared natural heritage. It is important that it be passed on, with all of its native wildlife, for the benefit of the future generation."

Other feedback, however, was less charitable. Some respondents to the National Park Service's environmental scoping process likened the grizzly bear to an ominous predator. "Why would we want to reintroduce something as unreliable and dangerous as grizzly bears?" asked one concerned citizen. Another chimed in with a similar sentiment: "If an individual entertains the

National Park Service ✪
March 24, 2018 · 🌐

Once a major part of the North Cascades ecosystem, grizzly bears have nearly been eliminated from the area. The U.S. Department of the Interior has announced moving forward with plans to restore the bear and support biodiversity of the North Cascades region. Learn more: https://on.doi.gov/2IKwD0c

Image: Grizzly bear in Yellowstone, NPS/Lori Wilkinson

⭕⭕ 1.5K   77 comments 165 shares

👍 Like   💬 Comment   ↪ Share

Figure 6.4. This Facebook post from the National Park System details the original plan to reintroduce grizzly bears to the North Cascades National Park ecosystem. The park service and other government agencies have several venues for public feedback about the plan, which focuses on the natural heritage and biodiversity of the area. (National Park Service/Facebook.)

foolish romantic ideal that wilderness needs to have deadly predators, let them hike in Alaska!" And others pointed to the incompatibility of human-kind and wildlife: "Humans and grizzlies are incompatible when forced to share the same terrain! One or the other has to give way!" Of course, some citizens used this process to register their displeasure in snarkier tones. For one citizen, the program represented the environmental aspirations of coastal urbanites from the city of Seattle: "I am OK with the grizzly bear repopulation, as long as Western Washington gets their fair share; in particular King County (where Seattle is located)." Ultimately, this environmental scoping program highlighted the realities of reintroduction in terms of a divided public sentiment. The process reinforced grizzly bear dystopias and utopias that are commonplace in popular culture and sometimes the news media: violent encounters between bears and humans and bears and other wildlife, accidental encounters, and even magical encounters with the predators. However, other aspects were left understated. These include the relatively low number of violent human/bear encounters, the challenges of sustaining a small population of grizzlies amid encroaching pressures from industry and tourism, and the long-term aspect of reintroduction and grizzly survival through a vibrant ecosystem.

TACTICS AND TOOLS: WRITING THE PUBLIC OP-ED

One of the most powerful writing tools for the public found in the green communicator's toolbox is the *op-ed*. As a platform, the op-ed is one of the few venues where a green communicator can be heard from directly in a national media outlet like the *New York Times* or the *Washington Post.* Op-eds also allow their authors to persuade, to inform, and to debate in other venues, such as regional newspapers, industry publications, and niche websites. The op-ed is not the exclusive venue of CEOs, academics, and professional communicators. Rather, it is a format where citizens are invited to share a well-informed and articulated argument about a specific issue or news item. While still subject to media gatekeeping, it is a more interactive forum that counts on public participation.

But what exactly is an op-ed? The term *op-ed* stands for "opposite the editorial page," indicating that the contribution of information or opinion comes from a citizen or communication professional outside the media entity. More specifically, it is a news article that offers the opinion of a named writer who is typically not affiliated with a news outlet's editorial board. If you scan the op-ed page of your local newspaper, or the opinion section of a specialized online news site, you will typically find signed articles expressing organizational or personal viewpoints on a range of topics.

The significant upside of the op-ed is that it allows your voice to be heard on a major journalistic forum, and it provides an ideal venue for *thought leadership*. That is, it allows you or your organization to showcase expertise, innovations, or services. The Harvard Kennedy School's Communication program notes that op-eds and columns share some common characteristics. First, they are typically short—usually about eight hundred words. Second, they feature a clearly defined point of view. And third, they distinctly represent a writer's clarity of thinking and their unique voice.

Strategic communications expert Fraser Seitel (2013) offers a succinct strategy for crafting op-eds consisting of five key writing components: 1) the grabber, 2) the point, 3) the chain of evidence, 4) the summation, and 5) the goodbye zinger. The *grabber* is your article's opener, and it needs to capture the attention of your audience. This is similar to the lead in newswriting. The *point* is the articulation of your main argument. After this you will provide your *chain of evidence*, which showcases your expertise in the topic: research, statistics, history, quotes, and even personal anecdotes.

You will typically end your article with a *summation* of your work, followed by a memorable closing sentence that captures the spirit of your argument, which is also known as the *goodbye zinger*. The zinger need not be cute, but it should deliver a dynamic message, conclusion, or parting quote that resonates with the reader. This might also come in the form of a final insight, an anecdote that brings the op-ed's argument full circle, or a call to action that implores the reader to engage with the organization, issue, or cause.

DISCUSSION QUESTIONS

1. What are ways that crowdsourcing has been used in your own community to tackle local issues related to housing, transportation, or energy consumption?
2. Paradigm shifts help people think differently about a specific issue. What are some recent examples of this at the national or international level?
3. What is the role of op-eds in the current media landscape, and why are they so important when it comes to public issues?
4. Can you think of an example of citizen science from your own neighborhood? For example, have local citizens been recruited to keep tabs on migrating birds, or monitor invasive species of plants in local parks?

KEY TERMS

Citizen science
Civic engagement
Crowdsourcing

Ecosystems
Op-ed
Paradigm shift
Public input
Public scoping
Socio-ecological model
Volunteerism

KEY EVENTS, LOCATIONS, AND ORGANIZATIONS

David Suzuki Foundation
Micro-Mappers
North Cascades National Park
Olympic pipeline explosion
Pipeline Safety Trust
U.N. Office for the Coordination of Human Affairs
U.S. National Park System

REFERENCES

Bronfenbrenner, U. (2005). *Making Human Beings Human: Bioecological Perspectives on Human Development*. Thousand Oaks, CA: Sage.
Foster, J. B., Clark, B., and York, R. (2011). *The Ecological Rift: Capitalism's War on the Earth*. New York: NYU Press.
Fraisl, D., Hager, G., Bedessem, B., et al. (2022). Citizen science in environmental and ecological sciences. *Nature Reviews Methods Primers*, 2(1): 64.
Kilanowski, J. F. (2017). Breadth of the socio-ecological model. *Journal of Agromedicine*, 22(4): 295–97.
Le Bon, G. (1897). *The Crowd: A Study of the Popular Mind*. London: T. Fisher Unwin.
Manning, R. E. (2011). *Studies in Outdoor Recreation: Search and Research for Satisfaction*. Corvallis: Oregon State University Press.
Olen, S. M. (2022). Citizen science tackles plastics in Ghana. *Nature Sustainability*, 5(10): 814–15. Seitel, F. P. (2013). *The Practice of Public Relations*. New York: Pearson Higher Ed.

Chapter Seven

Media Relations

This chapter focuses on the practice of media relations as a key mode of environmental strategy and public communication. Learning objectives of this chapter include the understanding of media relations approaches, including media framing and strategic advocacy, as well as the construction of narratives for the media through sourcing and contextual or storytelling variables. The examples provided in this chapter demonstrate the breadth and impact of media relations as a long-standing and effective approach for environmental persuasion and advocacy.

CONSTRUCTING THE ENVIRONMENTAL
MEDIA NARRATIVE

Thriving in environmental strategic communication requires a nuanced understanding of media production and practice. Media relations allows the green communicator to navigate news and popular culture to bolster organizational outreach and advocacy. It allows an organization or issue to reach out to mass media outlets with audiences numbering in the thousands if not millions of people. It also provides for outlets in which one can provide not only information but also persuasion. The changing of hearts and minds often takes place in our daily transmission of television newscasts, long-form interview podcasts, newspaper op-eds, radio talk shows, and magazine features. To find success in this complex landscape of green media relations, one must be well versed in multiple media formats of both digital and analog varieties. This ensures that the communication is strategic but also efficient, especially where limits on resources are a factor. For example, campaigns or initiatives that require national policymaking or a public sentiment shift might require a special push in well-known media institutions like the *Washington Post* or *Wall Street Journal*. On the other hand, a region- or industry-specific cause or topic might be better served with an industry or community publication, or perhaps a specific channel of social media.

Green media relations requires not only the ability to secure attention from journalists and media producers, but also the knowledge to help influence the construction of their stories. A good example of this comes from the Keystone XL Pipeline proposal debates that took place over the course of a decade in the state of Nebraska. During this time frame, leading voices on both sides of the debate looked to shift the overall coverage to their organizational viewpoint. For example, a *New York Times* column on November 8, 2014, authored by staff columnist Gail Collins, initially highlighted the idea of how the pipeline would create jobs and economic activity. However, a countering voice in the same article—Jane Kleeb, the founder of Bold Nebraska—slammed the notion of jobs creation with a stark warning about the danger posed to Nebraska's drinking water supply by a potential oil spill. "When you start to mess with Nebraska water, you definitely have a fight on your hands," said Kleeb. This quote helped pivot the story from one that amplified the point of view of the pipeline backers to one that represented a perspective aligned with environmentalists as well as some Nebraska farmers and ranchers.

HOW TO MAKE NEWS IN GREEN COMMUNICATION

The example of Collins's Keystone XL column highlights an important media relations reality: In recent decades, environmental advocates and like-minded communicators have become a well-established source for news stories. While stories about wildlife protection, climate change, and urban design will often feature data and information sourced from government and other institutional authorities, they will also source perspectives and added analysis or insight from other scientists, academics, nonprofit groups, nongovernmental organizations, activists, and other thought leaders.

To this end, green advocates engage in a process known as *media framing*. Media framing is a strategy that can help the cause of green organizations and advocates by improving communication between the news media and communities whose stories are underreported. For example, a news story about the expansion of an urban freeway system might be framed by the automobile lobby as a means to reduce commute times for stressed-out workers. Effective alternative frames might be offered up by cycling groups (focus on bike lanes infrastructure instead), parks enthusiasts (invest in greenspace to improve quality of life), or housing experts (find affordable ways for workers to live closer to their place of employment). In this sense, various organizations are vying for their frame to be best represented in a wide array of media forms, including news but also popular cultural programming such as television shows, feature films, books, and podcasts.

Media frames depend on successful engagement with journalists and an ability to roll with a dynamic media landscape that is more than ever shaped by partisanship, polarization, and political ideology. Getting one's message through amid this chaotic and cluttered situation is easier said than done, especially for smaller organizations or unorganized advocacy groups. However, when they are provided the economic and cultural resources, even disadvantaged voices can get through to influential editors and reporters and gain basic attention or even sympathetic coverage (Ryan, Carragee, and Meinhofer, 2001). That said, other troubling trends in the news media—including sensationalism, lack of quality control, and the preference for soft news or entertainment fluff—means that environmental communicators have their work cut out for them. Advocates need to be prepared for their interactions with media; they must understand local, national, and international media ecosystems; and they must work to improve their articulation of media frames.

According to the cognitive linguist and philosopher George Lakoff (2010), emotion is often overlooked as a driver of influence in media stories about environmentalism and climate. According to Lakoff, language can be used in ways that go beyond logic and reason to activate existing ideologies or worldviews on the part of publics. At the same time, emotions are an integral aspect of normal human thought processes.

In turn, communicators can start thinking about communication that repositions public discussion about the issue at hand in order to have the desired outcomes in media coverage and ultimately in public policy. To expand on this latter point about transferring public opinion into action with an example, the American Lung Association might be thrilled that their clean air advocacy for electric vehicles has resulted in a glowing feature story on a television program like *Good Morning America*. However, their ultimate goal with such efforts is for publics to shift their views and behaviors on gas versus electric-powered transport, or for lawmakers to consider new incentives for the manufacture and uptake of e-vehicles.

This is where framing stories for media again becomes a consideration for communicators, who might connect their public relations or press outreach to a range of human emotions such as surprise, joy, grief, or even anger. This view of framing topics for traditional or social media, and for public audiences, emphasizes the role of rhetoric previously described in chapter 4. One rhetorical model that helps conceptualize the construction of media

Table 7.1.   The strategic framing taxonomy for social or environmental advocacy (Gilliam and Bales, 2001)

Strategic advocacy element	Description
Numbers	The use of data or statistics to address or highlight an issue or problem; data can also make an issue more relevant, or more understandable
Messengers	Involving citizens, celebrities, or organizational members as spokespersons or advocates; they bring personal experiences, perspectives, actions, and environmental knowledge to an issue
Visuals	The use of photos, illustrations, maps, cartoons, charts, and other graphical representations; this also includes the proliferation of political memes online
Tone	The degree to which advocacy is strident or oppositional in tone; advocates can choose a hopeful or cooperative demeanor, or they can emote anger and conflict
Metaphors and simplifying models	Models or figures of speech that help make sense of more complex issues; popular metaphors might compare environmental topics to war, religion, finance, personal health, or American history
Context	Recognition of the problem or opportunity within the boundaries of time, space, and community; contextualizing issues as they pertain to a community's heritage, location, and larger society

engagement for issue advocates is the *strategic framing* taxonomy developed by Gilliam and Bales (2001). The strategic framing taxonomy encourages communicators to integrate rhetorical elements into their advocacy. These elements are numbers, messengers, visuals, tone, metaphors and simplifying models, and context (see Table 7.1)—and they are instrumental in helping organizations communicate alternative frames.

Climate change, for example, might not be captivating for readers of *Sports Illustrated* if the issue is presented in terms of pronouncements from a global science conference or academic journal. But it would certainly warrant attention if it were presented in terms of the number of athletic competitions canceled due to volatile weather conditions; a team's engagement with the topic through the visual branding of a stadium or on-field messaging; or an athlete's metaphorical engagement with climate change through individual advocacy and action on the playing field. Recent advocacies by high-profile professional athletes such as LeBron James, Aaron Rodgers, and Naomi Osaka provide helpful cases in point.

Rhetorically imbued messaging plays a powerful role in this regard. According to environmental rhetorician Robert Cox, ecological or scientific information in a vacuum doesn't always translate into newsworthiness for media practitioners. But when this information is attached to emotional appeals, tropes, narrations, and argumentation, it can play a much more influential role in environmental news controversies (Cox, 2013).

Additionally, a rhetorically based taxonomy like strategic advocacy framing helps create "reframes," described by George Lakoff (2014) as having the power to help publics reconsider previously held conceptions. Used cars, for example, were once diminished by some journalists as bad for the environment because they were inefficient on gas mileage or seen as emitting excessive particulate matter. However, a view from the International Institute for Sustainable Development holds that extending the life of energy-efficient used cars is sometimes more sustainable than the expensive and resource-intensive manufacture of new vehicles. In other words, there is much more complexity to this discussion, requiring closer analysis of global regulations, manufacturing materials, and supply chains. Because news reporting can be steeped in old conventions or stereotypes, newly developed or counterintuitive frames by organizations like the International Institute for Sustainable Development can help counter a dominant narrative and refresh or balance out the public's perspective. To this end, a key goal for green public relations and media advocacy should be message development that translates policy positions for citizens and considers the target audience's existing knowledge and beliefs (Gilliam and Bales, 2004).

BECOMING A RELIABLE SOURCE

A key takeaway from the discussion on media framing earlier in this chapter is the pivotal role of organizational sources. Anders Hansen (2018), a professor of communication at the University of Leicester in the United Kingdom, maintains that much production of green media hinges on activist sources, whose role is to make environmental or scientific claims while trying to influence what is communicated to the public. News media typically supplement their existing coverage of topics like climate volatility with these contributing perspectives from individual and organization-based sources. What might a source's contribution take the form of? Eco-activists who interface with the media might provide commentary on existing stories with interviews and quotes; the provision of data or new research; the sharing of photographs, video, or maps; or they can direct media to further expertise within their organizations. Advocates might highlight social or health trends to indicate an underlying problem or grievance, or they can profile a personality or cause that situates the issue in a positive (or negative) light.

The most important action, however, is the preparing of story ideas that are compelling for media outlets, and for dealing with reporter requests for comment or information when an organization is involved in a major event or crisis. This is known as *newsworthiness*. According to earlier research from University of Nevada sociologist Marilyn Lester, being newsworthy has a direct impact on whether an issue succeeds or fails in making the news (Lester, 1980). For example, a national water quality report issued several years ago might not be of interest to your local television news affiliate or city blog. However, if that same kind of report were to be published tomorrow, and if it featured important information about local human health impacts, it is more likely that you would soon be hearing from a reporter looking for expert comment, follow-up, or a full interview.

Communicators need to generate new stories in order to establish both media coverage and public interest. This is an important takeaway for environmental activists in particular. It is unlikely that reporters will somehow stumble across what environmental advocacy or conservation groups are doing or saying. Rather, the movement of an argument from a group or individual to the media is likely to involve research, strategizing, and the use of specific tactics. These might include press releases, informal media pitches, social media outreach, formal press conferences, media advisories, and the strategic distribution of special reports or research.

One thing that is very clear is that the prolific use of these tactics does work over time. For example, research focused on news coverage of Nike's manufacturing practices overseas showed that the larger presence of activists in various stories helped sway ensuing coverage to a more critical perspective (Greenberg and Knight, 2004). The activists used a large repertoire of media tactics to make this happen, including demonstrations, student protests, and even fashion shows. All of these things fit the necessary criterion of "newsworthiness." Similarly, another media analysis showed that the ability of nongovernment organizations and community activists to highlight newsworthy information such as chemical dumping, industrial leaks, and human health outcomes motivated media to publish more stories about industrial pollution (Barnett and Svendsen, 2002). This strategy, emphasizing the importance of finding an audience for a story to ensure it is recognized, conjures up the famous question from Mann and Twiss's book *Physics* (1910): "If a tree falls in the forest, does anybody hear?" The famous query highlights an important concern for green communicators. The deliberation of environmental problems requires an audience. It's the job of the environmental communicator to raise awareness and educate publics on key issues so that they don't exist in a vacuum.

LYNDA MAPES AND THE SOUTHERN RESIDENT ORCAS

Perhaps no wildlife story is more emblematic of contemporary environmental challenges than the Southern Resident orcas of the Pacific coast. The extended family of killer whales, comprising the J, K, and L pods, spends the summer and fall traversing the Salish Sea, which includes the Strait of Georgia, Puget Sound, and the Strait of Juan de Fuca. In winter and spring, these killer whales range the open coast from California to Alaska. Their population has experienced significant declines in recent years, some of which has been attributed to environmental degradation and climate change.

The future of the whales is the focus of a multitude of scientist and government efforts. That makes transmitting this information into a cohesive, understandable story for the public that much more important. One critically important journalism project about the orcas, produced by *Seattle Times* reporter Lynda Mapes and her colleagues at the newspaper, promises a healthy future for environmental journalism not only in the United States but also internationally. The *Times* project, titled "Hostile Waters: Orcas in Peril," is an ambitious, multipart initiative that has featured in-depth reporting alongside rich videography, photography, and an array of maps and illustrations.

The newspaper series' popularity reached a crescendo in 2018 when it reported on a grieving mother orca that carried her dead calf over a distance of one thousand miles. A year later, the series won the Kavli Science Journalism Gold Award from the American Association for the Advancement of Science. The work of the series has continued to resonate with citizens of the Pacific Northwest and beyond, who have turned to Mapes's work for a synthesis of scientific discovery, climate investigation, government action, and the ongoing health of the whales.

Mapes herself has received much feedback in the form of emails and letters about the importance of this journalistic work at the *Times* from across the continent and overseas. The plight of the Southern Resident whales has in many ways stood in for the global ecological challenges facing humankind, especially because it touches so many of the contemporary issues threatening the planet: climate change, warming oceans, the diminishing health of rivers and salmon populations, the impact of growing port traffic, and maritime pollution. The cross-border ocean habitat serves as a microcosm for the planet, and that has the world paying close attention to stories about the orca pods. "The Salish people [the region's earliest inhabitants] don't observe a border, and very intelligently so," said Mapes. "The issue of climate and fish doesn't observe a border."

Mapes asserts there is a need for more environmental reporting in her larger Pacific Northwest region of coverage. She points to the example of the Trans Mountain Pipeline expansion project, which would carry refined and crude oil from Alberta to the nearby British Columbia coast before it is shipped to Asia; and the growth of ports, including the Ports of Metro Vancouver, located just minutes north of the Washington state border. "All of that [shipping] is going through the San Juan Islands and orcas habitat," she said. "This is a fragile area that the orcas need that is in dire risk of an oil spill or worse. It's a delicate place that everybody wants access to. The economic reality of our joint fate is very important."

The heft of Mapes's reporting for the *Seattle Times*, along with her colleagues, has aligned with larger bets on environmental journalism by media enterprises on both sides of the border. However, such endeavors take time and money, both of which are increasingly rare as newspapers and other journalism outlets face declining budgets and reduced staffing. To cover the plight of orcas and other Salish Sea wildlife, Mapes's reporting has required border crossings, ferries, float planes, and other marine transit.

Environmental reporting thus requires extra resources to facilitate travel to remote locations and the ability to track down and analyze complex ecological stories. To report on the region's orcas during 2018, Mapes recalls the difficulty getting to Hansen Island's Orcas Lab during the height of British Columbia's wildfire season, and the special logistics required to get there. "You have to beg rides with scientists, but you want to cover orcas because that is what you do," she said. "It's a lot of work, a lot of hustle; when you add Canada to the equation it's even more, but it's worth it."

Ultimately, Mapes makes a bold case for the growth of environmental journalism at major media companies like the *Seattle Times*. Her output, along with that of her journalistic colleagues across the country, serves as a catalyst for larger action pertaining to conservation, sustainability, and environmental protection on the part of politicians, policymakers, and publics. "There is only one way to do this. You show up; you personally witness and generate the research with . . . a team of editors and reporters. What we put in the paper is put in the paper because we know it to be true, period. It is work that we stand behind because we did it ourselves. We are the base of the information food chain."

PREPPING THE MEDIA FOR A ROAD TO THE ARCTIC OCEAN

One of the benefits of mass media campaigns is that they convey concepts, experiences, and geographies to larger audiences that might not be able to experience them firsthand. Such is the case with one of Canada's latest infrastructure projects in the polar north. Canada's 137-kilometer (85-mile) Inuvik to Tuktoyaktuk Highway—built atop permafrost and traversing a polar landscape dotted with thousands of lakes and streams—was completed in 2017. It received broad media interest as a result of a concerted effort to explain the project to the majority of Canadians who live thousands of miles south.

Such projects do not arrive without their fair share of friction, particularly given the special ecological considerations of the global Arctic and sub-Arctic regions. For example, some citizens questioned the need for such infrastructure based on potential geological or climate impacts, while others took issue with the taxpayer costs involved. This is why the country devoted time and media-geared resources to ensure that it could provide a firsthand perspective and make its government representatives available to better explain the project.

At the opening of the highway, Canada's Governor General joined the Minister of Infrastructure, the Minister of Indigenous Relations, and the leader of the Northwest Territories, along with other political dignitaries, at the Arctic community of Tuktoyaktuk to mark the milestone moment for northern Canada. But it was the strategic issuance of a media release, a back-grounder, quotes, and quick facts that would help reporters quickly digest the story in terms of its political and economic implications.

In opening the highway, Canada's federal government proclaimed that its investment would create stronger communities through physical and economic mobility, enhanced tourism, and long-term resiliency to climate change. In the years leading up to its construction, Canadians debated the merits of bridging the Arctic coastline to the rest of the country. Former Canadian prime minister Stephen Harper, for example, explained the high-way in terms of both Arctic sovereignty and as a "road to resources." The latter description served to alienate some Canadians, who were skeptical of the highway's ultimate objectives. That's why it became important for government communicators to stress the road project's localized dimensions, including its employment of hundreds of Northwest Territories residents.

The national *Globe and Mail* newspaper described the highway in terms of bringing "new opportunities and new stresses to the North by opening a small, isolated community to the outside world." And a story from the national broadcaster, the CBC, juxtaposed the aspirations for tourism and economic growth against the downsides of such a project—highlighting, for example, a vodka-smuggling operation busted by the Royal Canadian Mounted Police on the new roadway. It also described the north end of the coastal community of Tuktoyaktuk as the final stop on a summer road trip:

"That's where tourists have set up their RVs and tents, and where many will head to dip their toes into the Arctic Ocean, or do a polar plunge."

That's why the provision of perspectives, background information, and quotes from political leaders became so important in this process. For example, in a quote from a Government of Canada news release, Amarjeet Sohi, the Minister of Infrastructure and Communities, explained the Inuvik-Tuktoyaktuk Highway as "a key piece of infrastructure that will have a long-lasting, positive impact on the lives of Northerners." According to Sohi, the investment "will help ensure that the people of Tuktoyaktuk have year-round access to essential services and a reduced cost of living." Similar comments from the country's leaders tied the polar highway to community needs and quality of life concerns. Though the highway's completion still fostered healthy debate, that kind of messaging from several project champions was important in forming a cohesive narrative that could help Canadians understand an investment that they might not be able to experience firsthand.

MEDIA CONCEPTIONS OF WILDLIFE

For communicators in the realms of biology, wildlife protection, and the animal world, the media can pose a key problem. Because of the often-relentless focus on newsworthiness and the driving of audience interest, news media outlets tend to dwell on stories that focus on conflict and surprise. It is commonplace to read headlines about animals in distress, or wildlife attacks on human populations. Less common is a focus on the long-term challenges facing animal populations.

One approach to better understanding how animals are represented in media coverage is Kellert's (1994) wildlife attitudes framework, which positions animals such as grizzly bears and wolves as contested symbols in wildlife discourses, informing mediation, dialogue, and ultimately public policy (see Table 7.2). A variety of factors help shape perceptions of predators such as bears, including the animal's presumed aesthetic value, size, assumed intelligence, likelihood of inflicting property damage, perceived dangerousness, and its cultural/historical relationship with a local human population (Kellert, 1980).

Public attitudes toward bears and their conservation are part of a broader scholarly conversation about the public's wildlife values and their perceptions of specific species. According to Kellert, the public's values can directly impact public policies regarding animal conservation, including the management of bears. For better and for worse, such views are informed by local

Table 7.2. Kellert's Basic Wildlife Values (2014)

Term	Definition
Aesthetic	Focus on physical attractiveness and symbolic appeals of animals
Dominionistic	Emphasis on the mastery and control of wildlife, typically in sporting situations
Ecologistic	Concerned with the interconnectedness of wildlife species and the natural habitat
Humanistic	Focus on the affection for individual wildlife species with anthropomorphic attributes
Naturalistic	Emphasis on direct experience with wildlife in outdoor recreational settings
Negativistic	Focus on the avoidance of wildlife due to fear, hostility, or indifference
Scientistic	Emphasis on the biological functioning of animals
Utilitarian	Focus on the practical value of wildlife or animal habitat

histories, but also through public deliberations and the mediation of wildlife through the news media, advertising, and even cinematic productions such as 2005's *Grizzly Man*, 2015's *Backcountry*, and 2023's *Cocaine Bear*.

Media treatments of grizzly bears, wolves, sharks, and other high-profile wildlife predators can therefore contribute to improved but also distorted understandings of ecological issues, and in particular mold discourses about specific wildlife species. Research about the conservation of elephants and rhinos in Zimbabwe shows how this works in the news media. In Western media coverage about both species, there was a documented spillover of metaphorical frames about political and economic events into the discussion of wildlife management efforts. For example, stories about rhino protection often included references to political instability or conflict in Zimbabwe. This *spillover effect*, one that wildlife and environmental communicators should be mindful of, created a hazier understanding of on-the-ground events. In other words, the public often understands the plight of wildlife through lenses of politics and current affairs (Gandiwa et al., 2014).

This has been the case in the rural United States, where wolf attacks on livestock in western states like Oregon, Idaho, and Montana are often presented symbolically as a long-standing conflict between Republican and Democrat, or red state versus blue state interests. As for Zimbabwe and the plight of elephants and rhinos, the documented media spillover effect caused some support from international donors to be withdrawn. However, this occurred even as populations of both species stabilized or even grew during the studied time frame.

CASE STUDY: HOW *DEADLIEST CATCH* CAPTAIN
HELPED REFRAME CLIMATE DEBATE

In spite of the saliency of globally impactful news issues such as poverty, human health, and environmental protection, Americans on the whole remain cautious of what they learn from the media. According to Edelman's (2021) Trust Report, which examines the relationship between global publics and institutions such as government, business, and the media, affinity for news reporters has hit all-time lows. For example, in a measurement of trust in spokespersons for business information, journalists as a profession ranked dead last—well behind scientists, CEOs, NGOs, and even politicians. Media institutions, as a result, are increasingly aware of the importance of featuring opinion leaders who might enjoy greater standing in building public engagement where traditional journalists have fallen short. That's why entertainers, athletes, and musicians enjoy special clout when it comes to social or environmental issues that on the surface might appear to fall outside their expertise.

A case in point comes from a 2017 climate forum hosted by the all-news television network CNN and former U.S. vice president Al Gore. Gore is a highly recognizable political figure and well-regarded expert on climate change. Yet one of his best-known guests did not hail from the lofty ranks of journalism, politics, or academia. Rather, the televised program featured hard-nosed crab fisherman Keith Colburn, the captain of the *Wizard* vessel on the Discovery Channel's long-running reality program *Deadliest Catch*. The colorful captain of the F/V *Wizard* has not been shy about discussing the impacts of climate change on the Alaska fishery. For example, he has noted that water temperatures play an outsized role in the life cycles of crabs, their predators, and all other life-forms in the Bering Sea. A volatile climate has also made the industry much more unpredictable for the Alaska fishing fleet, which deals with more intense and dangerous storms. Of course, *Deadliest Catch* has also provided plenty of evidence of the immediate effects of a changing climate. Warming oceans have rendered traditional fishing grounds unproductive and decades-old maritime expertise obsolete. And that sends some fishing vessels into more dangerous territories to meet their fishing quotas.

For over two decades, *Deadliest Catch* has provided a loyal viewing audience with firsthand perspectives of Alaska crab fishing on the Bering Sea. With its emphasis on maritime adventure, conflict, and resources extraction, the program commodifies the polar region by showcasing the accumulation of profits from the Alaska fishery. But it also highlights a counterintuitive environmentalism that conveys the connection between larger global issues and regional industries that rely on natural resources.

As a former politician, Al Gore was likely well aware of Colburn's influence. *Deadliest Catch* enjoys a loyal fan base across North America (and internationally). Perhaps ironically, reality programs like it have created their own kind of reality—one that has real implications for public perceptions and even policy for the region. To draw from the media theorist Marshall McLuhan, it is worth understanding not only what is communicated within these programs, but also the contexts—ecology, history, economy, technology—in which they are produced, transmitted, and received. *Deadliest Catch* provided Gore and the public with a relevant entry point for discussions about the health of the Bering Sea and Alaska's fishing industry, as well as the planet's future.

For CNN viewers who might understand climate change conceptually but not in terms of the nautical or maritime reality, the decision to include Colburn on a panel with Gore proved to be an inspired decision. Gore's environmental expertise can only be so effective with a mass news audience. But by inviting the crab fishing captain to the policy discussion, the climate forum's organizers sent a signal that the climate debate is intended for all citizens, not just traditional environmentalists, scientists, and policy experts. It comes as no surprise then that climate change politics now loom large within popular television and streaming programming. Indeed, as this book pointed out earlier, many actors, musicians, and television personalities have emerged as high-profile spokespersons on issues like climate change, wildlife conservation, and sustainability.

TACTICIAN'S TOOLBOX: GO LOCAL WITH A MINI CAMPAIGN

One of the daunting challenges at the outset of any formal public communication campaign is establishing appropriate resources and time for the communication task ahead. A full communication program with a time frame of one month or longer requires commitment on your part as a strategic communication professional, but also from your organization or client. One way to establish a strong rapport with a smaller organization, such as a small not-for-profit, and build long-term trust is through a mini campaign. This is a low-impact approach to test-drive new ideas, reach out to different stakeholders, or launch a new innovation. The various tactics and ideas that you read about in this book can easily be integrated into your campaign, and many of them won't cost you a thing to implement.

In the environmental space, there is no shortage of local organizations looking for strategic communication or public relations help. You might already be involved with an organization devoted to the protection of wildlife, the conservation of local lands, or the mitigation of climate impacts in your neighborhood or metropolitan area. Think about some of the tactics you have read about in this book, including press releases, op-eds, videography, photographs, feature articles, and social media hashtags. All of them give you a unique approach as you attempt to persuade, collaborate with, or engage your publics on green topics.

At the outset of your campaign, you should provide your client or organization with a basic summary document explaining what communication challenge or opportunity exists and how you intend to address it through public engagement or media. Be sure to lay out the larger strategy but also the specific tactics that will move the campaign forward. The beauty of the mini campaign is that it is scalable, so it can also be used for larger organizations or expanded into a larger communication program. For example, you might develop a mini campaign proposal for a metropolitan zoo or aquarium in your home state or city that is trying to promote a conservation program. Or you could look to one of the latest watershed protection programs that is being promoted publicly by your regional or county land trust.

What are some other tactics that might help you round out a mini campaign? Along with some of the major initiatives described above, you could also layer in public service announcements, aerial videography, letter-writing campaigns, or even a one-off special event. In the spirit of civic engagement, you could even organize a special event, research seminar, or a citizen advisory group. Conducting early-stage research about your client and the public issue at hand will help you assess the scope of your work and the kind of tactics you decide to deploy.

DISCUSSION QUESTIONS

1. Do you agree with the findings of Edelman's Trust Report? Do its findings suggest a greater role for organizational spokespersons from different walks of life?
2. What are some examples from your own region or state of wildlife being rhetorically framed by the media or situated as a political wedge issue?
3. Why are public attitudes so important not only in the shifting of dialogue but also in public policy?

KEY TERMS

Activist sources
Emotional appeals
Magazine features
Media framing
Media relations
Newsworthiness
Podcasts
Public attitudes
Reframes
Sources
Spillover effects
Strategic framing taxonomy
Target audience
Wildlife attitudes framework

KEY EVENTS, LOCATIONS, AND ORGANIZATIONS

Bold Nebraska
Edelman Trust Report
Inuvik-Tuktoyaktuk Highway
International Institute for Sustainable Development
Keystone XL Pipeline
Seattle Times' "Hostile Waters" series
Trans Mountain Pipeline

REFERENCES

Barnett, C., and Svendsen, N. V. (2002). Making the environment news: Reporting industrial pollution in Durban. *Rhodes Journalism Review*, (21): 54–55.

Cox, R. (2013). *Environmental Communication and the Public Sphere*. Thousand Oaks, CA: Sage.

Edelman. (2021). Trust Barometer Global Report. Online Fieldwork in 28 Countries between October 19 to November 18, 2020. Retrieved from: https://www.edelman.com/trust/2021-trust-barometer.

Gandiwa, E., Zisadza-Gandiwa, P., Muboko, N., Libombo, E., Mashapa, C., and Gwazani, R. (2014). Local people's knowledge and perceptions of wildlife conservation in southeastern Zimbabwe. *Journal of Environmental Protection*, 5: 475–81.

Gilliam, F. D., and Bales, S. N. (2001). Strategic frame analysis: Reframing America's youth. UCLA Center for Communications and Community.

Gilliam, F. D., and Bales, S. N. (2004). Strategic frame analysis and youth development. *Handbook of Applied Developmental Science: Promoting Positive Child, Adolescent, and Family Development Through Research, Policies and Programs*, 1: 421–36.

Greenberg, J., and Knight, G. (2004). Framing sweatshops: Nike, global production, and the American news media. *Communication and Critical/Cultural Studies*, 1(2): 151–75.

Hansen, A. (2018). *Environment, Media and Communication*. New York: Routledge.

Kellert, S. R. (1980). *Knowledge, Affection, and Basic Attitudes toward Animals in American Society: Phase III*. U.S. Department of the Interior, Fish and Wildlife Service.

Kellert, S. R. (1994). Public attitudes toward bears and their conservation. In *Bears: Their Biology and Management*, Vol. 9, International Association for Bear Research and Management, 43–50.

Lakoff, G. (2010). Why it matters how we frame the environment. *Environmental Communication*, 4(1): 70–81.

Lakoff, G. (2014). *The All New Don't Think of an Elephant!: Know Your Values and Frame the Debate*. White River Junction, VT: Chelsea Green Publishing.

Lester, M. (1980). Generating newsworthiness: The interpretive construction of public events. *American Sociological Review*, 984–94.

Mann, C. R., and Twiss, G. R. (1910). *Physics*. Chicago and New York: Scott, Foresman and Company.

Ryan, C., Carragee, K. M., and Meinhofer, W. (2001). Theory into practice: Framing, the news media, and collective action. *Journal of Broadcasting & Electronic Media*, 45(1): 175–82.

Chapter Eight

Advanced Writing and Visual Media Tactics

PROJECTING ENVIRONMENTAL MOMENTS

The ability to negotiate the sphere of environmental strategic communication requires not only a deep understanding of ecology, media, and public engagement. It also requires a special attention to the art of writing alongside sophisticated visual communication tactics. Environmental public communication is an applied calling. Emphasis is placed not only on strategy, but also on tactics. This includes traditional activities like news releases, media pitches, advisories, statements, speeches, and white papers. But it also involves visual and digital media endeavors such as photography for social media, videography, and spatially oriented communication such as mapping. The successful green communication professional should be able to do the following as part of their day-to-day activities:

- Write materials that are directed to journalists and other audiences as required by the organization
- Underpin communication output with a larger strategy in order to target appropriate audiences and to meet an organization's longer-term goals and objectives
- Communicate for a variety of traditional and digital media, including print, broadcast, and social channels
- Evaluate and edit external communication or public relations materials directed to the media or public
- Articulate the mission of the organization and the contribution it can make to society but also to the immediate quality of community life
- Engage with internal and external stakeholders in the service of relationship-building, information exchange, storytelling, or persuasion

IT'S ABOUT THE CONTENT *AND* THE MEDIUM

At the heart of much environmental public relations is strategic narrative. That's why rhetorical techniques such as storytelling play such a pivotal role. Environmental media is highly sensory. Audiences process information about the natural world and ecological problems with their senses. In turn, the production of environmental content uses a wide variety of communication tactics in order to advocate, inform, and replicate those sensory experiences. Kevin Deluca, a professor of communication at the University of Utah and an expert in environmental rhetoric, points to the emotional heft of "image events" that are crafted by environmental organizations and subsequently disseminated through television and other electronic communication. Drawing from the example of Greenpeace, Deluca points to how the organization's communicators infused their campaigns with high drama to reorient issues such as commercial whaling and ocean dumping of nuclear wastes for a mass audience at home (Deluca, 2005).

Greenpeace's strategic communication ethos draws directly from the Canadian media theorist Marshall McLuhan and his adage of "the medium is the message" (Dale, 1996). That is, in the projection of an environmental moment through a vehicle like photography, film, or digital media, the medium or media technology is at least as important as the embedded environmental message. Television and streaming video, for example, are bound to generate attention, controversy, and conflict by the way they project images in quick succession. And viewers come to expect this. For example, people often turn to their mobile devices or television screens in the wake of a natural or human-caused ecological disaster because of the sheer power of imagery.

USING WHITE PAPERS TO SHARE
RESEARCH WITH THE PUBLIC

Consider yet another prominent tactic that fuses topical information or news events with organizational persuasion: the white paper. Governments, nonprofits, and technology firms all use this tactic to communicate complex issues and policies to industry or public audiences. Often found on organizational websites, white papers are textual and graphical—they situate research, data, visuals, and storytelling into one easy-to-digest strategic communication document. Thus, white papers exist as a combination of organizational expertise and advocacy, even as they tailor the style of writing for organizational peers as well as stakeholders, journalists, politicians, and even the general public (Perez, 2011).

Like other advanced media tactics, the production of a white paper starts with conducting research about your organization's key industry, area, or issue in conjunction with the organizational objective or goal. For example, if you are writing a paper about the need for greater civic investment in a metropolitan parks system or regional watershed, you probably will be seeking and collecting general data about the issue, as well as details that account for history, trends, and current concerns or opportunities. A white paper not only conveys how your organization engages an environmental or social challenge or opportunity, but also allows your organization to highlight certain services or programs where it is already enjoying significant success.

Many communicators choose to include data visualizations with their research reports, media publications, or white papers. Drawing from data that has either been collected or drawn from your organization or a credible third party (such as a think tank, government body, university, or a dedicated

White Paper on Water Sustainability Management, by the Sierra Club Napa Group

August 26, 2022

Sierra Club Napa Group
White Paper on Water Sustainability Management

Summary

Far from exhaustive, this list of necessary actions is essential to beginning a path to a sustainable water management system within Napa County. Decisive leadership is required to address the crisis we are heading toward. Basic actions that need to be taken by the Board of Supervisors include:

1. Growth limits
The county cannot permit new and expanded water use

Figure 8.1. This white paper on water sustainability management was published by the Sierra Club Redwood Chapter and the Sierra Club Napa Group. The paper listed a number of necessary actions deemed essential to manage water within Napa County. (The Sierra Club.)

research service such as Pew Research), practitioners use software programs like Microsoft Excel or IBM's SPSS Statistics to transform primary data about an issue or project into further analysis, and this information can be conveyed via a pie chart, histogram, or bar chart. Some organizations even develop more aesthetically pleasing charts and graphics in computer design and graphics programs such as Adobe Photoshop and Illustrator. In this sense, the visual communication of data is literally taken to an art form.

The success of the white paper lies in its ability to reach appropriate publics or stakeholders. Some organizations publish white papers in thematic sections of their websites, while others will give them an extra push via the media. For example, in April 2022 the U.S. Environmental Protection Agency distributed a white paper on measures that could mitigate carbon emissions from combustion turbines. The white paper was included as part of a larger EPA subsection devoted to stationary sources of air pollution. Similarly, the Sierra Club Redwood Chapter released a 2022 white paper on water sustainability management on the public news and blog section of its website (see Figure 8.1).

LETTING DATA TELL THE STORY

The emphasis on integrating key data into the larger organizational narrative is well deserved. Data, like other narrative elements, helps tell the story of an issue, industry, or organization. To use the example of reef sharks conservation, you might feature data that shows public opinion around a contended issue such as shark fishing. You could also show the number of sharks in a given jurisdiction, such as the Florida Keys, in 2024 versus 2020 versus 2010. Or you could show annual fishing data (number of violation citations broken down by type of incident, for example). Again, this is data that informs and supports the information and message that you are trying to communicate. Remember: Your white paper's message will be delivered to key decision-makers connected to your organization, including industry and government leaders. And that is what makes the confluence of data, narrative, and strategic messaging so important with this influential tactic. It is also a reminder that text is especially powerful in environmental communication when it coexists with informational or rhetorical visuals such as graphics, photographs, and maps.

The onset of the COVID-19 pandemic in 2020 provided a timely reminder to the fields of environmental communication and advocacy that nuanced, high-quality reporting was of paramount importance to the news and public information industries, especially with global news audiences struggling to make sense of a then-unknown virus. Yet the pandemic also revealed gaps in the ability of journalists and professional communicators alike to grapple with large sets of environmental, healthcare, and scientific data in terms of not only providing key insights but also reporting out to mass audiences in understandable and contextually relevant ways. Increasingly, media practitioners recognize the need to understand, efficiently navigate, and create statistical knowledge to communicate with audiences and stakeholders. This isn't just true for a long-standing issue like a health pandemic. Rather, it exists for a myriad of environmental and human health topics: climate change, air pollution, wildlife conservation, and more. The consequences of not being able to communicate data effectively have negative impacts on public perceptions of newsroom competencies and journalistic ethics. Data that is cast aside or interpreted in biased ways exacerbates public mistrust of media institutions.

The arrival of big data to the journalism industry has raised questions about how media practitioners represent such data for publics (Lesage and Hackett, 2014). To this end, how can public communication professionals best synthesize and highlight complex sets of data to be of greatest benefit to their audiences and stakeholders? The aforementioned media coverage of COVID-19 in mainstream and local media outlets has put renewed pressure on newsrooms, government officials, health advocates, and the medical industry to communicate such data efficiently and ethically. While the production/collection and interpretation of large data sets is not the sole activity of the journalism or public relations professional, the ability to communicate the meaning of statistical data to other practitioners and broader publics requires basic understanding of data research, production/analysis, and best practices in data visualization.

So where does one start on the data communication journey? Having a foundation in basic statistics is an important start. An introductory university course is a best bet, but if that's not an option, it's worth looking into any number of books devoted to beginning statistics. In conjunction with this, professionals turn to software tools like the previously mentioned Microsoft Excel and IBM SPS Statistics to collect, analyze, and share data sets. Another software tool, Tableau, also offers a compelling opportunity for data-fluent communicators to share data insights visually with sophisticated graphics.

DRONE VIDEOGRAPHY FOR ANCIENT ECOLOGY

Among the range of visual technologies available to the environmental communicator, aerial videography is among the most technologically powerful and aesthetically dramatic. And while communicators once relied on expensive helicopter or airplane flights to secure the best footage, they can now rely on personal technology in the form of drones. The growth of drones is due to a number of factors, including their affordability and relative ease of operation. They provide environmentalists with an important new tool in the battle to protect endangered wilderness areas and monitor contended ecological sites such as industrial agricultural sites or mining industry tailings ponds. Like their reporter counterparts in the news media, environmental advocates use drones for communication activities such as reporting, monitoring, and image capture in remote or distant areas.

A good example of this comes from Canada's Central Walbran Valley. As one of the largest unprotected old-growth forests on the West Coast, the Central Walbran is considered one of North America's most impressive rainforests. It is also a popular destination for recreation and outdoors enthusiasts, including hikers, campers, anglers, hunters, and mushroom pickers. This aesthetic, recreational, and ecosystem value means that it holds a special place for area residents on Vancouver Island as well as recreational tourists. Over the past few decades, this serene geography has become of significant interest for advocates on account of its bountiful forest of western redcedar, Sitka spruce, and western hemlock. Sustained protests against logging in this area in the early 1990s helped lay down a foundation for the well-known Clayoquot Sound protests of 1993, which occurred farther north near Tofino, British Columbia. Today, increasingly rare old-growth forests continue to be the focus of protection efforts across North America.

Enter the Ancient Forest Alliance, which is a self-described nonprofit organization working to protect endangered old-growth forests to "ensure a sustainable, value-added, second-growth forest industry." The Alliance doesn't just conduct its public communication through press releases, media pitches, and letter-writing campaigns in order to influence policymakers and journalists. Rather, it interfaces directly with nature to bring the story of the rainforest straight to the public. For example, it documents record-size heritage trees with professional photos and videos; it organizes public forums and slideshows to showcase the value of the forests but also the work of the organization; and it focuses on outreach with organizations that aren't always part of the conversation about environmental protection, such as local businesses, unions, and faith groups. The organization also situates social media as a key vehicle for educating the public about the plight of Canada's rainforests.

But drone videography has arguably been the organization's most effective advanced media tactic. During September 2015, the Walbran Valley was set for logging by a Canadian forestry company, with some of these heritage trees at risk of being harvested. Such a logging event would have had significant impacts not only on the forest itself but also the larger valley ecosystem, including wildlife and watersheds. In a bid to save the old-growth forest from permanent damage at the hands of logging, the AFA used drones to document the scope of this project and capture views of some of the most inaccessible parts of the rainforest.

TJ Watt, an activist and photographer with the AFA, used a drone equipped with a GoPro camera to capture otherwise unseen images of massive trees in previously hard-to-reach sections of the forest. The footage eventually formed the basis of a successful media campaign via television news as well as social media video channels like YouTube. As Watt said in an interview with *The Province* newspaper, drones serve as "a new tool in our tool box because for many people these trees might as well be on the moon. They were out of sight and mind for most. But the drones let us raise environmental awareness about these remote endangered areas where companies believe they can log with little scrutiny . . . we're going to bring the forests to the people."

The organization's first video from 2015, titled *Save the Central Walbran Valley—Canada's Grandest Ancient Forest at Risk*, featured both aerial and ground-level footage of the 500-hectare (1,235-acre) Central Walbran Valley. In addition to striking imagery of ancient western redcedar trees and aerial

The Walbran Valley's "Castle Grove" - Canada's Finest Old-Growth Cedar Forest

Figure 8.2. Videography from the Ancient Forest Alliance, seen here on their YouTube channel, has helped put a larger spotlight on threatened landscapes like southern Vancouver Island's Castle Grove, which is known as among the largest and most dense stands of ancient redcedar trees in Canada. Seen here is the "Castle Giant," which is part of the Lower Castle Grove. The sixteen-foot-diameter western redcedar is one of the largest of its kind in Canada. (Still from YouTube.)

vistas of the valley, the video also included images of its members interfacing with the forest and the trees. The second video, released in the summer of 2016, highlighted Canada's second-largest Douglas-fir tree, dubbed "Big Lonely Doug." The video, distributed on AFA's YouTube channel, drove home the message that old-growth forests are key to the survival of endangered wildlife, water, and climate stability, but also First Nations culture and local tourism. The follow-up video about the same tree is now the organization's most watched video with roughly 2.4 million views. The Ancient Forest Alliance's productions about "Big Lonely Doug" have therefore turned the fir tree into a Canadian icon and a symbol of the rainforest conservation movement. A key to driving more widespread audience interest was the organization's prolific use of media relations. The Ancient Forest Alliance regularly reached out to major Canadian news organizations to provide compelling environmental imagery but also expert interviews detailing the organization's ongoing concerns. Images of the ancient rainforest were not only viewed by a YouTube audience, but also millions of viewers of traditional TV news programs.

TACTICS AND TOOLS: STORYTELLING THROUGH AERIAL IMAGERY

As the example of the Ancient Forest Alliance demonstrates, visual communication is a powerful force in environmental advocacy. But you don't need pricey drone videography equipment to tell stories from the air. One low-cost and highly sophisticated means to producing aerial environmentalism is through readily available software technologies like Google Earth.

A sophisticated example of this is the Keystone Mapping Project developed by a California landscape photographer named Thomas Bachand. This internationally recognized photography and multimedia project uses the aerial mapping of the Keystone XL Pipeline proposal to examine larger environmental issues of land use, climate policy, and corporate transparency. According to Bachand, "a map can become so indelibly associated with a place, so as to define it—from who can own it, to how it is perceived and used" (Bachand, 2023, para. 3).

Using Google Maps and Google Earth, he created aerial maps of the controversial petroleum pipeline proposal for the Great Plains with milepost markers, waterbody crossings, water and gas wells, and more. The self-described author/photographer and web developer has tied the project to larger social issues playing out over the environment. "Not only do these maps describe the countryside as seen from space and the path of the pipeline through it, but also impacts to individuals, communities, and the environment," he wrote. "From our virtual perch we see how our dependency on fossil fuels and the forces of economics, business, government, politics, and foreign policy shape how we both perceive and engage with the landscape" (Bachand, 2023, para. 5).

Not all Google Earth projects are going to be as meticulously researched and photographed as the Keystone Mapping Project, however. Increasingly, environmental newsrooms and advocates are using Google Earth to tell stories about specific geological phenomena or geographies of special interest. Using Google Earth's narrative capabilities, a communicator can tell the story of metropolitan growth, the migratory pattern of birds, the relationship of a coal mine to a local watershed, or even a melting glacier.

Mike Reilley, an expert in Google Earth who teaches SPJ/Google News Lab programs, stresses to his journalism students that a program like Google Earth can help answer the "where" questions when they are seeking answers to the broader who, what, when, where, why, and how (Reilley, 2017). At the Global Investigative Journalism Network, he focuses on three Google Earth products: Google Earth Pro, Google Earth Engine Timelapse, and Google Earth for Chrome. He encourages students to follow official social media sites like @GoogleEarth and @GoogleNewsLab to see professional examples and to get information about program capabilities and updates.

Based on this notion of the power of visual storytelling and communicating in green advocacy, communicators can get started by choosing an environmental advocacy topic or site to form the basis of a Google Earth storytelling project. For example, a communicator might choose to focus on a national park, a chain of islands, a transboundary region, or even a Superfund site like Hanford. Advocates might also look to specific industrial, mining, or energy projects, as well as transportation and logistics venues such as maritime ports and airports. For the public interest communicator telling an aerial story about the environment, it's a good idea to think like a journalist. Just like other public communication and mass media tactics, Google Earth and other aerial visual projects should be relevant, informative, and newsworthy.

CASE STUDY: MIKE SATO KEEPS HIS COMMUNITY INFORMED ABOUT THE SALISH SEA

The story of the Salish Sea on the North American West Coast presents a compelling communication case study in terms of the marine system's naming and its subsequent coverage in the media. The naming is in recognition of the transboundary nature of the watershed's ecology and wildlife. It also pays homage to the ecosystem's Coast Salish tribal communities and their long-standing history in the region. At least one nonprofit enterprise is focusing on this intersection of community, governance, industry, and marine biology. The *Salish Sea News and Weather*, published by Salish Sea Communications, tracks numerous stories across the Salish Sea transborder ecosystem for its thousands of email and social media subscribers. The publication's weekday content is a curated aggregation of news articles about wilderness areas, industrial projects, beach cleanups, climate change topics, and border-specific issues. The newsletter's founder, Mike Sato, is also the managing editor of Bellingham-based *Salish Current*, a nonprofit news site that serves northwestern Washington State.

The origins of *Salish Sea News and Weather* go back to 1997, when Sato began *Puget Sound News and Weather* as part of the membership organization People for Puget Sound to track environmental stories. After leaving the organization in 2012, he renamed the publication *Salish Sea News and Weather* and expanded aggregation and curation of news articles to both sides of the British Columbia/Washington State border. While coverage is focused primarily on the Salish Sea bioregion, it also looks to interconnected issues playing out across the Pacific Northwest, from salmon runs in the Columbia River to debates over wolves in Montana and Idaho. Between its blog and email services, the publication reaches policymakers in science, government, higher education, and transportation. Sato believes that the nonprofit model, which treats news like a public good, is the future for news in the transboundary Cascadia region.

Similarly, with the *Salish Current* Sato is looking to adjoin hyperlocal issues in Washington's State's northwest quadrant to macro-political, economic, and environmental topics. The open-access format publication contains original news content as well as a weekly newsletter that highlights original reporting and a curated aggregation of news from northwestern Washington State. Sato points to the recent closure of an aluminum manufacturing facility in Washington State's northwest corner as an example of the kind of story that requires in-depth and multidimensional journalistic attention and community reporting. "We want to create a community forum [with *Salish Current*] with people who are thoughtful and can communicate different issues around a subject."

TACTITIAN'S TOOLBOX: ACE THE MEDIA INTERVIEW

Congratulations! Your media-pitching to your network of editors, reporters, and bloggers has paid big dividends, and you have just heard some good news from the television network affiliate in your city: Its environmental beat reporter is planning to attend your organization's public awareness event. As part of the visit, the reporter wants to conduct a proper, one-on-one interview with you that will be part of a larger news package airing later in the day. A positive story in the media could have major ramifications for your organization's public awareness, lobbying, or fundraising efforts. This means your role as a spokesperson is key to the big-picture success of your organization.

You will want to get your talking points in order before everything else. But it also means you'll want to lay down a foundation for overall interview success. When reporters conduct interviews with organizations, they are looking to add expertise, opinion, and insight to the stories they are producing or writing. But spokespersons need to make sure they are also engaged in the outcomes from this interviewing process.

One simplified approach to navigating the media interview is championed by marketing communications expert Kari Hernandez, the co-founder of Ink. According to Hernandez, a "rule of three" draws upon a tradition of Roman rhetorical device in postulating that concepts and words that come in three are more impactful and memorable (Hernandez, 2023). For example, "life, liberty, and the pursuit of happiness" represent three unalienable rights from the Declaration of Independence that are etched into American politics and history. In environmental parlance, that rule of three might translate into health outcomes, biological features, or geological phenomena. For example, the three R's of responsible waste management—reduce, reuse, and recycle—provide a simple and memorable framework for citizens and businesses. The rule of three was also used by Great Plains pipeline opponents to build public awareness of the potential hazards of petroleum infrastructure. During the peak of its activism against pipeline company TransCanada, the organization Bold Nebraska regularly appealed for protection of three domains—"land, air, and water"—in media stories to highlight the different ways that oil spills could harm local communities.

Hernandez also points out that the rule of three can help spokespersons retain control during a media interview. That's because if you try to bring too many facts or concepts to an interview you probably won't remember them all when it's your time to talk (Hernandez, 2023). Furthermore, the reporter probably won't remember more than three of your concepts, nor will they have the chance to relay more than three big ideas in their story. By sticking to three, you'll be able to prioritize which strategic messages are communicated not only to the reporter, but also to the larger public.

Ready to participate in your media interview? Now that you are versed in the "rule of three," here are ten quick pointers to make the rest of your interview a success:

1. Remember that you are always on the record, even when cameras and recording devices aren't turned on. That means you should be mindful of what you communicate outside of your formal interview. You should be helpful and professional with your journalistic colleagues, but don't engage in gossip, speculation, or anything else that you wouldn't want to air on the nightly newscast.

2. Dress appropriately for the interview. If you are appearing on camera, you will want to look the part of a spokesperson and align with your organization. What to wear then? It depends on whether you are representing a government agency, a green investment firm, or an environmental advocacy group. The key is to remember that you are representing your organization.

3. Visual backgrounds matter, and not only for superficial reasons. Yes, backgrounds can convey a sense of expertise, acumen, or human interest. But more importantly, you'll want to avoid backgrounds that feature distracting lighting, sounds, or movement. Make sure that the reporter, and the audience, can focus on you and your message—not what's going on behind you.

4. Be in the moment during your interview. This goes back to the rule of three. By simplifying your messaging, you'll be able to have a genuine conversation with the reporter and focus on their questions, while articulating your own organizational insights with eloquence and thoughtfulness. Being in the moment means that you are not worried about what the reporter is going to ask next, or worse, what you are going to be doing after the interview.

5. Be conversational. By going into your interview with a friendly, chatty, authentic demeanor, you'll find yourself less stressed, more relaxed, and better able to navigate any moments of conflict or tension that arises during the dialogue.

6. Always be truthful with reporters. Ethics is at the heart of successful environmental advocacy and public relations. And if you can't answer a question because you don't have the answer or because of legal ramifications, it's perfectly acceptable to relay that to the reporter. But never distort or manipulate data or information to sway a reporter to your organization's point of view.

7. Avoid the phrase "no comment" if you can't or won't answer a particular question. You might indicate to the reporter that you don't know the answer or need more time to find the information in question. But the words "no comment" send a message that you are obscuring or outright hiding key information.

8. Avoid name-calling or emotionally charged conflict with a reporter if an interview takes a turn for the worse. It is important to keep your cool at all times. If and when tensions do arise, take a deep breath, go for that drink of water, and remember that you are representing your organizational colleagues in not only your messaging but also your demeanor.

9. Remember that you are *not* Google. Even though you probably know about as much if not more about your organization or issue as anyone, you simply can't have every data point, historical fact, and research result memorized for instant dissemination. Not only is it perfectly acceptable to admit that you "don't know" in an interview, it is expected. Simply tell the reporter that you will follow up via email with the specific data or information they are looking for, and then do so accordingly.

10. Know that this is ultimately an interview for you and your organization or issue as much as it is for the reporter. After all, you are taking valuable time out of your schedule to assist the reporter in getting their story right. But it's just as important that the interview results in a valuable impact for your organization.

DISCUSSION QUESTIONS

1. They say that a picture tells a thousand words. What is a picture that changed the way you engaged with nature or helped you reconsider an ecological issue?
2. What are some of the ethical and legal challenges facing operators of drones not only for the purposes of journalism, but also for activism and public communication?
3. How might communicators use Google Earth to tell stories about green issues or causes?

KEY TERMS

Aerial videography
Data visualization
Drone activism
Image events
Media interviewing
Rule of three for interviews
Spatial communication

Videography
White paper

KEY EVENTS, LOCATIONS, AND ORGANIZATIONS

Ancient Forest Alliance
Central Walbran Valley
Google Earth
Google Maps
Keystone Mapping Project
Salish Current
Salish Sea News and Weather

REFERENCES

Bachand, T. (2023). Keystone Mapping Project. Retrieved online from: https://key-stone.steamingmules.com/about/.

Dale, S. (1996). *McLuhan's Children: The Greenpeace Message and the Media.* Toronto: Between the Lines.

DeLuca, K. M. (2005). *Image Politics: The New Rhetoric of Environmental Activism.* London: Psychology Press.

Hernandez, K. (2023). Three reasons your messaging isn't pulling through. INK Communications: Brand Strategy. Retrieved from: https://ink-co.com/insights/three-reasons-messaging-isnt-pulling-through/.

Lesage, F., and Hackett, R. A. (2014). Between objectivity and openness—The mediality of data for journalism. *Media and Communication*, 2(2): 42–54.

Perez, M. (2011, May 17). White papers: What you need to know. PR Newswire.

Reilley, M. (2017). Bring the world to the classroom with Google Earth tools. Mediashift. Retrieved from: http://mediashift.org/2017/08/bring-the-world-to-the-classroom-with-google-earth-tools/.

Chapter Nine

Digital Environmentalism

This chapter focuses on the growing realm of social, online, and digital media within environmental strategic communication. Learning objectives of this chapter include the contextualizing of digital and social media as a forum for persuasion, interaction, and sharing; the role of specific channels like X (formerly Twitter) and Instagram; and the growth of this area through specific approaches like podcasting, gaming, and social media hashtags. The examples provided in this chapter demonstrate the breadth of trajectory of digital media within environmentalism, and the ability of social media channels to support advocacy, collaboration, and community.

A TRANSFORMED MEDIA LANDSCAPE

When Andrew Dessler, a professor of atmospheric sciences at Texas A&M University, appeared on an episode of the popular *Joe Rogan Experience* podcast, the media took notice. Dessler, who has provided expert comment to media outlets like CNBC and MSNBC, took a slightly different view of climate change than the MMA fighter turned media powerhouse. Asked by Rogan if he would engage in a debate with skeptics about the science of climate change, Dessler gave the comedian a flat-out "no": "My feeling is that I won't debate the science. So the science is set," he said bluntly. "The temperature is warming, humans have caused it."

During the podcast, Rogan countered by providing the perspective of a previous guest, Steve Koonin, a physicist at New York University, holding that climate change science remained unsettled and was exaggerated by the media. The brief but telling exchange prompted thousands of opinions from online commentators on places like YouTube and Twitter, along with coverage from several media outlets, including *Fox News*, which ran a headline declaring, "Climate scientist tells Joe Rogan he refuses to debate dissenters on climate change." However, while some conservative-leaning publications took Dessler to task for his position, other outlets celebrated the climate science professor's public appearance.

Climatewire, a news service focused on environmental policy, noted that Dessler's two-hour podcast provided the rare opportunity to connect with an online audience of eleven million people and provide the issue with greater depth and exploration. The Dessler interview "was a comprehensive, two-hour exploration of climate science that Rogan's massive audience rarely gets to hear." Dessler, according to *Climatewire*'s Scott Waldman, may have even won Rogan over, thanks in part to his explaining the science of the Texas freeze that prompted devastating blackouts, and the benefits of reducing fossil fuels: "By the end of the episode, Rogan appeared assured by the scientific research Dessler had presented—particularly around their home state of Texas and its reliance on renewable energy." The series of media events involving Rogan, Dessler, and Koonin finally led to an impressive climate change debate during the summer of 2022, in which the two professors sparred over the view that "climate science compels us to make large and rapid reductions in greenhouse gas emissions." It represented a milestone in the evolution of podcasting as one of the most influential media for intellectual exchange on pressing environmental and social topics.

More than ever before, people are turning to social or digital media to receive their news and information about the world they live in. According to a 2022 report from the Pew Research Center, about a quarter of U.S. adults say they get some of their news from podcasts. Furthermore, according to Pew Research, podcasts are enjoyed by Americans from all walks of life. The uptake of podcasting by Americans shows few differences in terms of ethnic background or political affiliation. In fact, roughly one in three adults under the age of fifty admit to getting some of their news from the podcasting format. That's why podcasts like Rogan's long-form interviews, or the *Office Ladies*, featuring *The Office*'s Jenna Fischer and Angela Kinsey, have vaulted into such prominence in American public life. These programs have an ability to not only relay perspectives and information that is compelling to Americans, but also reframe the way citizens think about public issues.

ENVIRONMENTAL PODCASTS INFORM, EDUCATE, AND ENTERTAIN

With so many podcasts to choose from, it might be daunting for an environmental communicator to come up with a short list of go-to programs. In 2022, Earth.org's Deena Robinson came up with this list of the twenty-two best environmental podcasts, ranging from topics such as environmental science to climate change to greenwashing.

1. *Outrage and Optimism*
2. *Sustainababble*
3. *Big Closets Small Planet: Michael Schragger*
4. *A Matter of Degrees*
5. *Sustainable(ish)*
6. *The Wild*
7. *Wild Lens' Eyes on Conservation*
8. *Jane Goodall: The Hopecast*
9. *Think Sustainably*
10. *Global Goals Cast*
11. *Climate Rising*
12. *Mother Earth News and Friends*
13. *Yale Climate Connections*
14. *The Food Fight*
15. *The Nature Podcast*
16. *So Hot Right Now*
17. *The Climate Briefing*
18. *Women Mind the Water*
19. *How to Save the Planet*
20. *What Could Go Right?*
21. *Climate One*
22. *Forces for Nature*

INFLUENCERS IN THE DIGITAL AGE

A strong grasp of individual and group influence has obvious implications for green communicators, particularly where the introduction of products, policies, and innovations is concerned. Yes, we want our environmental messages to be amplified and to resonate with the public. But we also want the public to be driven to some form of action, whether it is the purchasing of sustainable products or voting for a political candidate. This is known as citizen or consumer *mobilization*. A challenge for both environmental practitioners and those who study environmentalism is to understand the work of opinion leadership in the digital space—since interpersonal communication takes on different features online. This gap between in-person and virtual interaction was exacerbated during the COVID-19 pandemic, with more people utilizing digital social spaces like Facebook, Instagram, and Zoom, whereas they might have previously engaged in person.

In the digital space, communication channels play a key role in the dissemination of green messages that are positive or negative. That's because social media are driven by networks of individual users. In their *influentials hypothesis*, consumer researchers Duncan Watts and Peter Dodds (2007) argue that argument quantity should go along with quality: It's better to have more opinion leaders getting behind a cause or an idea than less. That's why social media channels like Twitter, which aggregate opinion from a wide range of citizens, have become so important. Networks of influence succeed not just because of charming or chatty individuals, but rather from a "critical mass of easily influenced individuals influencing other easy-to-influence people" (Watts and Dodds, 454). This in part underpins the success of the many online "influencers" who we are familiar with today on Instagram and TikTok.

But the upside of exchanging information online is the concept of *self-efficacy* in environmental persuasion. Self-efficacy is understood as the perception that one can perform a behavior or influence others' behaviors to achieve a greater goal (Dalrymple et al., 2013). For example, you might consider yourself capable of championing for more park space in your city because of your own communication or civic engagement skills. However, you might also be confident about your goal for more parkland because of the existing goodwill and pro-environmental stances of your local city council and fellow citizens. Through this concept of self-efficacy, it is easy to understand the imperative for our institutions, such as government and the private sector, to instill confidence in their stakeholders and communicate their values to the world. But it's also easy to imagine why individuals might feel they have more power online, where the barriers to effective communication are removed, and the ability to connect with others through tweets, reviews, videos, and podcasts is much greater.

VIEWS, REPLIES, AND RETWEETS

It would be impossible to overestimate the impact of X (or Twitter) in the early part of the twenty-first century. From groundbreaking social movements to some of the most contested presidential campaigns in political history, Twitter has provided a robust forum for the exchange of social and environmental worldviews, ideologies, and messages. It is also a critical venue for the shaping of public opinion. However, beyond the most well-known opinion leaders, celebrities, politicians, and corporations, this influence of the medium is not always apparent. After all, many users on Twitter only have a handful of followers and seldom communicate on the platform. Others might have hundreds or even thousands of followers, but they close their discussions by way of strict privacy settings.

To understand Twitter, then, and by extension other social media that serve environmental communication, one must understand the mechanics of these channels. Twitter, for example, allows for wider distribution of messaging through its built-in tools that allow users to cluster, reply to, or rebroadcast the back-and-forth exchange of information. This can be an especially powerful tool for environmentalists, who toggle between online and offline environments. For example, live-tweeting at environmental protests can serve multiple purposes, including communicating to other members, publicizing efforts for journalists, and amplifying protest for a much larger constituency in the social media environment. This is known as *digital activism*.

One of the advantages of digital media over other forms of communication is this multiplicity of capabilities built into these formats. A key advantage of Twitter over an offline tactic like a newsletter or poster is its ability for members to amplify messages through retweeting. This function allows advocates or protesters who aren't present within an organization, or at a high-profile event, to convey the significance of an issue or an event by pushing the message out to their own networks and followers. In certain cases, this can transform a message's impact from one that is seen by a few dozen faithful devotees of an organization to millions of citizens around the world. In such a case, a message might be viewed as trending regionally or nationally, or enjoying virality across multiple digital channels.

However, popular social media like Twitter, Instagram, Facebook, and TikTok offer no guarantee of successful message distribution for communication professionals. There are numerous accounts of Twitter messaging programs that have been hijacked by outside or even oppositional interests, which results in publics becoming distracted, confused, or even hostile. The chaotic nature of social media provides an important and ongoing reminder that environmental public communication is best served by authentic social media engagement that lays out strategy and objectives, and that is defined by results serving online and offline environments.

According to communication strategist Ginni Dietrich, digital and social media are part of a larger informational ecosystem understood as a merger of earned, paid, owned, and shared media. The first three categories refer to the well-established outputs of public communicators. Earned media refers to placement and publication in journalism and media outlets; paid media is advertising, though Dietrich points specifically to digital advertising like Facebook, as well as sponsored content and email marketing; and owned media represents the in-house media that a communicator or organization has control over. It is the shared category, driven by digital networks, that represents the newest and arguably most energized space, however. According to Dietrich, shared media has become for organizations the main source of internal and external communication. It is content that establishes engagement and community (Dietrich, 2014).

Let us use as an example the case provided from Chapter 3 ("Case Study: Transboundary Advocacy Highlights Concerns for Water and Wildlife"). The coalition of cross-border watershed advocates in the Pacific Northwest not only distributed press releases and advisories that eventually turned into prominent stories in major newspapers (earned media), but they also published their own stories and articles on their website and digital media channels (owned media). On top of this, the coalition even purchased advertisements with metropolitan news publishers in Canada (paid media). Finally, they encouraged supporters to be participants in the advocacy by sharing messages in online forums, rebroadcasting hashtags like #SavetheSkagit, and engaging in online forum discussions (shared media).

There is overlap between the categories: for example, the area where shared and owned media is the domain of publishing platforms and content curation and distribution. And the crossroads of shared and earned media is where community thrives in all of its forms—engagement, brand ambassadorship, advocacy, and user-generated content. Finally, the area where earned, owned, paid, and shared media meet represents an organization's larger reputational efforts, including trust, credibility, and thought leadership.

VISUAL RENDERINGS OF NATURE AND SELF

Social media platforms do more than facilitate social exchange between individuals or organizations and their audiences in the digital arena; they also mediate users' experiences of production, sharing, and interaction (Hochman and Manovich, 2013). In other words, these media directly shape the nature of our daily interactions. That helps explain why some social media platforms feel more exciting or combustible, while others feel slower-paced or cautious. While tonality drives the social media experience for environmental communicators, the content itself is a major factor in how social media conversations are consumed.

View more on Instagram

♡ ◯ ⬆   ⬚

14,642 likes

Add a comment...   ◎

*Figure 9.1.   The social media hashtag of #VanLife has been especially
popular on Instagram, where enthusiasts of the outdoors and recreational
vehicles share images of their travels and breathtaking landscapes from
around the world. The author of this post, Foster Huntington, helped
popularize the #VanLife concept in 2011 when he traveled across the
United States in a camper van and began posting about his adventures
on a popular Tumblr account. Foster, a native of Skamania, Washington,
has since authored a book about the van lifestyle, appropriately called*
Van Life: Your Home on the Road. *(@fosterhunting/Instagram.)*

While social media channels like Twitter and Facebook offer the ability to win hearts and minds with the deployment of primarily textual information in conjunction with visuals, other channels like Instagram and TikTok are driven by visual content. Like Twitter and Facebook, Instagram is a social networking service that allows for the exchange of ideas and information between users, and for subsequent organization of these ideas through clustering mechanisms. The primary engine that drives Instagram's popularity, however, is the ability to upload photographs and video, which are then organized by hashtags and geographic tagging. This content can also be edited with filters, which allows users to imbue their contributions with aesthetic, emotional, or intellectual personalization.

As a medium immersed in the visual (much like TikTok or YouTube), Instagram serves as a conduit for self-representation, and this is true for individuals and organizations. According to one study, users of the service have five primary social/psychological motives when using Instagram: self-expression, social interaction, archiving, peeking, and escapism (Lee et al., 2015). This helps explain why many people interested in ecological topics spend so much time with this channel and others like it. The concepts of "peeking" and "escapism" align with appeals to outdoor recreation and engaging with nature. Furthermore, motives such as "self-expression" and "social interaction" underscore the potential for environmental learning, advocacy, and behavioral modeling with larger audiences.

A long-running example in the Instagram sphere comes from the hashtag #VanLife, which highlights the lifestyles of van enthusiasts across the globe and their travels to often remote and ecologically noteworthy destinations. The online movement has been understood as a digital tribe of sorts, with members using Instagram (and other visual digital media) to not only engage and document in a nomadic fashion, but also emphasize eco-lifestyle values such as minimalism and mobility (Gretzel and Hardy, 2019).

GOING TO THE #VW DARKSIDE

"May the force be with you" is not an expression heard often at climate policy summits. But for street activists looking to change hearts and minds at a prominent London intersection in 2011, the expression from the *Star Wars* film franchise spoke volumes about the powerful intersection of popular culture, digital activism, and the climate. During a London rush hour, members of Greenpeace dressed as white-armored Stormtroopers marched onto the city's Old Street with "The Imperial March" song playing in the background. Behind them, Darth Vader banners were hurled over digital billboards

PRWeek

Greenpeace's spoof of Volkswagen's Star Wars ad removed from YouTube

LucasFilm has forced YouTube to remove Greenpeace's spoof of Volkswagen's 'Star Wars' style advert.

by Sara Luker

Figure 9.2.   Greenpeace's campaign against Volkswagen using Star Wars *characters like Darth Vader attracted the interest of industry publications like PR Week, but it also caught the attention of LucasFilms, which forced the environmental advocacy group to remove its* Star Wars–*themed advertisements from YouTube. (Sara Luker/PRWeek.)*

proclaiming a message of "Volkswagen: The Darkside" and #VWDarkside. Greenpeace's eco-friendly Stormtroopers were looking to shame automotive manufacturer Volkswagen into backing European climate laws intended to mitigate carbon emissions. As this theatrical performance played out on the streets of London's Old Town, the hashtags #OldStreet and #Stormtroopers began trending globally on social media.

Greenpeace's campaign moved quickly from digital media like Twitter and Facebook to traditional media platforms. The next day, a prominent city newspaper published a photo of Darth Vader and the Stormtroopers admonishing Volkswagen at the event, with accompanying text explaining the politics of climate change regulation in the European Union. Meanwhile, supporters across digital platforms were encouraged by Greenpeace to join a "Jedi Rebellion" by engaging their local political leaders or signing online petitions devoted to the cause. By lobbying for climate action through the activation of Hollywood appeals, Greenpeace showed an uncanny ability to time their campaign with broader interest in the popular culture generated by the *Star Wars* franchise. There is one other element that worked to Greenpeace's advantage: urban space as a stage for the transmission of popular environmental appeals. Greenpeace's demonstration connected directly with audiences in London's Old Town by tapping into the vibrancy and interactivity of the city, juxtaposing a setting of density and congestion with the perils of vehicular emissions.

GAMING PERSUASION

It is not just the social space that attracts environmental communicators. Because video games provide a simulation of fictionalized or real-world scenarios, they are sometimes held up as an opportunity for optimal civic engagement and interaction about ecological/political topics. Common elements with some games (though not all) include civic action, consideration of controversial topics, and participation in groups for sharing interests and information (Kahne, Middaugh, and Evans, 2009). The popular game *SimCity*, for example, provides an open-ended urban planning environment that considers government and societal issues such as housing, taxation, parks, and transportation. Because such games, in addition to being popular, can be deeply engaging, they are positioned to influence a wide range of attitudes and behaviors (64). There has also been a growing interest in games simulating specific social outcomes or promoting a healthier lifestyle. This genre of persuasive games that strive for human health or social impact requires appropriate strategic planning, however. Organizations should know their target group and their main objectives before commencing with the design of a game. And according to gaming researchers, they should use game design elements that will compel and engage audiences, and include subject experts from an early design stage to ensure that the game's content is persuasive but also technically and informationally sound (Brox, Fernandez-Luque, and Tøllefsen, 2011).

Ian Bogost, an award-winning game designer and media studies professor, points to the use of computers to carry out different versions of existing written and oral discourses, such as letters transforming into emails, and conversations becoming instant messaging sessions. The gaming expert has called the digital rhetorical approach within computer software "procedural authorship" (Bogost, 2010). He draws from the example of a video game directed at an international restaurant franchise, which teaches players about corruption and excess in the fast-food industry. Bogost calls this genre of game the "anti-advergame"—created to disparage a company rather than support it, and forcing the player to make difficult moral choices as consumers.

CASE STUDY: PETA, PIXELS, AND ANIMAL ADVOCACY

In November 2014, the animal rights group People for the Ethical Treatment of Animals (PETA) established a first in the popular video game *Minecraft*: It established an "Animal Utopia" where digital animals such as wandering sheep and pigs could be protected from the harmful actions of other players. This intersection of advocacy and video-gaming is notable in that it leveraged the game itself to convey a social or environmental message. Digital activists have been prolific users of social media channels, but until the past decade they had been largely absent from the video-gaming sector. For organizations that are using video games as a vehicle for social change, there has remained some questions about the effectiveness of gaming as a tool of public outreach and engagement.

PETA's foray into *Minecraft* culture might have caught some gamers off guard. *Minecraft* is not a lightning rod for political controversy in the way that some other video game titles are. But PETA is no stranger to gaming culture. The organization previously promoted its animal and wildlife protection message with games parodying other popular titles and iconic gaming characters, including *Mario Kills Tanooki* and *Pokémon Black and Blue*.

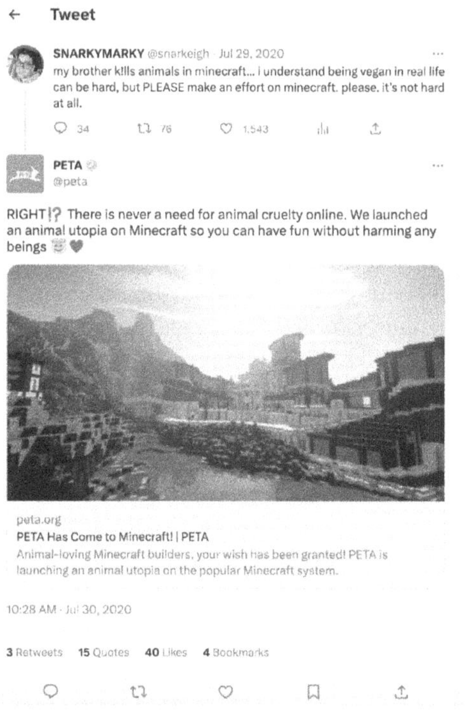
Tweet
SNARKYMARKY @snarkeigh · Jul 29, 2020
my brother k!lls animals in minecraft... i understand being vegan in real life can be hard, but PLEASE make an effort on minecraft. please. it's not hard at all.
34
76
1,543
PETA
@peta
RIGHT!? There is never a need for animal cruelty online. We launched an animal utopia on Minecraft so you can have fun without harming any beings
peta.org
PETA Has Come to Minecraft! | PETA
Animal-loving Minecraft builders, your wish has been granted! PETA is launching an animal utopia on the popular Minecraft system.
10:28 AM · Jul 30, 2020
3 Retweets 15 Quotes 40 Likes 4 Bookmarks

Figure 9.3. PETA's interest in Minecraft *has captured interest from video game enthusiasts as well as animal rights activists. The organization has been an advocate for animal rights on the popular game title as early as 2014, when it launched its "Animal Utopia" to protect wandering farm animals within the creative/adventure 3D game. (@snarkleigh, @peta/Twitter.)*

This movement into gaming reflects a recognition on the part of organizations that audiences increasingly spend recreational time in digital environments that are shaped by gaming ecosystems. PETA has also provided input for gaming industry developments, and notably commended Nintendo's launch of the *Nintendogs* game, a puppy simulator for Nintendo systems. The game was previously awarded with PETA Europe's "Best Animal-Friendly Video Game" prize—indicative of PETA's reach in the gaming sphere, both as a producer but also as an industry observer. Animal advocates aren't alone in embracing video game technology for political and environmental messaging.

CASE STUDY: REI'S #OPTOUTSIDE FOSTERS ONLINE/OFFLINE ENGAGEMENT

The November shopping "holiday" known as Black Friday has long been associated with larger conversations in the United States about rampant consumerism. The Friday following the U.S. Thanksgiving has come to be associated with the beginning of the holiday shopping season and invokes the scene of consumers lining up for discounted television sets and many other consumer goods.

The day, not surprisingly, has long been in the crosshairs of anti-consumerism activists. Vancouver, B.C.-based *Adbusters*, for example, has promoted a "Buy Nothing Day" on the same Friday since the early 1990s to address issues of overconsumption in society and their negative impacts on communities and the environment. In 2011, outdoor clothier Patagonia ran a full-page ad in the *New York Times* with a seemingly counterintuitive message also aimed at overconsumption on Black Friday: "Don't buy this jacket." Such activities highlight how the day has become a flashpoint in the ongoing debates over consumerism. Perhaps not ironically, consumers themselves have taken up the rallying cry against Black Friday. News narratives often situate the shopping stampedes across the country—seen sometimes as unruly crowds fighting over home appliances and electronic devices—as the inevitable embodiment of greed, envy, indulgence, and waste.

Seattle-based outdoor retailer REI entered the same conversation with a Black Friday campaign of its own in 2015. With over twenty million members, REI is the largest consumer cooperative in the United States, and describes itself as a "passionate advocate for the outdoors . . . committed to creating access to inspiring outdoor places across the country" (REI. com, 2017, para. 1). Members pay a one-time membership fee, which gives them a share in the cooperative's profits through an annual member refund, as well as a vote in the organization's annual board elections. It also gives them a commercial attachment to the great outdoors through the opportunity to buy clothing and equipment for pursuits that include hiking, cycling, and camping.

Founded in 1938 by mountain climbers Lloyd and Mary Anderson, the roots of the organization are in serious alpine sports such as climbing, mountaineering, and backpacking. In recent decades, the REI retailing model has moved into more mainstream activities, including family camping, kayaking, hiking, and cycling. This includes the retailing of sporting clothing geared for these activities, but also for everyday casual wear. The growth of this market in the United States has fostered long-term growth for REI, which in 2020 alone laid claim to over $2.75 billion in sales. This revenue windfall allows the company to annually donate millions of dollars across four hundred

Figures 9.4 and 9.5.   Sustainability advocates like SGP Partnership have used the #OptOutside hashtag to recommend REI's values of social responsibility and outdoors conservation. The hashtag, which was first used by the outdoors apparel retailer in 2015, has helped to advance REI's outdoors mandate while engaging its employees and members, and raising awareness of the outdoor co-op's brand nationally. Similarly, recreation groups like the Washington Trail Association have partnered with REI to raise awareness of #OptOutside and encourage hikers to explore new trails. (@ SGPPartnership/Twitter.) (@WTA_hikers/Twitter.)

not-for-profit organizations and distribute hundreds of millions of dollars in dividends to its membership.

Sustainability has been an oft-stated organizational goal for REI. The cooperative works with suppliers to enhance the environmental sustainability of its product offerings and utilizes alternate energy to power its retail operations. It also claims the first distribution center in the United States to be certified as LEED Platinum and Net Zero Energy, both key benchmarks for sustainability. In addition, REI makes large donations to nonprofits across the United States that are focused on environmental impact, social change, and ecological conservation.

REI advocates on behalf of its outdoors-minded membership with a motto of "purpose before profits." This mission was apparent when the co-op launched #OptOutside—an organization-wide public communication campaign with a hashtag moniker intended to simultaneously advance its outdoor mandate, engage its employees and members, and raise awareness of the REI brand nationally. Unlike other national retailers, REI closed all of its stores on Black Friday, encouraging employees and members to instead use the extra time to participate in outdoor activities.

For environmental communicators, the two-way nature of social media allows stakeholders to express themselves—and the nature of their relationship to an organization—in a multitude of ways. In the case of #OptOutside, this relationship with the company was expressed through not only digital messaging between the cooperative and its membership, but by physical action. Motivated by the hashtag, members and followers of the organization visited a variety of outdoor spaces, from remote mountain ranges and lakes to local city parks and greenbelts. Audiences communicated what they saw and experienced at these spaces through words and images conveyed online. This included wildlife sightings, weather conditions, and geological features as well as their relationship with the REI mission and the cooperative's outdoor products. For individuals who engaged with REI's #OptOutside campaign, Black Friday served as a catalyst for brand ambassadorship and outdoor advocacy.

DISCUSSION QUESTIONS

1. PETA was one of the first organizations to integrate environmental activism into gaming. Are there other examples like this from either gaming companies or environmental organizations?

2. What made the #OptOutside campaign so successful, and how might other organizations facilitate an offline/online dynamic with their social media programs?
3. Why are hashtags, retweets, and information networks so important in social media? How do they build support for green programs and causes?

KEY TERMS

Citizen mobilization
Consumer cooperative
Digital environmentalism
Gaming persuasion
Hashtag
Influentials hypothesis
LEED Platinum
Net Zero Energy
Retweet
Sustainability

KEY EVENTS, LOCATIONS, AND ORGANIZATIONS

Adbusters
Climatewire
#OptOutside
People for the Ethical Treatment of Animals
REI
#VanLife

REFERENCES

Bogost, I. (2010). *Persuasive Games: The Expressive Power of Videogames*. Cambridge, MA: MIT Press.
Brox, E., Fernandez-Luque, L., and Tøllefsen, T. (2011). Healthy gaming—video game design to promote health. *Applied Clinical Informatics*, 2(02): 128–42.
Dalrymple, K. E., Shaw, B. R. and Brossard, D. (2013). "Following the leader: Using opinion leaders in environmental strategic communication." *Society & Natural Resources*, 26(12): 1438–53.
Dietrich, G. (2014). *Spin Sucks: Communication and Reputation Management in the Digital Age*. Indianapolis: Que Publishing.

Gretzel, U., and Hardy, A. (2019). #VanLife: Materiality, makeovers and mobility amongst digital nomads. *E-Review of Tourism Research*, 16(2/3).

Hochman, N., and Manovich, L. (2013). Zooming into an Instagram City: Reading the local through social media. *First Monday*, 18(7).

Kahne, J., Middaugh, E., and Evans, C. (2009). *The Civic Potential of Video Games*. Cambridge, MA: MIT Press, 111.

Lee, E., Lee, J. A., Moon, J. H., and Sung, Y. (2015). Pictures speak louder than words: Motivations for using Instagram. *Cyberpsychology, Behavior, and Social Networking*, 18(9): 552–56.

REI.com. (2017). About REI. Retrieved from: http://newsroom.rei.com/company -information/about-rei/.

Waldman, S. (2023). Meet the climate scientist taking on Joe Rogan and QAnon. *E&E News: Climatewire*. Retrieved from: https://www.eenews.net/articles/meet -the-climate-scientist-taking-on-joe-rogan-and-qanon/.

Watts, D. J., and Dodds, P. S. (2007). Influentials, networks, and public opinion formation. *Journal of Consumer Research*, 34(4): 441–58.

Chapter Ten

Corporate Social Responsibility

This chapter focuses on the impact of corporate social responsibility and related concepts on environmental strategic communication. Learning objectives of this chapter include the contextualizing of corporate social responsibility within the public communication work of organizations; emergent approaches such as socially responsible investing (SRI) and environmental, social, and governance (ESG); and connecting such efforts to sustainability, environmental responsibility, and community engagement. The examples provided in this chapter demonstrate the breadth of environmental and social responsibility approaches and how they align with stakeholder, shareholder, and corporate governance objectives.

COMPANIES COMMIT TO ENVIRONMENTAL AND SOCIAL VALUES

Can the aluminum industry really make a difference in the global push to reduce greenhouse gas emissions? It is a question you might contemplate next time you're using up that roll of aluminum foil to prepare a plate of chili cheese fries or wrap a gyro. Pittsburgh-based Alcoa, a company that invented the aluminum business 135 years ago, seems to think it indeed can make a difference. The company wants aluminum to be an integral, affordable part of modern life. At the same time, it wants the mainstream uptake of aluminum products to be aligned with emergent standards for the reduction of carbon emissions.

As a bauxite mining company (bauxite ore is the world's primary source of aluminum), Alcoa isn't the first company that comes to mind when one thinks of leading the industry charge to meet aspirational climate standards. Indeed, the mining company has often played the foil (no pun intended!) to other green leaders from the realms of clean energy, green consumer brands, and environmental nonprofits. But the times are changing, and companies from the ranks of mining, oil and gas, and transportation are among those that are attempting to align with a broader global interest in reducing the ecological footprint of industry.

In 2021, Alcoa announced a new endeavor to reach net-zero greenhouse gas emissions by 2050, a target that would coexist with existing targets, including the reduction of GHG emissions from its smelting and refining operations by 50 percent by the end of the decade. Alcoa president and CEO Roy Harvey pointed to his company's environmental, social, and governance practices, noting that this specific endeavor was an extension of the company's decarbonization pathway. This journey also included collaborations with leading consumer brands like Apple and Audi to develop carbon-free aluminum production capabilities. Clearly the company is driven by green objectives that are having an impact not only on the company's supply chain but also on production processes and even the overall corporate mission.

Alcoa's foray into carbon emissions reduction is an example of corporate social responsibility (CSR). Through CSR strategies and tactics, companies large and small are recognizing their commitment to environmental and social value that go well beyond profit motives. Simply articulating a green-friendly message isn't good enough, however. Companies that espouse the tenets of CSR are expected to align their communication with real action, and vice versa. That translates into improved manufacturing processes, transparency of sourcing raw and secondary materials, and being attuned to the needs of employees and community members.

Make no doubt about it, CSR has emerged as a defining force in the business world and in many of our social institutions. But what is it, and why has it been so successful in transforming the way people think about the businesses immersed in their communities and in the global economy? According to the World Business Council for Sustainable Development, corporate social responsibility is defined as the commitment by businesses to contribute to economic progress while improving the quality of life for employees and their families along with the larger community and society (Dahlsrud, 2006).

Given its role as a driving force for social and environmental change within the global economy, it is not surprising that CSR has served as a catalyst for communication and sustainability careers. According to Lindsay Hooper, the executive director of the Cambridge Institute for Sustainable Leadership, careers in CSR and corporate sustainability require competencies in communication, marketing, leadership, and engagement. In a 2021 *Financial Times* article, Hooper also indicated that collaboration was a critical skill set, since success in CSR often means bringing people together from different backgrounds, whether public policy, local activism, or specific functions such as corporate finance.

What are the different forms that corporate social responsibility can take? They can range from carbon reduction programs to community wellness and human health activities. This engagement will often depend on the nature of the organization, the way it is structured as a business or organizational entity, and its unique situation in terms of workforce, customer markets, and citizen stakeholders.

The CSR initiatives for a multinational company like Nike, for example, might seek to address environmental and social issues at the international, national, regional, and hyperlocal levels. Other companies might implement CSR programs based on a prioritization established by stakeholders or a pressing need by an adjacent or surrounding community. Every firm will have different standards and programs to achieve these goals, though it is common to find an overlap of CSR missions and objectives between organizations.

THE EVOLUTION OF A STAKEHOLDER SOCIETY

There is a necessary alignment of corporate social responsibility with communication and marketing functions. Companies will often look to in-house communication counsel to provide direction for sustainability outreach, community engagement, and relationships with not-for-profit organizations. However, CSR is not window dressing for companies looking to establish a better reputation with the media or the general public.

As an ethical practice that is immersed in management, communication, and engaged strategy, CSR provides a conduit by which companies actively listen to their constituents, engage in appropriate two-way dialogue, and evolve their practices, products, or business model as a result. Thus, for a consumer products company, CSR might lead to changes in product sourcing, supply chain management, or retail packaging that provides an environmental benefit.

That's not to say that CSR forgoes attention to the bottom line. Many management scholars argue that CSR aligns with a company's propensity for growth and profit. And CSR programs should continue to flourish, as they provide a platform for engaging publics not only on pressing topics such as the climate and environmental pollution, but also in areas like human rights, education, and health.

Archie Carroll, professor emeritus at the University of Georgia and a leading CSR expert, argues that CSR will only continue to expand along with

Figure 10.1. Carroll's CSR pyramid highlights the responsibilities of businesses to society (Michel Awkal/Wikimedia Commons.)

the public's expectations of companies: "More than likely, we will see new realms in which to think about business responsibilities to our stakeholder society, particularly at the global level, and in new and emerging technologies, fields, and commercial applications," he wrote in his summary of CSR's evolution over the past several decades. "In this context, it appears that the CSR concept has a bright future because at its core, it addresses and captures the most important concerns of the public regarding business and society relationships."

In 1979, Carroll developed a four-part definition of corporate social responsibility, with organizational CSR commitment focused on economic responsibility, legal responsibility, ethical responsibility, and philanthropic responsibility. This original explanation was recast in 1991 as a CSR pyramid to show how these building blocks relate to one another, and to show that the infrastructure of CSR relies on sound economic fundamentals and sustainability (Carroll, 2016).

CRITICAL TRENDS FOR ENVIRONMENTAL
PUBLIC RELATIONS

CSR has evolved to become a function of public relations practice in the realms of sustainability, ethics, and stakeholder relations. There are two major drivers of studies of corporate social responsibility as a function of corporate communication and public relations. One involves stakeholders' perception, including employees and customers. For example, an examination of CSR responses in the fast-food restaurant industry found that publics were more responsive to generic social issues advocated through CSR programs than those advocating strictly for public health (Kim and Ramos, 2018).

Customers perceive CSR in a positive light and as an outcome of mutually beneficial motives. For example, in the telecommunication sector of Ghana, the thrust of CSR and stakeholders' emphasis is more broadly directed at society rather than a specific stakeholder group like shareholders or customers (Welbeck et al., 2020). Fine-tuning a CSR program therefore requires multiple organizational inputs and long-term refinement.

Corporate social responsibility also serves as a compelling vehicle for persuasion. Ashli Q. Stokes, a professor of communication studies at the University of North Carolina Charlotte, explained in her research the constitutive or binding implications of CSR activities (2017). These programs foster process and dialogue for organizational change by bringing people together under an umbrella of specific ideas about social and environmental reform. This view of CSR as a constitutive or binding form of rhetoric that brings stakeholders together shows how firms align their profit-seeking motives with efforts to meet societal expectations (Stokes, 2017). For international context, public diplomacy provides another way of understanding CSR efforts, as companies' efforts are also intended to meet the informal or legal expectations of government leaders or nation-states as well as other foreign companies (Ingenhoff and Marschlich, 2019).

MARKET SHAREHOLDERS AS CSR STAKEHOLDERS

Elon Musk is arguably the world's most famous entrepreneur. His Texas-based company Tesla, which trades on the New York Stock Exchange, has revolutionized the electric vehicle market and in the process brought sizzling growth to the sector while delivering enormous profits to the company's shareholders. As Tesla rose through the years to become a $1 trillion company based on the value of its public shares, new discussions arose about how the company was meeting its environmental responsibility mandate.

Driss Lembachar, a transportation research investment analyst at Morningstar's Sustainalytics, told CNBC during the fall of 2021 that while Tesla's growth and profitability achievements were impressive, the company had more work to do in an area known as ESG. The acronym ESG stands for Environmental, Social, and Governance. These three categories are now an integral part of a public company analysis for many would-be investors, especially as they look to future risk but also growth opportunities. That's why, even as Tesla's stock approached the breathtaking benchmark of $1,000 per share, some investment experts were more concerned about the company's focus on a range of social impact, governance, and green criteria that would cement the company's ESG reputation for the long term.

According to the Chartered Financial Analysts (CFA) Institute, one of the vital areas for ESG investing is climate analysis. For example, the institute has called on government leaders to implement laws and regulations related to carbon pricing so that there are similar standards between jurisdictions and ease of access for global participants.

There are five recommendations that the CFA makes in terms of helping with climate analysis, and all are immersed in the traditions of public and financial communication. These are:

1. That carbon price expectations are included in analyst reports to assist with climate risk analysis.
2. Investment professionals should disclose climate-related risks, and align with guidelines offered by the Sustainability Accounting Standards Board and the Task Force on Climate-related Financial Disclosures.
3. Investment professionals should provide more engagement with stakeholders on climate-related issues in order to address immediate and potential climate risk.
4. Greater education within the financial analyst community about climate change in order to best serve clients.
5. Increased collaborations and engagements between investors and policymakers to ensure allocation of capital to climate change.

Not everybody is on board with the ESG business approach, especially as some companies clamor to jump aboard the bandwagon to impress Wall Street investment firms or individual investors. Some observers have pointed out that companies might overpromise in terms of what they can deliver for the environment or social causes. Others note that, because of its top-down nature, ESG is more likely to force a company's hand in moving to environmental or social action, as opposed to corporate social responsibility, which tends to be the purview of company leadership and employees as opposed to outside forces. Related to this is the view from some skeptics that the embrace of ESG by publicly traded companies is driven by motivations of shareholder gains or corporate profits, thus watering down the legacy of traditional corporate social responsibility, which has historically been driven by grassroots organizational culture and leadership.

More broadly, a critique of this stakeholder capitalism is that it risks downplaying financial performance, which impacts investors and employees, in favor of external pressures from lobbyists or political groups in conjunction with institutional investors and hedge funds. A related concern is that external pressures from some lobbyists might pit an organization's stakeholder groups against one another, thus forcing organizations with bipartisan constituencies or aspirations into partisan political positions.

Despite the growing pains associated with ESG in particular, expect both it and CSR to be around for a while, even as both evolve with the times. Demographics are a big part of this story. In a 2020 interview with *Forbes*, ESPN's vice president of corporate citizenship, Kevin Martinez, articulated two key dimensions driving the evolution of corporate social responsibility at his company. Martinez said that "the generational shift happening with the employee base is very real—younger workers are demanding their companies be more than profit focused. And stockholders are now more educated than ever on the synergy and influence that CSR has on brand reputation, business continuity and innovation" (Hessekiel, 2020). This intertwined relationship between corporate management, employees, customers, community stakeholders, and shareholders lies at the heart of corporate social responsibility's trajectory in the years ahead.

STAKEHOLDERS, SHAREHOLDERS, AND STOCK INDEXES

In understanding CSR and corporate governance, shareholder and stakeholder viewpoints are typically aligned with business ethics because they help managers and executives make appropriate decisions for their organizations. Shareholder theory emphasizes the relationship between the stock owner and manager, and highlights the role of company leaders in managing corporate funds on behalf of their shareholder base. Stakeholder theory also includes the relationship between manager and stockholder, but it emphasizes many other parties worthy of consideration by the corporation beyond formal capital investment, including customers, employees, and the local community (Smith, 2003). This theory balances profit maximization with the legitimate interests of all stakeholders, thus fostering the firm's long-term viability.

The stakeholders versus shareholders debate is a long-simmering one. Even though the shareholder view has been around for many decades and has a long tradition in the U.S. economic system, prioritization of shareholders became more apparent in the 1970s thanks to economist Milton Friedman's argument that profit was the paramount goal for the social responsibility of business. This view extended into the 1980s thanks to corporate volatility and the merger and takeover activity that gained momentum during this time (Smith, 2003). In short, shareholders wanted a bigger say in how their companies were managed. This would eventually have major ramifications for the environment.

Management and CSR thinkers have advocated for the shifting of language about shareholder prioritization to one of company value, while also recommending a public-facing changing of attitudes and behaviors on the part of company executives. In other words, corporate leadership should feel free to articulate an embrace of stakeholders even in the face of arguments warning of takeovers or mitigated shareholder returns in the short term. However, executive decisions in this realm are not strictly motivated by external variables. Personal values also play a role in where a company positions itself. Corporate senior leadership, including directors and CEOs of public corporations, have historically favored shareholders, but they also base decisions on entrepreneurial values such as achievement and self-direction (Adams, Licht, and Sagiv, 2011).

Ultimately, the bottom line plays a big role in the ability of companies to appease external stakeholders, and there is a significant difference between companies enjoying financial success and those struggling to get by. More profitable firms were more likely to broadcast information about their ESG activities than those with negative earnings, in great part because criticism of ESG activities is lessened when a company is already enjoying success. The flip side of this is that underperforming companies are bound to be less transparent about their ESG and CSR actions.

THE EMERGENCE OF SRI

Investment analysts and CSR scholars point to the emergence of Socially Responsible Investment (SRI) stock indexes as a means to monitor company CSR standards. Performance indexes, which include the DJSI family and FTSE4GOOD series, signal compliance with standards to stakeholders, and their growth is a reflection of their ability to incentivize corporate sustainability performance for those companies wishing to be included in the index (Salvioni and Gennari, 2017). This embrace of CSR and sustainability

Table 10.1.   SRI vs. ESG vs. Impact Investing (via Pitchbook)

Socially Responsible Investing (SRI)	*Environmental, Social, and Governance (ESG)*	*Impact Investing*
Investors engage in various actions such as stock screening, divestment, activism, and more to achieve desired social/ environmental outcomes	The metrics by which a company is measured for environmental and social variables beyond traditional financial/ accounting frameworks	A process in which investors look to funds and companies attuned to both measurable environmental/ social impact and financial returns
Most commonplace within open markets where investors can engage with publicly traded companies such as the New York Stock Exchange	Often used by market funds to assess performance by publicly traded companies; however, more private companies are being assessed through ESG measurement	More prominent with private market investment; access is more limited for smaller investors

standards on the part of public markets is reflected more recently in the rise of Social Stock Exchanges (SSEs) such as the South African Social Stock Exchange, the Social Stock Exchange in London, and the Social Venture Connection in Canada. Such trading venues point to investors who embrace value creation over the long-term rather than short-term speculation.

Shareholders are rewarding CSR programs by examining multiple approaches. They consider variables such as local impact and public awareness, which are made larger through public relations and media publicity activities. Media coverage of corporate social responsibility initiatives with impact on local employees and communities are positively associated with both shareholder value and future operating performance (Byun and Oh, 2018). This relationship between local CSR impacts and the valuation of shares aligns with the view that stakeholder awareness and shareholder endorsement are intertwined.

One challenge facing CSR, however, is the contemporary nature of shareholding, which emphasizes ownership through institutional channels such as mutual funds and related investment vehicles. An example is retirement savings, which are frequently composed of expansive mutual funds that feature a range of stock holdings and other financial assets. This means that most individual shareholders have little control or knowledge over daily corporate activities, which leaves managers with a critical role of educating shareholders (Spurgin, 2001).

For those companies with a greater degree of institutional ownership, CSR performance is improved in various areas, including financially material categories. This arises in part because institutional shareholders provide an external influence over CSR activities through their proposals for social impact (Chen, Dong, and Lin, 2020). Furthermore, the presence of institutional investors holding both debt and equity claims in the same company, also known as dual holders, can lead to an increase in CSR performance (Lopatta et al., 2020).

There is a growing focus on the importance of disclosure within CSR communications, which is driven by shareholder activists. The term *disclosure* refers to the action of relaying relevant company information to stakeholders or government agencies in a transparently, timely fashion. Companies facing pressure about their CSR disclosures in areas such as human rights or climate change are more likely to focus on disclosure statements rather than the CSR action itself. Furthermore, CSR practices can actually deteriorate when accountability requirements reshape the motivations of NGOs and the disarticulation of social movements (Michelon, Rodrique, and Trevisan, 2020).

ECOLOGICAL MODERNIZATION

Let's return to business and technology rock star Elon Musk. In 2021, the serial entrepreneur eclipsed the $200 billion mark to become the richest person in the world. A year later, he bought the social media company Twitter. Much of Musk's wealth owes to the incredible success of Tesla, the Austin, Texas–based manufacturer of electric vehicles and other clean energy products. Musk is not the exception but rather the rule when it comes to the growth of green capitalism. The rapid growth of pro-environmental technologies, industries, and consumer products has been one of the remarkable stories of the contemporary global economy. These developments—which also include alternative energy products, carbon emission credits, and sustainable consumer goods—play a significant role in mitigating our societal ecological footprint and in raising awareness of pressing issues such as climate change mitigation and wildlife conservation.

This trend is increasingly noticed by some environmentalists, who have challenged it through a perspective known as ecological modernization theory. This view holds that environmentalism capitalism maintains the economic status quo rather than enacting the changes necessary to promote more long-lasting and meaningful environmental change. According to political scientist and environmental policy expert Frank Fischer, the process of "ecological modernization translates the otherwise radical climate-oriented call for societal change into business-friendly reform-oriented tasks, emphasizing the use of markets, cost-benefit analysis, green marketing, and the search for the technological fix" (2017, 8).

Similar to Fischer's position, John Foster, an environmental sociologist at the University of Oregon, points to the role of language and communication in establishing "consensual nature of ecological modernization discourse" (2012, 217). Drawing from the philosopher Kenneth Burke, he points to a vocabulary of motive that is ultimately directed by politicians, CEOs, and cultural influencers. To this end, media emerges as a critical conduit for extending influence on the part of not only journalists but also national governments, corporations, international bodies, and issue advocates. Foster's critique situates this dialogue of innovation and sustainability as conforming with existing government and business interests, and suggests that environmental interests are easily co-opted in the name of profit and power.

Some caution about making these charges is warranted, however. Fisher and his research collaborator Freudenburg (2001) argue that ecological modernization has to be viewed on a case-by-case basis, depending on national and contextual factors. For example, government partnership is necessary to the success of environmental initiatives in some countries more than others. But the larger point Foster makes still holds up across national and cultural contexts. There are always going to be conflicting interests at play when the financial stakes are so high in the environmental economy, and the often glowing stories that accompany these sometimes financially lucrative developments play a significant role in holding up this ecological modernization.

CASE STUDY: PATAGONIA'S SOCIAL RESPONSIBILITY THROUGH DOCUMENTARY FILM

When U.S. senator Patty Murray and Washington State governor Jay Inslee announced a process to restore salmon runs in their Pacific Northwest state, including a potential removal of four dams on the Lower Snake River in southeastern Washington, they were building on a foundation of advocacy and activism that included a coalition of environmentalists, tribal communities, conservationists, and outdoor recreation enthusiasts. The removal of these hydroelectric dams would have a significant impact on salmon populations, which in turn are related to the health of human communities but also the struggling orca populations in the Salish Sea. As Alyssa Macy, a member of the Confederated Tribes of the Warm Springs and CEO of the Washington Environmental Council/Washington Conservation Voters explained in a statement to the media, "The loss of salmon is an existential threat to Native Nations, fishers, business owners, economies, and communities. Salmon is a critical part of life for people across the state."

Figure 10.2.   Patagonia's 2014 documentary DamNation *offered a new look at the impacts of hydroelectric dams across the United States, and their long-term impacts on wildlife, including salmon. The successful film inspired students at Whitman College in Walla Walla, Washington to start a student advocacy group called Rethink Dams in order to raise greater awareness of the issue. (Patagonia.)*

One company that provided this movement with a significant push over the past decade was outdoor apparel maker Patagonia. In 2015, university students at Whitman College in Walla Walla, Washington, started a student advocacy group inspired by the Patagonia-produced documentary *DamNation*. Their organization, named Rethink Dams, was established to bring student support to the movement to decommission the controversial dams in the state's southeast corner, and to bring that message to other university students and community members.

That diffusion of a message was embedded into Patagonia's *DamNation* documentary push from the very beginning. The film enjoyed an acclaimed first screening at the South by Southwest festival in Austin, Texas, before it was distributed to audiences at regional film festivals, university campuses, community centers, and even Patagonia stores. It also collaborated with like-minded civic organizations to spread the word of its anti-dam message. In Eugene, Oregon, for example, the screening of *DamNation* was hosted by the Western Environmental Law Center and the environmental group Save Our Wild Salmon.

Long before *DamNation*, Patagonia embraced the concept of social and environmental accountability, a philosophy that has been espoused by founder/owner and outdoor conservationist Yvon Chouinard. For example, the company established the Tools for Grassroots Activists Conference in 1994. More recently, the company makes a CSR splash every year during the Thanksgiving holiday and subsequent Black Friday shopping activity with its "Don't buy our products" campaign. Patagonia has sought to discourage the kind of unbridled consumerism that takes place on the Friday after the U.S. Thanksgiving holiday—the so-called Black Friday shopping event—by funding advertisements proclaiming, for example, "Don't buy this jacket."

DISCUSSION QUESTIONS

1. What are some examples of corporate social responsibility from the consumer brands that you are most loyal to? Do these CSR initiatives ring true to you?

2. Do you agree or disagree with the premise of ecological modernization theory—that some solutions to environmental problems seek to facilitate economic growth and a company's bottom line at the expense of real change?

3. Patagonia's *DamNation* is a good example of documentary activism. How have other documentaries weighed into pressing topics of public concern?

KEYWORDS

Climate analysis
Community engagement
Corporate governance
Corporate social responsibility
CSR stakeholders
Decarbonization
Disclosure
Ecological modernization
Environmental, Social, and Governance
Impact investing
Product sourcing
Public diplomacy
Shareholders
Socially Responsible Investment
Stakeholder capitalism

KEY EVENTS, LOCATIONS, AND ORGANIZATIONS

Alcoa
Chartered Financial Analysts (CFA) Institute
DamNation
Patagonia
Social Stock Exchange (London)
Social Venture Connection (Canada)
South African Social Stock Exchange
Sustainalytics
Tesla
World Business Council

REFERENCES

Adams, R. B., Licht, A. N., and Sagiv, L. (2011). Shareholders and stakeholders: How do directors decide? *Strategic Management Journal*, 32(12): 1331–55.

Byun, S. K., and Oh, J. M. (2018). Local corporate social responsibility, media coverage, and shareholder value. *Journal of Banking & Finance*, 87: 68–86.

Carroll, A. B. (2016). Carroll's pyramid of CSR: Taking another look. *International Journal of Corporate Social Responsibility*, 1(1): 1–8.

Chen, T., Dong, H., and Lin, C. (2020). Institutional shareholders and corporate social responsibility. *Journal of Financial Economics*, 135(2): 483–504.

Dahlsrud, A. (2006). How corporate social responsibility is defined: An analysis of 37 definitions. *Corporate Social Responsibility and Environmental Management*, 15(1): 1–13.

Fischer, F. (2017). *Climate Crisis and the Democratic Prospect: Participatory Governance in Sustainable Communities*. Oxford University Press.

Fisher, D. R., and Freudenburg, W. R. (2001). Ecological modernization and its critics: Assessing the past and looking toward the future. *Society & Natural Resources*, 14(8): 701–9.

Foster, J. B. (2012). The planetary rift and the new human exemptionalism: A political-economic critique of ecological modernization theory. *Organization & Environment*, 25(3): 211–37.

Hessekiel, D. (2020). Changemaker interview: Kevin Martinez, VP, Corporate Citizenship, ESPN. Retrieved from: https://www.forbes.com/sites/davidhesse kiel/2020/11/14/changemaker-interview-kevin-martinez-vp-corporate-citizenship -espn/?sh=7676f395441a.

Ingenhoff, D., and Marschlich, S. (2019). Corporate diplomacy and political CSR: Similarities, differences and theoretical implications. *Public Relations Review*, 45(2): 348–71.

Kim, Y., and Ramos, M. L. Z. (2018). Stakeholder responses toward fast food chains' CSR. *Corporate Communications: An International Journal*.

Lopatta, K., Bassen, A., Kaspereit, T., Tideman, S. A., and Buchholz, D. (2020). The effect of institutional dual holdings on CSR performance. *Journal of Sustainable Finance & Investment*, 1–20.

Michelon, G., Rodrigue, M., and Trevisan, E. (2020). The marketization of a social movement: Activists, shareholders and CSR disclosure. *Accounting, Organizations and Society*, 80: 101074.

Pitchbook (2021). The key differences between SRI, ESG and impact investing. Retrieved from: https://pitchbook.com/blog/what-are-the-differences-between-sri -esg-and-impact-investing.

Salvioni, D. M., and Gennari, F. (2017). CSR, sustainable value creation and shareholder relations. *Symphonya: Emerging Issues in Management*, 1: 36–49.

Smith, H. J. (2003). The shareholders vs. stakeholders debate. *MIT Sloan Management Review*, 44(4): 85–90.

Spurgin, E. W. (2001). Do shareholders have obligations to stakeholders? *Journal of Business Ethics*, 33(4): 287–97.

Stokes, A. Q. (2017). A rising tide lifts all boats? The constitutive reality of CSR in public relations. In B. Brunner (ed.), *The Moral Compass of Public Relations*, New York: Routledge, 62–76.

Welbeck, E. E. S., Owusu, G. M. Y., Simpson, S. N. Y., and Bekoe, R. A. (2020). CSR in the telecom industry of a developing country: Employees' perspective. *Journal of Accounting in Emerging Economies*.

World Business Council. (2009). Corporate social responsibility. Retrieved from: http://old.wbcsd.org/pages/edocument/edocumentdetails.aspx?id=82&nosearchco ntextkey=true.

Chapter Eleven

Community, Accessibility, and Diversity

This chapter focuses on the importance of aligning environmentalism with objectives of community engagement, accessibility to all citizens, and integrating diverse voices and publics. Learning objectives of this chapter include the contextualizing of community, accessibility, and diversity within environmentalism, and the tracing of key figures who helped shape the trajectory of these areas. The examples provided in this chapter demonstrate the variety of approaches used to connect underserved or underrepresented publics with the larger mission of environmental strategy, persuasion, and advocacy.

WHEN ECOLOGICAL DISASTER STRIKES A COMMUNITY

The working-class Ohio community of East Palestine was left reeling in early February 2023 when a train operated by the Norfolk Southern Railway Company derailed, causing thirty-eight rail cars to careen off the tracks. The accident, which caused a toxic fire to burn for several days, proved to be catastrophic for the local area. Thousands of people living in the area had to leave their homes while government officials worked to defuse a major explosion. The situation deteriorated further when Ohio's governor approved the intentional burning of the hazardous materials, which created a massive black cloud in the sky seen from miles away.

The incident created a worst-case scenario for local residents, and it left a legacy of environmental degradation hovering over multiple communities in the Ohio-Pennsylvania borderlands. Roughly a dozen of those rail cars were carrying hazardous materials such as vinyl chloride, butyl acrylate, ethyl-hexyl acrylate, and ethylene glycol. Being exposed to these chemicals can cause a number of significant human ailments, including cancer, damage to organs, and development problems for fetuses.

The event not only proved to be a devastating blow to the local residents of East Palestine, a community that has suffered from population decline and the shrinking of local industries, but area farmers farther out also bore the brunt of this ecological tragedy. In the weeks after the derailment, agricultural leaders in Ohio and Pennsylvania pressed both Norfolk Southern and the U.S. Environmental Protection Agency to expand the sampling radius for toxic chemicals and other contaminants within the soil.

Michael Leppert, a communication consultant writing for the *Indiana Capital Chronicle*, referred to the East Palestine rail derailment as a lesson for all Americans. Why? Because it presented not only a worst-case environmental scenario for transportation and freight security, but also a classic example of how *not* to engage with community in the wake of an ecological disaster. According to Leppert, the moment that Norfolk Southern decided to be a "no-show" at a town meeting at a local high school, it relegated itself to being the deserved focal point for local angst. "Taking care of this village and its people should be the uninterrupted priority for a large group of stakeholders for the foreseeable future," he said. "Everyone watching this experience, from near and far, should absorb the lessons it's teaching about governing and communicating. With empathy" (Leppert, 2023, para. 14).

Nearly two months after the incident, the U.S. Justice Department filed a lawsuit against Norfolk Southern, citing the unlawful pollution of watersheds and violation of the Clean Water Act. Yet the damage inflicted on the community could not be undone by government litigation. "It should have been clear that the company felt the village's pain," wrote Leppert (2023, para. 12). The abandonment felt by area residents wasn't exclusively focused on company officials, however. In the early days of the disaster, East Palestine residents clamored for greater attention from the national media and the White House.

By winter's end, though some national news outlets had arrived to report on the tragedy to national and international audiences, area residents were still waiting for a visit from U.S. President Joseph Biden. This had the effect of leaving people in the region feeling disillusioned about the recovery effort and the attention afforded to their plight (Zito, 2023). Simply put, this kind of disaster would have certainly received more attention if had occurred in closer proximity to influential national politicians and media practitioners.

GRAPPLING WITH ENVIRONMENTAL INEQUALITIES

The East Palestine saga underscores a long-standing problem in American life. Smaller or marginalized communities are more vulnerable to the risks of ecological disaster or degradation, and they can often fall under the radar of government oversight or media watchdog activity. This reality is not only true of rural communities, but also applies to distinctions of class, ethnicity, and physical ability. Many of the ecological efforts one learns about from the national news or even in regional media focus on famous geographic locations or the pristine landscapes of national parks or secluded maritime zones, or they pertain to wealthy urban centers.

Some communities, it turns out, are afforded better environmental protection than others. And impoverished communities are likely to receive less regulation and less attention. That's why it's important for policymakers and members of the public to broaden their scope of what qualifies as an environmental space. If you take a few minutes to consider your own local neighborhood or community, you will find a multitude of places where environmental advocacy and communication is needed or is already happening. For example, there are local schools, hospitals, recreation centers, libraries, small businesses, and even shopping malls that are impacted by environmental outcomes, from the air quality of government buildings and workplace sites to the carbon output associated with maintaining programs and services.

You will also see a range of community members—children, the elderly, those with physical disabilities—who interface with their physical environment in different ways. Making sure that citizens are equally served by environmental policymaking and advocacy is easier said than done, however. Historically, the environmental movement has not always drawn from a diverse range of community members in a way that reflects the compositions of American communities and their environmental struggles. In some quarters, at least, environmentalism is seen as the lofty pursuit of a homogenous group that is predominantly white-collar, upper-middle-class, and politically progressive. In the past, this has led to charges of elitism or classism from some quarters. This charge has also extended to organizations. Leadership in the environmental movement is typically the domain of the university-educated, with preference extended to Ivy League or liberal arts graduates from prestigious institutions on the East and West Coasts.

Another critique is that environmental advocacy doesn't reflect the composition of our society in terms of ethnicity. Part of this criticism is grounded in a broader concept called *environmental racism*, which argues that the impacts of environmental problems like pollution and climate change disproportionately impact communities of color. The term environmental racism was coined by Benjamin Chavis, an African American civil rights leader who described it as "racial discrimination in environmental policy-making, the enforcement of regulations and laws, the deliberate targeting of communities of color for toxic waste facilities, the official sanctioning of the life-threatening presence of poisons and pollutants in our communities, and the history of excluding people of color from leadership of the ecology movements" (Vittal, 2021, para. 2).

By looking at environmental challenges through this lens, one might better understand how modern societal issues—urban decay, construction of highways through immigrant neighborhoods, the removal of needed recreational greenspace, air pollution from industrial activity—have historically harmed marginalized communities and continue to do so. At an international level, such a lens is also helpful in understanding environmental inequities between the Global North and Global South, with developing nations facing a disproportionate degree of environmental and human health challenges such as air pollution, contaminated drinking water, drought, and disease.

DISPROPORTIONATE IMPACTS IN
ENVIRONMENTAL HISTORY

Regardless of location, environmental problems are exacerbated for those with physical or mental disabilities. Elizabeth Wright, a disability rights activist and Paralympian athlete, refers to this as *eco-ableism*, which stems from environmental activists overlooking those who don't have the same abilities. According to Wright, eco-ableism isn't easily apparent. In fact, it emerges as a blind spot for well-meaning policymakers. She notes that "eco-ableism is often hidden by the very spectacle of positive sustainable solutions to climate and environmental problems." Not only do disabled populations have limited access to resources and services, says Wright, but they might also be dealing with long-term compromised health, which makes them more vulnerable to variables like climate change, pollution, and disease.

Another demographic that is disproportionately impacted by environmental injustice is North America's Indigenous and First Nations peoples. Decades of failed government policy have left many tribal communities to deal with unacceptable living conditions and health outcomes. One of the key challenges for environmental public communicators is to engage tribal nations in a way that does not exploit or exacerbate their situation or living conditions. A key to Indigenous community success and long-term community sustainability is the ability for tribes to navigate complex economic and ecological issues with a high degree of autonomy. The incursion of outsiders can backfire, even when the intentions might be in the right place. Historically, this interplay of Eurocentric values and ideology with the fate of Indigenous nations had transformative impacts upon Indigenous groups in the Americas. In his book *Catlin's Lament: Indians, Manifest Destiny and the Ethics of Nature*, environmental philosopher and author John Hausdoerffer of Western Colorado University describes how George Catlin—who sought to celebrate Native Americans during the nineteenth century with his paintings and shows—simultaneously helped usher in the demise of many of their communities by emphasizing the inevitability of American settlement, and also by positioning them as the "other" vis-à-vis European settlers.

Mark Spence, a historian with the National Park Service, is more charitable toward Catlin's legacy. In his book *Dispossessing the Wilderness: Indian Removal and the Making of the National Parks*, Spence argues that it was only Catlin who argued in favor of having Native American settlements integrated into a national park system—a mindset dismissed by most ecologists and bureaucrats of his time as impractical. But Spence notes that in national parks such as Death Valley, Native American tribes are indeed being allowed by the federal government to coexist in their ancestral lands.

But the centrality of tribal communities to America's environmental history raises the broader perspective of intersections with class, ethnicity, and geography in the United States. Another environmental historian, Connie Chiang, has demonstrated that prominent contemporary civic institutions serving the environment, such as aquariums and zoos, must face up to their own complicated legacies in American history. These civic institutions hold a unique place as often beloved community destinations that communicate messages about animals, botany, and wild spaces. But there is more to their story than positive public engagement.

In her book *Shaping the Shoreline: Fisheries and Tourism on the Monterey Coast*, Chiang shows how the California coastline served as an intersection of labor and leisure as well as ethnicity and class. It was here where Asian Americans and Japanese immigrants were discriminated against and a focal point of turn-of-the-twentieth-century rioting. Chinese fishermen were also the subjects of relocation, political bias, and violence. Local fishermen were resentful not only of Chinese fishing techniques (such as trawling versus the traditional hook on a line) but also their processing techniques (such as the drying of squid on the docks or shoreline). Chiang's research serves as an important message for those communicators working with aquariums in particular. The modern aquarium or zoo might showcase the diversity of organisms in a region's waters, but they have too often overlooked the diversity of peoples who labored upon those same waters, shorelines, and marine spaces.

A key driver in the effort to foster environmental protection and sustainability across the widest possible swath of communities is the environmental justice movement. According to the Sierra Club, environmental justice helps explore the linkages between environmental conditions and social justice as well as facilitating dialogue, understanding, and action in critical ecological areas (Sierra Club, 2023). According to the organization, the environmental justice movement took hold during the 1980s as a result of environmental degradation and dangerous living conditions in U.S. minority and low-income communities. A notable example was from Warren County, North Carolina, where PCB-contaminated soils were dumped in a facility located near a Black community, despite the protests of local residents (Sierra Club, 2023). What eventually followed was a national report on the racial and socio-economic dimensions of communities with hazardous waste sites titled *Toxic Wastes and Race in the United States*. Authored by the Commission for Racial Justice for the United Church of Christ, the report found that minority and ethnic communities were disproportionately impacted by the placement of hazardous waste facilities, and this pattern held true at the national level (Lee and Chavez, 1987).

STAKING A CLAIM TO ENVIRONMENTAL JUSTICE

This growing approach to tackling environmental problems in the United States, especially as they pertain to disadvantaged or vulnerable communities, positions environmental justice as a means to address parallel social inequalities such as poverty and illness. According to the Natural Resources Defense Council (NRDC), environmental justice strives to "maintain a clean and healthful environment, especially for those who have traditionally lived, worked and played closest to the sources of pollution" (Skelton and Miller, 2016). According to the NRDC, statistics bear out that people of color and the poor are disproportionately impacted by America's most polluted environments.

A key figure in the evolution of environmental justice is Robert D. Bullard, a professor of urban planning and environmental policy at Texas Southern University. Sometimes described as the father of the environmental justice movement, Bullard has authored eighteen books on topics such as industrial activity siting, housing and transportation, and emergency response to natural disasters. He is also the co-founder of the Historically Black College and University Climate Change Consortium. One of his earlier publications, *Dumping in Dixie: Race, Class and Environmental Quality*, represented an important marker in understanding the impacts of industrial disposal and

← **Robert D. Bullard**

··· ✉ **Follow**

Robert D. Bullard
@DrBobBullard

Scholar, author of 18 books, co-chair of @NBEJN1, #HBCU Climate Change Consortium, director of @BullardCenter and father of environmental justice. #Actonclimate

⊙ Houston, TX ⊘ drrobertbullard.com ⊞ Joined February 2011

10.8K Following **32.4K** Followers

Figure 11.1. Considered the father of the environmental justice movement, Dr. Robert Bullard has authored eighteen books devoted to environmental health, climate justice, and industrial pollution. He is also the co-founder of the Historically Black College and University Climate Change Consortium. (@DrBobBullard/Twitter.)

associated toxins on African American communities. According to Bullard, the government must play a stronger role in protecting Black, minority, and working-class families from industrial polluters. "Zip code is a power predictor of health and vulnerability," wrote Bullard in a 2017 op-ed. "Environmental vulnerability maps closely with race and income. Many of the nation's environmental disparities and injustices have their roots in racial segregation and discriminatory zoning and land-use practices (Bullard, 2017, para. 3).

Another prominent leader in this space is Elizabeth Yeampierre, the co-chair of the Climate Justice Alliance (CJA), a consortium of over seventy organizations engaged in the climate movement in the United States and internationally. Through this alliance, Yeampierre focuses on localized organizing strategies and the mobilization of grassroots members to help communities move away from environmental degradation and toward what the CJA holds up as "resilient, regenerative and equitable economies."

Much of Yeampierre's environmental advocacy is focused on the hyperlocal dimensions of transitioning to a green economy and a low-carbon future, and the opportunity for gaining buy-in at a grassroots level. As Yeampierre said in an interview with the climate publication *Yale Environment 360*, "A just transition is a process that moves us away from a fossil fuel economy to local livable economies, to regenerative economies" (Gardiner, 2020, para. 21). Part of this process involves working with local political leaders and other on-the-ground stakeholders to help change the rules that uphold some of the traditional industrial economy approaches. The CJA identifies legal and societal roadblocks to environmental progress and looks for ways to rebuild the system of laws and regulations to move closer to a greener economy.

In her organizing and communication leadership work with the Climate Justice Alliance, Yeampierre must consider a wide range of variables that relate to community history, the context of local economies and politics, and the human rights inherent in environmental justice work. According to the champion for greener communities, "a just transition looks at the process of how we get there, and so it looks at not just the outcomes, which is something that the environmentalists look at, but it looks at the process—workers' rights, land use, how people are treated, whether the process of creating materials that take us to a carbon-neutral environment is toxic and whether it affects the host community where it's being built" (Gardiner, 2020, para. 22).

CASE STUDY: TETRA SOCIETY TRANSFORMS THE OUTDOORS FOR PEOPLE WITH DISABILITIES

It was a serious skiing accident that dramatically changed the life of Canadian Sam Sullivan at the age of nineteen. The spinal cord injury he sustained meant that he was unable to play active sports, let alone dress or feed himself. As a result, he sank into a deep depression. It was only after engagements with leaders in the disability community, and learning about disability sports, that he began producing newsletter stories about individuals with disabilities who achieved success in spite of their challenges.

Soon, Sullivan began focusing on nonprofit groups that could provide more accessibility for people with disabilities. Over the course of two decades and a professional rise through civic leadership roles, the quadriplegic advocate launched a succession of nonprofit groups serving not only western Canada but also people with disabilities across North America. One of those not-for-profit organizations, the Tetra Society of North America, helps people with disabilities navigate the physical environment through innovations.

gizmo ⊕

Tetra clients get out on the slopes in the Okanagan using a customized sit-ski.

TETRA SUPPORTS
STAYING ACTIVE
IN WINTER

As fall turns to winter, Canadians from Tofino, British Columbia to Cape Spear, Newfoundland, seek out activities suited to the changing of the seasons. For over 30 years, the Tetra Society of North America has been supporting people with disabilities looking to participate in skiing, curling, sledge hockey, and other winter recreation activities.

In our 34-year history, the modifications made to sit-skis are numerous. From adapting handlebars to altering seats and changing the way that skis connect to the bucket seats, volunteers across the country have seen it all. Tetra works both with individuals and sporting organizations. In Vernon, BC, for example, volunteers have worked with Community Recreational Initiatives Society (CRIS) to adapt sit-skis that can be used by people with a range of disabilities. These kinds of projects are being completed by tireless volunteers across the county.

Hockey is, perhaps, the quintessential Canadian winter pastime. Tetra volunteers design devices that support individuals with disabilities as they get out on the ice. Earlier this year, Tetra was contacted by a client in Newfoundland, Carter, who wanted to figure out how to get his hand into a hockey glove in a way that accommodated his disability. Long-time Tetra volunteer Dr. Leonard Lye took on the case, converting a

traditional hockey glove into a "hockey mitten". Now, Carter is often found "doing crossovers and learning to skate backwards", as part of his local team.

"Tetra has been a tremendous partner with SportAbility over the years". Jade Werger, Sport Development Coordinator with SportAbility, says: "With the help of Tetra volunteers, we have overcome equipment barriers to sport participation as well as providing upgraded equipment to athletes, enhancing their sport experience. Thank you, Tetra, for all of your work!"

Check out the Tetra website for many more examples of winter recreation projects being built across the country.

Tetra client Carter wears his new custom gloves during a hockey game in Newfoundland.

Figure 11.2. The Tetra Society of North America helps people with disabilities to navigate indoor and outdoor environments through engineering innovations. Its quarterly newsletter called Gizmo *spotlights individual success stories and the work of project volunteers and program coordinators. (The Tetra Society of North America.)*

Through the help of a longtime volunteer, Paul Cermak, the organization developed a series of modifications that would foster increased mobility, accessibility, and independent living for those with physical disabilities. Some of these modifications or constructions to date have been tailored for core activities like communication, personal care, or household chores. But others are geared for outdoor activities and sports to ensure that disabled individuals can access the same scenery, fresh air, and encounters with nature afforded to the able-bodied. Success stories to date have included devices for sailing, kayaking, and hiking, as well as all-terrain walkers. Because of these progressive technologies, individuals with significant disabilities have been able to access otherwise inaccessible spaces such as recreational waterways and hiking trails.

The Tetra Society's ongoing communication helps the organization expand its reach and increase the number of participants and volunteers. For example, the society's quarterly *Gizmo* newsletter highlights advances in adaptive sporting equipment and individual success stories, but also puts the spotlight on Tetra's new and long-serving program coordinators and project volunteers. The society also hosts the annual TetraNation video contest, which celebrates the organization's work while setting up a friendly competition between Tetra chapters across Canada. Like the *Gizmo* newsletter, the video program was established to celebrate the Tetra community's participants and volunteers, and to showcase the innovative solutions they help produce. The competition, which runs for five weeks, concludes during National Volunteer Week.

In a story published by the Disability Foundation, Sullivan noted that his advocacy and innovation work is motivated in part by his own story: "We have to improve our own lives from within, by finding interests and making connections," he said. "Accessible outdoor activities might sound like leisure, but in reality they help people who have experienced despair to move on and find value in their lives, realizing their own potential."

Even as Sullivan navigates a successful political career in western Canada, including a previous mayorship of the City of Vancouver, he continues to make the outdoors a more inclusive and diverse place. Through a network of twenty-seven local chapters across Canada, the Tetra Society of North America has drawn from the know-how of more than two hundred volunteers to build over two hundred custom assistive devices for daily living as well as outdoor recreation, sport, and mobility.

DISCUSSION QUESTIONS

1. Is the environmental movement diverse enough? How can it continue to expand its ranks while increasing not only diversity of identity but also diversity of ideas?
2. What is eco-ableism and why is it so important for millions of Americans as they interface with the environment?
3. What is an environmental justice issue from your own community or state, and how does it impact a group of citizens? How can communities overcome environmental discrimination?

KEYWORDS

Accessibility
Diversity
Eco-ableism
Environmental justice
Environmental racism
Indigenous sovereignty
Mobility

KEY EVENTS, LOCATIONS, AND ORGANIZATIONS

Climate Justice Alliance
HBCU Climate Change Consortium
Natural Resources Defense Council
Sierra Club
Tetra Society of North America
Yale Environment 360

REFERENCES

Bullard, R. (2017). African Americans need a strong and independent EPA. *Op-Ed News*. Retrieved from: https://www.opednews.com/articles/African-Americans-Need-a-S-by-Robert-Bullard-African-Americans_Black-History-Month_Civil-Rights-Violations_Climate-170221-71.html.
Climate Justice Alliance (2022). Climate Justice Alliance applauds senators who voted with communities. Retrieved from: https://climatejusticealliance.org/how-we-work/#3.

Gardiner, B. (2020). Unequal impact: The deep links between racism and climate change. *YaleEnvironment 360*. Retrieved from: https://e360.yale.edu/features/unequal-impact-the-deep-links-between-inequality-and-climate-change.

Lee, C., and Chavez Jr, B. F. (1987). *Toxic Wastes and Race in the United States: A National Report on the Racial and Socio-Economic Characteristics of Communities with Hazardous Waste Sites*. New York: Commission for Racial Justice, United Church of Christ.

Leppert, M. (2023). East Palestine's battle is a lesson for all Americans. *Indiana Capital Chronicle*. Retrieved from: https://indianacapitalchronicle.com/2023/03/07/east-palestines-battle-is-a-lesson-for-all-americans/.

Sierra Club. (2023). A history of environmental justice in the United States. SierraClub.org. Retrieved from: https://www.sierraclub.org/environmental-justice/history-environmental-justice.

Skelton, R. and Miller, V. (2016). The environmental justice movement. Natural Resources Defense Council. Retrieved from: https://www.nrdc.org/stories/environmental-justice-movement.

Vittal, P. (2021). It's time for the federal government to address environmental racism. Greenpeace. Retrieved from: https://www.greenpeace.org/canada/en/story/46929/its-time-for-the-federal-government-to-address-environmental-racism/.

Zito, S. (2023). After two centuries, a dairy farm family near East Palestine worries for the future. *Pittsburgh Post-Gazette*. Retrieved from: https://www.post-gazette.com/opinion/insight/2023/03/19/salena-zito-east-palestine-derailment-norfolk-southern-enon-valley-farmer/stories/202303190049.

Chapter Twelve

International Communication

This chapter focuses on the global dimensions of environmental advocacy and public communication. Learning objectives of this chapter include understanding concepts such as spatial communication, public diplomacy, and international public relations; and the tracing of key issues that demonstrate the importance of strategic communication within global environmentalism. The examples provided in this chapter highlight a range of opportunities and challenges facing the contemporary international communicator in addressing issues such as climate, environmental protection, and regional sustainability.

TIME AND SPACE IN INTERNATIONAL MEDIA

Think back to the last time you took an overseas flight for vacation or study. Or maybe you have been chatting online with an internet acquaintance from another continent. In either case, you have been engaged in a concept known as *spatialization*. Long-standing conceptualizations of space and time offer key insights for the environmental advocate in global contexts. Our day-to-day communication exists within a larger sphere of history and geography. Vincent Mosco, a communication scholar at Queen's University in Canada specializing in the political economy of media, champions the concept of spatialization as a means to understanding the role of government and corporations within global communication flows. That's because spatialization helps us understand not only the role of environmental media and communication in fostering new kinds of globalized media, but also the rise of various forms of media concentration and convergences: media production, capital markets, knowledge workers, corporate media campaigns, and more.

While this can take the form of global media conglomerates like Paramount Global, News Corp, or AT&T, it can also be understood through capital-intensive new-economy cities like London, Hong Kong, and New York (finance); Tokyo, Seoul, and San Francisco/Silicon Valley (technology); and Los Angeles and Mumbai (film and entertainment). Increasingly, the green economy sees robust economic activity flowing through these same cities, as well as cities that are specializing in green innovation such as Portland, Oregon, Vancouver, B.C., Melbourne, Australia, and Belo Horizonte in Brazil.

Mosco positions media spatialization alongside cross-country and international transportation activities such as aviation and rail. According to the media researcher, both transportation and communication minimize the time it takes "to move goods, people and messages over space, thereby diminishing the significance of spatial distance as a constraint on the expansion of capital markets." Spatialization therefore provides media companies with new ways of expanding their reach and disseminating their content globally. It allows banks to spread the risk emanating from one market (U.S. real estate mortgages or Canadian mining, as examples) around the world, and even fosters new, global opportunities for organizations ranging from environmental nongovernmental organizations (NGOs) to technology firms.

Given the increase in global media flows in the environmental space, it is important for communicators to consider their role in media spatialization. For example, how do environmental campaigns or projects emanating from the United States disrupt economic or social patterns in other parts of the world? Furthermore, does green media content such as environmental documentaries or news articles contribute to the profitability of global media giants at the expense of local communities and regional culture?

NATURAL RESOURCES AND NET ECONOMIC BENEFIT

According to the environmental sociologist John Foster and his colleagues Brett Clark and Richard York (2011), a key role of the government in free market nations has been to enhance the viability of for-profit organizations at home and abroad. This may sound like good news for boosters of business growth, but it also presents a paradox for nations seeking to balance the net economic benefit of their natural resources bounty with the protection of their ecologies and human populations. That is why nations like Brazil, Australia, and Canada, which are all blessed with a bounty of natural resources, must strive to balance economic activity with responsible ecological management.

This is not a new phenomenon, however. National governments have long served as conduits between their respective commercial interests and the natural resources within their own borders as well as those abroad. In less populated regions or countries, it is common to find economic activity primarily taking the form of resources extraction—a cornerstone activity of commodification. This can include fishing, logging, mining, and oil drilling. To this end, the staples theory tradition developed by the late geographer, historian, and international communication scholar Harold Innis emphasizes the outsized roles of natural resources commodification processes, including extraction and export, in a given society or nation-state.

Innis's work at the crossroads of geography and communication helps inform the relationship between nations when it comes to natural resources trading and extraction. As a doctoral student at the University of Chicago, Innis studied the development of the Canadian Pacific Railway, which served as a catalyst for agricultural and logging industries. Based on his investigations into the expansion of railroading across the North American West, as well as his travels across Canada's hinterland, Innis developed the staples theory to explain how a society's resources economy informed its social structures.

Staples theory holds that a country such as Canada existed *because* of its geography and the economic materials borne of it. Such staple products included wheat, fish, fur, lumber, and agricultural products. Cod fisheries, for example, dictated the terms of labor, settlement patterns, modes of transport, and styles of government. Furthermore, the exploitation of staples, typically located in Canada's "periphery," was crucial to sustaining the country's "core"—the southerly provinces of Ontario and Quebec, and the financial-government urban centers of Toronto, Ottawa, and Montreal. According to Innis, the staples trade was responsible for peculiar tendencies of Canadian development, including transcontinental railroads and financial institutions with headquarters in these eastern cities.

Yet these same dynamics can also be seen in other resource-rich nations. For example, cities like Houston and Dallas aggregate wealth from the surrounding oil and gas economy in Texas, while Kansas City's stockyards and manufacturing economy draws from the agricultural bounty of Great Plains states such as Missouri, Kansas, Iowa, and Nebraska.

Beyond Canada's borders, staples theory has come to provide a historical understanding of Canada's economy as an exporter of staples products to "metropolitan countries" like the United States, with these exports in turn helping shape the country's institutions and internal structures (Hayter and Barnes, 1990). Other scholars have referred to staples theory as the staples trap/resource curse because of the adverse ecological and societal impacts on hinterland and rural communities, as well as countries that are stuck in a cycle of exploiting natural resources in order to address financial deficits.

RELATIONSHIPS AND ETHICS MATTER
IN GLOBAL PUBLIC RELATIONS

Public relations scholars have provided similar perspectives highlighting the economic disparities between nations and what this means for communication practice. Dean Kruckeberg (1993), a professor of communication studies at the University of North Carolina at Charlotte, has called for a universal code of ethics applied globally to ensure that public communicators from more powerful countries are responsible and ethical when engaging with publics and workers in other international jurisdictions. Krishnamurthy Sriramesh, a professor of public relations at the University of Colorado, is another scholar of international public communication who has made important contributions that are highly relevant for environmental communicators. Sriramesh's (2008) research from organizations in India and China highlights the usefulness of testing symmetry theory in professional contexts. Noting that localized customs and contexts cannot be dismissed in terms of their influence, he has developed a non-Western model of public relations that takes into account unique relationship dynamics within cultures. These perspectives are marking out best practices not only for governments and corporate institutions, but also for grassroots activists and other publics (Sriramesh, 2008).

Increasingly, the international dimension of environmental communication is also influenced by journalists and media coverage. And one of the most important variables in assessing how climate change is represented in media coverage internationally is national context. From *Folha de São Paulo* to the *Times of India* to the *South China Morning Post*, a range of national-level contexts for climate change influence coverage in the media across Asia, the Americas, Africa, and Europe.

While examples of climate change challenging existing social structures, such as industry and government, are common, one can also see the issue of climate change reinforcing national narratives and perpetuating long-standing ideologies in those countries. The topics within this climate change coverage encompass a wide spectrum, and range from user-friendly sustainable development stories to coverage of resources extraction industries to the downright apocalyptic. A commonality for all of these stories, however, is that they are immersed in this tension between publics and citizens and their expert or authority counterparts.

PUBLIC RELATIONS, PUBLIC DIPLOMACY, OR PROPAGANDA?

This range of coverage internationally provides the strategic communicator with some important perspectives on how journalism is evolving to meet not only the needs of this complex issue, but also the tensions that exist between overarching national narratives, mythologies, and framings versus the media companies and industries that are driven by shareholders, technologies, and profit motives.

Because the coverage of climate change in global media is driven by media forms such as news stories, social media posts, and public relations campaigns—it is susceptible to being caught up in national and regional politics and culture. This dynamic creates a climate change paradox. Journalists hold the discursive or communicative power in these narratives because they, along with their editors, produce the stories. Yet they too are constrained by cultural, professional, and national variables. For example, a reporter may feel beholden to a community's industry, or to professional journalistic traditions within a country.

Increasingly, scholars are paying attention to communication about the climate that aligns with the objectives of national governments or industries. This ranges from advocacy in democratic nations to propaganda in countries where media is state-controlled. It can also include media that produces impactful national mythology-making, like what is sometimes seen in the United States when appeals to the environment are conflated with patriotism. Snowboarder Jeremy Jones, the founder of the nonprofit Save Our Winters, launched a campaign called the Outdoor State in 2019 to tap into this powerful combination of environment and nationalism. The Outdoor State campaign integrated online communities with bipartisan, pro-environmental resources to mobilize outdoor enthusiasts to vote on climate policies.

In other cases involving corporate or government messaging, imperatives of profit or politics might be at play. Furthermore, the sources that are represented in news stories dictate the way climate change or a related topic might be framed. Sophisticated sources representing vested specific interests are often well resourced and regularly seek out placement in high-profile stories. At the global level, this brings climate change coverage directly into the realm of public relations, public diplomacy, and even propaganda.

Ultimately, this scenario raises a significant question for environmental communicators who seek to reach consensus on climate or green issues at the international level. Are environmental advocates dealing with a potentially diminished role for internationalism and international structures, especially when it comes to climate change as a global policy issue?

It is commonplace to see China reaching out and being particularly aggressive about its image and communication with stakeholders, while the United States moves toward exceptionalism and mythmaking with a more isolationist approach. In other countries, we see climate change mediation that integrates the global reality of governmental intervention, corporate- and industry-level influence, and the hopeful mission of sustainable development, renewable resources, and long-term climate change mitigation.

CRAFTING NEWS PEGS FOR COMMUNICATION STRATEGY

The push to find environmental solutions through media in global contexts requires a strategic push, which is why it is hard to understate the power of the news peg in global media. A news peg is a story angle that makes a topic newsworthy. A good example of this process comes from China's September 2018 launch of the *Xuelong 2* polar research vessel, also known as *Snow Dragon II*, which set off a number of articles in the international press about China's larger polar strategy.

Similarly, the adventures of Hou Zhili provided another news peg for China's Arctic strategy a year later. Zhili is a graphic designer from China who turned a taste for adventure into a larger narrative of public diplomacy. Since his childhood, Zhili always wanted to paddle the entirety of the Ob-Irtysh River. According to the *China Daily*, he spent four years paddling various sections of the river spanning China, Kazakhstan, and Russia in an impressive, three-stage drifting journey.

The last leg of the Chinese kayaker's voyage to the Arctic Ocean—after a two-thousand-kilometer (1,243-mile) journey through Siberia—also provided a timely symbol of China's polar aspirations. Another story from China's government news service *Xinhua* detailed the journey of Zhili as he geared up to paddle the final 1,200 kilometers (745 miles) of his trip on the Ob-Irtysh river network, which connects Xinjiang in northwest China to the Arctic Ocean.

Zhili's maritime journey also provided a metaphor for China's significant polar interests, articulated through a 2018 white paper. Titled *China's Arctic Policy* and authored by China's State Council Information Office, the white paper formalized a series of statements from Chinese officials about the country's hopes and vision for the Arctic, including environmental and climate protection. At the same time, it called for greater international cooperation over shipping and infrastructure in the Arctic—described as a "Polar Silk Road."

China's Arctic Policy white paper emerged as an important media source in understanding China's mix of motivations and aspirations in the polar region, and served as a subsequent story angle—or news peg—for journalists from a wide range of publications, including CNBC, the *Financial Times*, and the *South China Morning Post*. All of these stories contributed to global media coverage that emphasized different facets of China's polar strategy. For example, China was sometimes featured as a scientific and economic innovator, even though in some stories it was portrayed as a threat to the geopolitical status quo. Sometimes, media coverage of the white paper took on themes that wavered from the document's original Arctic focus. Thus, publication of the government white paper provided the media with a crucial platform for pursuing this coverage in the first place.

China's Arctic white paper highlights how the country envisions its future in the international region—not as a remote or separate site of ecology and geopolitics, but rather as a strategic location for the country's future interests in logistics, resources extraction, scientific exploration, and climate policy. Media coverage of China's Arctic white paper, then, is the inevitable outcome of a journalistic process that ties larger stories to events, incidents, or publicity announcements and missives that editors consider newsworthy. China's publication of a foreign policy white paper served to both broadcast policy and promote the country's national interests in the polar sphere.

As both a public-facing document and a strategic communication medium, it invited mass consumption through media coverage, as national white papers exist as informational and publicity conduits between policy and publics. This sequence of media events hints at a China that is actively aware of how global media can influence and shape narratives abroad. From a public diplomacy and soft power perspective, the journalistic representation of international policy represents a strategic pathway and opportunity for nations intent on reclaiming media narratives, public opinion, and policy outcomes.

THE ARCTIC COUNCIL'S POLAR ENGAGEMENT

As an international region and ecology, the Arctic remains a compelling focal point for observing the previously mentioned staples theory because of the belief in some quarters that extractive industries can help Arctic regions and communities become more sustainable (Huskey and Southcott, 2013). During the 1920s, Innis was skeptical of the Canadian government's reach into the far north. As one scholar noted, "He was clearly calling for greater study of the northern economy in order to understand the next steps of state expansionism . . . given the agenda of governance in the North, even wildlife conservation could become an exercise in 'nationalism'" (Colpitts, 2013, 113).

Innis eventually led the University of Toronto's Arctic Survey, a research project supported by the Canadian Social Science Research Council with funding from the Rockefeller Foundation (Evenden, 1998). The 1944 survey was seen as a major milestone in the advent of northern studies in Canada, and Innis himself had a long-standing interest and expertise in Canada's Arctic. This focus helped pave the way for Innis's theory of international communication, which emphasized the roles of time and space in how communication manages relations between nations, and the outsized role of spatialization in disrupting nations and empires.

In recent years, scientists have refocused on the Arctic for other reasons. Given its vulnerability to climate shifts and environmental threats, the Arctic remains a geographic region of significant interest not only to the nations and citizenry of the polar north, but also the global community. The region has emerged as one of the planet's symbolic environmental battlegrounds and a flashpoint of global ecology, pitting broader themes of economic growth and technological expansion against environmental and community stewardship. This tension has helped elevate the region's prominence in the global community and has captured growing attention from world leaders. And it has aligned with the rise of the Arctic Council over the past quarter-century as an intergovernmental forum devoted to high-level policy dialogue and diplomacy.

Established in 1996 as a result of the Ottawa Declaration, the Arctic Council is an intergovernmental forum promoting "cooperation, coordination and interaction among the Arctic states, with the involvement of the Arctic Indigenous communities and other Arctic inhabitants on common Arctic issues, in particular issues of sustainable development and environmental protection" (Arctic-Council.org, 2023).

In order to further diplomacy and advance policy, the Arctic Council brings together senior officials from Arctic countries at least twice a year. Furthermore, the council's partners gather at ministerial meetings held every two years. All council decisions must be accepted by the consensus of all eight Arctic states, which are the United States, Canada, Russia, Iceland, Sweden, Finland, Denmark, and Norway. In addition to the core nations, the council fosters input from Permanent Participants (including organizations representing Indigenous peoples in the Arctic), working groups, and observers.

At the same time, many global and regional nongovernmental organizations, particularly in the realms of environmental and wildlife protection, seek to influence the Arctic Council through official channels as well as unofficial public relations activities such as representation in news stories.

In 2020, Iceland's Einar Gunnarsson, chair of the Senior Arctic Officials, highlighted four pressing issues for the council: the Arctic's people and communities, the region's marine environment, climate and energy issues, and strengthening of the Arctic Council itself (Gunnarsson, 2020). These themes of environmental protection and social impact are likely to permeate Arctic Council deliberations in the future.

Public communication is a key component of the Arctic Council's work. In addition to its member nations, the council is composed of a team that includes a director of communications, a public relations officer, a digital media officer, and several members of an Indigenous peoples' secretariat. This growth of public-facing communication reflects a recognition of the critical impacts of media and public engagement, particularly as the council grapples with a number of complex economic and environmental issues.

In the past, the forum's lack of formalized strategic communication to stakeholders resulted in communication that was either misaligned or nonexistent—with public relations efforts mostly directed to branding activities such as the production of websites and brochures (Breum, 2012). Recent years, however, have seen the Arctic Council make significant investments in public communication, including communication personnel. Furthermore, the Arctic Council has become an important subject, and source, for journalists covering the region (Chater and Landriault, 2016). In some cases, media

Figure 12.1. At the Arctic Council Ministerial Meeting in Fairbanks, Alaska held in 2017, U.S. Secretary of State Rex Tillerson signed the Fairbanks Declaration, in which the intergovernmental forum maintained its commitment to regional peace, cooperation, and environmental protection in the Arctic. (Arctic Council Secretariat/ Linnea Nordström/Wikimedia Commons.)

gravitate to what *isn't* communicated by the Arctic Council. For example, the absence of a joint declaration from the 2019 ministerial meeting in Rovaniemi, Finland—due in part to U.S. opposition to climate change language (Breum, 2019)—was widely reported by international news outlets, including *Xinhua*, *Reuters*, and the *New York Times*.

What these media discussions highlight in part is the growing interest in understanding both the aims and production of Arctic Council communication, including public dialogue, press relations, and official pronouncements. The council's official declarations—joint statements describing the outcomes of the organization's political meetings—become what are described as the *mediatization* of political action.

The Arctic Council's declarations serve an international media function, as they extend across time and geography to proclaim evolving Arctic Council priorities, including climate change, wildlife protection, responsible economic growth, and the future of traditional and Indigenous communities. This confluence of nation state interests, economic activity, and resources extraction potential—and its relationship to political dialogue—points to the importance of communication artifacts as vehicles for ecological deliberation, amplification, and even persuasion.

CASE STUDY: CLIMATE CHANGE IN THE AMERICAS ATTRACTS GROWING MEDIA ATTENTION

The year 2020 was marked by historic events that have changed the trajectory of environmental media and climate reporting in the United States, across the Americas, and internationally. The summer wildfires that ravaged parts of the United States provided a stark example of how natural disasters—caused in part by warming temperatures—could lead to displacement of populations, devastation to ecological assets, degradation of air quality, and most importantly, loss of communities and human life.

In confirming the link between climate volatility and the 2020 blazes, Niklas Hagelberg, a Senior Program Officer with the United Nations Environment Program, declared the state of events to be "America's new normal" (UN Environment Programme, 2020). During the same summer, Mexico and Canada experienced a number of wildfires in their western regions. South America would not be spared either. Large fires in Brazil brought on by agricultural practices as well as dry conditions engulfed more than 10 percent of that country's wetlands, and this came after the previous year's fire in the Amazon, which generated a backlash from the international community (Arrelega, Londono, and Casodo, 2020).

The wildfires were not an isolated event linked to climate volatility. In all of these countries, significant issues have arisen over the past decade that have activated political debate, media coverage, and public response. These include the construction of petroleum pipelines, clear-cut logging of once-pristine forests, mining of precious metals, and the continued reliance on fracking. Runaway carbon emissions arising from industrialization, urban growth, and transportation patterns in these countries continue to challenge policymakers and worry environmental advocates. Several of these climate issues, including continental petroleum pipelines and atmospheric issues like wildfire smoke and air pollution, create collective anxiety for the Americas and impact nations simultaneously.

Climate change thus situates the United States and by extension the Americas at the center of a planetary ecological challenge. The issue of climate change is particularly high stakes in the Americas because the Western Hemisphere is home to some of the world's largest economies and many of its most sensitive and threatened ecologies. For the environmental communicator, there is a special attention that needs to be paid to not only how stories about this situation are consumed in specific countries, but indeed how they are understood across the Americas. This is borne out in the growing coverage of climate-linked politics and events in Brazil, Canada, Mexico, and the United States, the largest countries of the Americas in terms of economic activity. Increasingly, government leaders and politicians are being proactive about engaging media to ensure that their citizens' national voice is heard by the international community. This becomes especially apparent when nations are trying to rally support for global agreement around a specific program, such as the Paris Accord.

To this end, climate change coverage in news media in the Americas also serves as a form of public diplomacy. Public diplomacy that is conducted through news organizations (such as when politicians strategically reach out to another nation's citizens through broadcast, print, and social media news stories) is also known as mediated public diplomacy. This form of diplomacy comprises a rich array of contributors, including networks of political actors involving not only state leaders but also corporations, nongovernmental organizations, nonprofits, environmental activists, and lobbyists. Because of these participants, the framing of climate change stories is often contingent upon the integration of officials, spokespersons, and organizational representatives. These strategic and public communicators help articulate climate change priorities within and between the nations of the Americas and the world.

As vehicles for information and narrative about climate change as a public policy issue, news media happen to wield significant power in terms of influencing reader perceptions and concerns about the issue (Boykoff, 2011). While climate change has garnered increasing attention within the field of mass communication, it remains understudied within the context of the Americas, and in particular Latin America and the Caribbean (Takahashi et al., 2018).

A previous examination of climate change coverage in Brazil and the United States, along with Argentina and Colombia, found stories in the latter two nations skewed toward themes of natural catastrophe, while U.S. and Brazilian media emphasized economic dimensions of the debate (Zamith, Pinto, and Villar, 2013). At the same time, coverage in Latin America is notable for the challenges faced by journalists and media organizations, including existing relationships between reporters and officials (Takahashi et al., 2018). However, understandings of climate change as an issue impacting the collective nations of the Americas are far less prevalent. Even with the economic cooperation between Canada, Mexico, and the United States, there is said to be "little public debate about regional options for better climate change and energy governance (Selin and VanDeveer, 2011, 295). The larger result of this mixed bag of communication is a confusing set of narratives about the climate across the Americas. The work of environmental advocates and communicators will be to streamline the multiplicity of competing storylines and find more ways to bring the international public into the larger dialogue.

CASE STUDY: #HIROSHIMA70, #OBAMAHIROSHIMA, AND THE MEDIATED LEGACY OF NUCLEAR WEAPONRY

At 8:15 a.m. on August 7, 1945, a B-29 bomber dropped an atomic weapon of mass destruction on the southern Japanese city of Hiroshima, killing 140,000 civilians, over half of them instantly. Ordered by U.S. president Harry Truman, the atomic bombing of Hiroshima represented the first use of nuclear weaponry in history, proving to be one of the seminal moments of twentieth-century history. It was followed two days later by a similar attack on the city of Nagasaki, this one killing 70,000 people. Less than a week after the attacks, Japan surrendered to the Allied powers to bring an end to World War II. The debate over the deployment of nuclear weapons, however, had only just begun.

The 1945 U.S. bombing of Hiroshima represents a key historical moment that continues to attract diverging media narratives about the legacy of World War II and ongoing implications for global militarization and nuclear technology/weaponry (Lifton and Mitchell, 1995; Takaki, 1996; Orr, 2001). Two relatively recent milestones—the seventy-fifth anniversary of the occasion of the bombing in 2020, and U.S. president Barack Obama's historic

May 2016 visit to the site—positioned social media as a key site for public discourse about the event and its implications for international diplomacy and global nuclear disarmament. Previous microblogging activity has done the same via the Twitter hashtags #ObamaHiroshima and #Hiroshima70, both of which helped foster a more internationalized and nuanced understanding of this pivotal world event.

"Hiroshima" as a word has come to be associated with the destruction of a city, but also the death and suffering of those victims of nuclear attack

← **Tweet**

Greenpeace e.V.
@greenpeace_de   ...

Hiroshima: Never Again! Greenpeace activists protest at the air base Büchel for the withdrawal of all nuclear weapons from Germany. #hiroshima75

12:11 AM · Aug 5, 2020

129 Retweets   **8** Quotes   **439** Likes   **1** Bookmark

Figure 12.2.   On the seventy-fifth anniversary of the atomic bombing of Hiroshima, Greenpeace activists launched a hot air balloon at a German air base to deliver a global message about nuclear disarmament. (@greenpeace_de/Twitter.)

(Boyer, 1995). This connection—between the ramifications of nuclear technology and weaponry and human health—is not something that Hiroshima's institutions or civilians have shied away from. The atomic bombing of Hiroshima, along with Nagasaki, represented the beginning of the Japanese population's engagement with radiation health issues, at the same time that universities in the two victimized cities developed particular expertise in this medical area (Clancey and Chhem, 2015).

On the fiftieth anniversary of the atomic bombing of Hiroshima, the cultural legacy of the event was thought to be ensured, with continued cultural works such as poetry, books, and documentaries underscoring its ability to stir the imagination in the United States and elsewhere (Boyer, 1995). However, less was known about how digital media would impact the aftermath of the fateful event from 1945. During the summer of 2015, on the seventieth anniversary of the Hiroshima bombing, social media users with a message of global peace and nuclear disarmament marked the occasion by tweeting their views with the hashtag of #Hiroshima70.

Not surprisingly, the mood was somber during the seventieth anniversary event. Japan's Prime Minister Shinzo Abe joined foreign delegates, including U.S. ambassador to Japan Caroline Kennedy, as well as tens of thousands of observers, to share a moment of silence in Hiroshima's Peace Memorial Park. Even as Abe laid a wreath at the ceremony to mark the occasion and mourn the victims, debates in traditional and social media revealed the bombing of Hiroshima to be a highly contested issue. Peace activists argue against the use of nuclear weaponry, even as a "last resort" in a conflict as devastating as World War II. Along with historians, environmentalists, war veterans, and the nuclear attack victims themselves, they have played an important role in shaping the narratives and, by extension, the debates related to the use of atomic weapons.

As Japan and the world memorialized victims of Hiroshima, a backdrop of world events corresponded with the anniversary in different ways. Negotiators had just recently reached a historic accord limiting Iran's nuclear ability in exchange for lifting oil and financial sanctions. Environmentalists continued to fret about the ongoing nuclear plant disaster in Japan's Fukushima prefecture, even as the Japanese government put a nuclear reactor back into service. Anti-war activists, meanwhile, continued to campaign against the production and proliferation of nuclear arsenals by a number of nations.

Amid these debates, the hashtag on Twitter emerged, offering a rallying cry for those either wishing to memorialize the bombing or adjoining a social, political, or environmental issue to the anniversary. On August 7, 2015, and during the days leading up to it, #Hiroshima70 emerged as a global touchstone for those opposed to nuclear proliferation or who wanted to highlight this tragic history to afford new lessons for government leaders today. This global movement eventually led to U.S. president Barack Obama's visit to the Hiroshima bombing site. The hashtag #ObamaHiroshima emerged as the digital media touchstone for his historic visit, the first visit to the site by a sitting U.S. president. And the momentum continued in the next decade with the establishment of the #Hiroshima75 hashtag, which continued with similar themes of global peace and nuclear disarmament.

The #Hiroshima70, #Hiroshima75, and #ObamaHiroshima hashtags were notable for engaging a diverse range of actors globally. The former was promoted by the municipal government of Hiroshima to remember the Japanese city's history and celebrate its recovery. Overseas, it was promoted by the New Zealand Red Cross and its "Target Nuclear Weapons" movement to call for the elimination of nuclear weapons. Despite such a diversity of perspectives, however, the hashtag worked because of the environmental and social messages it carried, and the number of people who engaged with the hashtag from around the world.

True to the aims of organizers from Hiroshima, many of the messages remembered the historic event itself, from linking to photos of the bombing to the endorsement of commemorative events during the summer of 2015. At the same time, global peace activists used the Hiroshima event to cast a message about the consequences of nuclear weaponry worldwide. They brought observers and social media participants into the discussion by localizing the events. The Hiroshima Generations application, supported by the United States-Japan Foundation, for example, proved to be highly popular because it allowed users to move the footprint of Hiroshima's nuclear disaster to one's hometown. Other means to further interest and knowledge included online links to media debates about how the event would be portrayed at the Smithsonian Institution in the United States, and even to potential mentions of the anniversary during the U.S. political primary debates.

DISCUSSION QUESTIONS

1. What interests of member countries are conveyed in an organization such as the Arctic Council?
2. How does the Arctic Council communicate economic objectives and aspirations in the context of climate change, ecological crisis, and the unique challenges facing the Arctic's traditional communities?
3. What is a news peg? How might a news peg be applied to an issue such as marine protection or wildlife conservation?

KEYWORDS

Core and periphery
National context
Net economic benefit
News pegs
Propaganda
Public diplomacy
Space and time
Spatialization
Staples theory

KEY EVENTS, LOCATIONS, AND ORGANIZATIONS

Arctic Council
#Hiroshima70
Ob-Irtysh River
Paris Accord
Polar Silk Road
United Nations Environment Program

REFERENCES

Arctic-Council.org. (2023). About the Arctic Council. Retrieved from: https://arctic-council.org/about/.

Arréllaga, M. M., Londoño, E., and Casado, L. (2020). Brazil fires burn world's largest tropical wetlands at "unprecedented" scale. *New York Times*. Retrieved from: https://www.nytimes.com/2020/09/04/world/americas/brazil-wetlands-fires-pantanal.html.

Boyer, P. (1995b). Exotic resonances: Hiroshima in American memory. *Diplomatic History*, 19(2): 297–318. Retrieved from: http://doi.org/10.1111/j.1467-7709.1995.tb00659.x.

Boykoff, M. T. (2011). *Who Speaks for the Climate?: Making Sense of Media Reporting on Climate Change*. Cambridge, UK: Cambridge University Press.

Breum, M. (2012). When the Arctic Council speaks: How to move the Council's communication into the future. In *The Arctic Council: Its Place in the Future of Arctic Governance*. Gordon Foundation. Retrieved from: https://gordonfoundation.ca/wp-content/uploads/2017/03/2012_ArcticCouncilGovernance_WEB.pdf.

Breum, M. (2019). For the first time ever, an Arctic Council ministerial meeting has ended without a joint declaration. *Arctic Today*. Retrieved from: https://www

.arctictoday.com/for-the-first-time-ever-an-arctic-council-ministerial-meeting-has
-ended-without-a-joint-declaration/.

Chater, A., and Landriault, M. (2016). Understanding media perceptions of the Arctic
council. *Arctic Yearbook*, 5, 60–72.

Clancey, G., and Chhem, R. (2015). Hiroshima, Nagasaki, and Fukushima. *The Lancet*,
386(9992): 405–6. Retrieved from: http://doi.org/10.1016/S0140-6736(15)61414
-3.

Colpitts, G. (2013). Review. *Canadians and the Natural Environment to the Twenty-
First Century*, by Neil S. Forkey. *Environmental History*, 18(4): 805–7.

Evenden, M. (1998). Harold Innis, the Arctic Survey, and the politics of social science during the Second World War. *Canadian Historical Review*, 79(1): 36–67.

Foster, J. B., Clark, B., and York, R. (2011). *The Ecological Rift: Capitalism's War
on the Earth*. New York: NYU Press.

Gunnarsson, E. (2020). Together towards a sustainable Arctic: One year into the
2019–2021 Icelandic chairmanship. Arctic-Council.org. Retrieved from: https://
arctic-council.org/ru/news/one-year-into-the-2019-2021-icelandic-chairmanship/.

Hayter, R., and Barnes, T. (1990). Innis' staple theory, exports, and recession: British
Columbia, 1981–86. *Economic Geography*, 66(2): 156–73.

Huskey, L., and Southcott, C. (2016). "That's where my money goes": Resource
production and financial flows in the Yukon economy. *Polar Journal*, 6(1): 11–29.

Kruckeberg, D. (1993). Universal ethics code: Both possible and feasible. *Public
Relations Review*, 19(1): 21–31.

Lifton, R. J., and Mitchell, G. (1995). *Hiroshima in America: Fifty Years of Denial*.
New York: Harper Perennial.

Orr, J. J. (2001). *The Victim as Hero: Ideologies of Peace and National Identity in
Postwar Japan*. Honolulu: University of Hawaii Press.

Selin, H., and VanDeveer, S. D. (2011). Climate change regionalism in North America. *Review of Policy Research*, 28(3): 295–304.

Sriramesh, K. (2008). Globalization and public relations. In *Public Relations
Research: European and International Perspectives and Innovations*. Wiesbaden:
VS Verlag fur Sozialwissenschaften, 409–25.

Takahashi, B., Pinto, J., Chavez, M., and Vigón, M. (2018). *News Media Coverage of
Environmental Challenges in Latin America and the Caribbean*. London: Palgrave
Macmillan.

Takaki, R. T. (1996). *Hiroshima: Why America Dropped the Atomic Bomb*. New
York: Back Bay Books.

UN Environment Programme. (2020). Yes, climate change is driving wildfires.
UNEnvironment.org. Retrieved from: https://www.unenvironment.org/news-and
-stories/story/yes-climate-change-driving-wildfires.

Zamith, R., Pinto, J., and Villar, M. E. (2013). Constructing climate change in the
Americas: An analysis of news coverage in US and South American newspapers.
Science Communication, 35(3): 334–57.

Chapter Thirteen

Greening the Field

Communication and Sport

This chapter focuses on the intersection of green communication and sport, including professional sporting leagues and global events like the Olympics and World Cup. Learning objectives of this chapter include the integration of sustainability into sport communication and understanding the "greening" of sport through specific activities and programs like environmental report cards and sustainability branding. The examples provided in this chapter demonstrate how sport has become a growing stage for the dissemination of environmental appeals through fan engagement, thought leadership, and the fostering of sustainable design and infrastructure.

FROM CARBON-NEUTRAL WORLD CUP TO "GREENEST EVER" OLYMPICS

In the lead-up to the 2022 World Cup of Football in Qatar, the host nation's embassy hosted a virtual event in partnership with the U.S. Chamber of Commerce to proclaim the carbon neutrality of the soccer tournament. The goal of this announcement was to highlight both the climate-friendly nature of the athletic competition and the sustainability philosophy at the heart of infrastructure and organization operations. In addition, it outlined Qatar's arsenal of sustainability tactics to deliver a fully carbon-neutral showcase for the global sport of soccer.

For mass-mediated international events like the World Cup, the Olympics, and the NFL Super Bowl, a public-facing commitment to the welfare of the planet is increasingly not only an expectation of host cities and government bodies, but even of the fans and athletes themselves. While Qatar's goal of hosting a carbon-neutral World Cup spoke to newfound support for climate initiatives on the part of the sporting community, it was not the first time a major event has made this commitment. The Olympics has aspired to similar goals in the past.

In 2010, the David Suzuki Foundation noted in an Olympics climate report card that "Olympic bids now typically include aspirations to be the 'greenest Games ever' and this appears to be encouraged by the International Olympic Committee (IOC). However, when it comes to making sure that environmental commitments are met, there is little evidence of strong IOC engagement." That concern over the Olympics has shifted significantly in recent years, with the IOC now leading the way in terms of delivering a sustainability strategy, a sustainability report, and a carbon footprint methodology that aims to accurately assess the Games' overall ecological footprint.

The goals of the Olympic Games closely align with FIFA (Federation Internationale de Football Association) in terms of staging an event that simultaneously energizes the host city or country with economic opportunities while paying close attention to an array of environmental impacts related to sourcing, supply chain, infrastructure, travel, and operations at the competitions. But one of the most valuable aspects of delivering a sustainable Olympics, World Cup, or Super Bowl is the public and media attention that is already focused on these events.

A successfully staged event with transparent ecological reporting can serve as an aspirational role model for governments, corporations, and communities around the world. The popularity and internationalism of the World Cup and Olympics in particular mean that they serve as a unique medium for disseminating messages and best practices about environmental protection and mitigation of greenhouse gases. They can also highlight global standards such as the U.N. Sustainable Development Goals, which address concerns over global poverty, inequality, and human health.

That brings us back to the excitement of the World Cup. The Qatar World Cup plan was based on a longer promise of sustainability by the host country, including its being one of the first countries to ratify the U.N. Framework Convention on Climate Change in 1996. As Beau Waters, Market Director of Sports & Entertainment at Jacobs, noted at the climate-neutral announcement, "The World Cup has been a catalyst for increased attention and awareness around sustainability in the region and it has been an important component driving many global sporting events to Qatar."

RIDING THE GREEN WAVES OF SPORT

The emergent green ethos that permeates events like the World Cup and Olympics primarily connects sport to sustainability through event logistics,

Table 13.1. Waves of Green in Sport (Brian McCullough, Michael Pfahl, and Sheila N. Nguyen)

Wave 1	Wave 2	Wave 3
Initial awareness	Awareness becomes knowledge	Knowledge becomes strategy
Education established	Education is disseminated	Education continues and develops outreach
Simple activities	Advanced activities	Sophisticated activities

but it also points to the transformation of perceptions and attitudes through team- and league-based advocacy. This echoes the view from sustainability researchers that two prominent potential roles for sporting entities are to reduce their ecological footprint and to raise environmental awareness (Trendafilova et al., 2014). Similarly, sport management scholars Brian McCullough, Michael Pfahl, and Sheila N. Nguyen refer to this marriage of ecology and athletics as "the green waves of environmental sustainability in sport" (2016, 1040). A first wave is generated due to the need to take action because of internal or external pressures, such as the activism of players or input from fans or community members. A second wave sees a series of green actions in which awareness translates into longer-term learning or attitudinal change. Finally, a third wave sees environmental action become embedded into the ethos of the sporting event, league, or team through outreach, education, and long-term strategy.

THE KRAKEN CLIMATE PLEDGE

Professional sport is big business in the United States. Every week, Americans devote countless hours to watching their favorite teams compete in leagues like the NFL, MLB, and NBA. Top players regularly earn contracts in the hundreds of millions of dollars, while cities are known to spend billions in expenditures on glitzy, state-of-the-art stadiums. The NHL is no exception, and over the last decade has grown further by expanding into new hockey markets such as Las Vegas and Seattle.

In the latter city, the establishment of the Seattle Kraken professional ice hockey franchise has marked an intriguing new era for professional sport. After the NHL Board of Governors voted unanimously in 2018 to approve the expansion team for the 2021–2022 season, the team launched a series of engagements that offered fans the ability to weigh in on the development of a variety of branding materials, including hockey jerseys and team colors. Perhaps most symbolically, they also engaged with management about the

Release the Kraken: NHL Seattle announces team name is Seattle Kraken

KING 5 Seattle   [Subscribe]   🖒 189   👎   ↗ Share   ↓ Download   ⋯
272K subscribers

23K views 2 years ago
The 32nd NHL franchise will be called the Seattle Kraken, team owners announced Thursday morning. The team, led by majority owner David Bonderman, spent 18 months researching and considering more than 215,000 fan votes and 1,200 suggested team names. Show more

Figure 13.1.   The Seattle Kraken's new brand was launched in 2020 at the construction site of the team's home, Climate Pledge Arena. The hockey team's name, jersey, and logo were introduced at the launch event by Heidi Dettmer, Seattle Kraken's former vice president of marketing and broadcast. The team commenced play during the 2021–2022 season. (Still from YouTube.)

team's new name and moniker, which ultimately emerged as the Kraken—an homage to the city's nautical and ecological mythology, and its connection to the Salish Sea.

The Kraken name launched nineteen months after the franchise was approved, and was chosen from a list of 1,200 prospective names amid a process that was explained as "grueling, onerous, and tedious" (Rizzardini, 2021, para. 3). According to team ownership, the team spent over a year and a half engaged in research to establish the best name, including the identification of more than 1,200 names from 215,000 fan submissions. A Kraken logo was simultaneously designed in partnership with Adidas (Cotsonika, 2020).

Ultimately, the Kraken moniker—which references the mythical sea creature that is found in multiple popular culture venues, including the movie

Pirates of the Caribbean—was deemed to be the fitting choice, in light of Seattle's nautical heritage and association with maritime industries such as fishing and shipping. It also positions the team as a steward of the Salish Sea, one of the continent's more complex marine ecosystems.

The name's "reveal" became a public event unto itself. The launching of the Kraken moniker in 2020 also featured the team's long-awaited logo and team colors, as well as a sneak preview of the team's home venue, Climate Pledge Arena. The logo, a stylized "S," was presented as a throwback to the Seattle Metropolitans legacy, and features a tentacle and red eye to conjure up the specter of the sea monster. The establishment of a marine creature as team mascot also helps conjure up the ecological identity of the Kraken's larger hockey territory that extends from Oregon to Alaska. Through the stylized logo and moniker, hockey fans might also picture oceanic imagery of nearby orca pods, salmon runs in Washington watersheds, or even the crab fishery of the Bering Sea.

Yet it is the team's commitment to environmental and social impact that helps the Kraken stand out from other NHL franchises. Whether it's ongoing support of climate initiatives, or community outreach to ensure diversity in hockey, the team is making the most of its opportunity to integrate social impact with on-ice action. The Kraken launched its first season at the uniquely branded Climate Pledge Arena, a stadium name established and paid for by online retailing behemoth Amazon. The naming of Climate Pledge Arena, the first arena to earn zero carbon certification, marked one of the few times that a corporation used a stadium naming rights opportunity to further an environmental or social objective instead of merely driving attention to the company's own brand identity.

While at Climate Pledge Arena, fans can marvel at the 1,800-square-foot green wall that highlights the hockey arena's green mission. At the home opener, the *New York Times* reported on fans who stopped to "snap selfies in front of thousands of plants growing in the vertical bedding, which is made from recycled plastic bottles" (Belson, 2021). The *Times* also reported on fans taking in the scene of solar panels, wind turbines, and the proclamation of "World's First Net Zero Carbon Arena" inside the arena concourse. The Kraken's growing popularity in the Seattle region is a testament in part to the team's spirited play on the ice. But it's also the result of the team's off-ice identity, which reflects the city's environmental aspirations. More professional sporting teams are looking to follow this template that features excellence on the ice or field combined with ecological and social impacts connecting the fan base to the franchise.

ORGANIZATIONAL PROFILE: GREEN SPORTS ALLIANCE

Founded in 2010, the Green Sports Alliance was established as a forward-thinking collaboration between the late philanthropist Paul Allen's Vulcan Inc. and the National Resources Defense Council (NRDC). The trade organization strives to be a convener of stakeholders from across the sporting landscape, including professional teams but also leagues, corporate sponsors, government partners, and of course the athletes and their fans.

Its inaugural members and partners included the NFL's Seattle Seahawks, the NBA's Portland Trailblazers, the NHL's Vancouver Canucks, and Major League Soccer's Seattle Sounders FC. They were joined by the Bonneville Environmental Foundation, Green Building Services, and Milepost Consulting. The organization dubs itself as promoting "healthy, sustainable communities where we live and play. . . . We share resources, experience, and expertise to raise awareness of what's environmentally possible in sports, business, and society."

So how does a hub for sustainable pro sports activity create lasting, meaningful impact? In 2021, it partnered with Major League Baseball's Colorado Rockies, Change the Course, and the Colorado Water Trust to help promote the protection of water resources in the state of Colorado and across the American West. The high-profile initiative came after the Colorado River's driest twelve-month period on record. The partnership focused on restoring thirty million gallons of water to an ecologically sensitive stretch of the river known as 15 Mile Reach in order to support endangered fish as well as downstream communities.

Green Sports Alliance also presents an annual award, the Environmental Leadership Award, for green leadership in professional sport. One previous winner, the United States Tennis Association, received the honor for sustainability and community impact. The award also provided an opportunity to recognize tennis legend Billie Jean King, who spurred on the green movement at New York City's National Tennis Center (which hosts the annual U.S. Open tournament) and who co-founded GreenSlam, which incentivizes tennis promoters, venues, and gear producers to commit to sustainability objectives.

These activities are emblematic of the vision, and legacy, of the late entrepreneurial legend Paul Allen, who championed the green sports movement before it was on the radar of most pro sporting organizations. Allen, who co-founded Microsoft in 1975, owned both the Portland Trailblazers and Seattle Seahawks and was focused on a number of ecological issues, including the impacts of plastic on ocean life, the potential for renewable energy sources, and LEED certification for new building construction. As a supporter of more sustainable approaches in the professional sport industry, Allen helped provide the industry with self-awareness and also new solutions for reducing its footprint.

CASE STUDY: GREENING THE TOKYO OLYMPICS

Of all global sporting events, few can compete with the public spectacle that is the Olympic Games. The Tokyo Summer Olympics was no exception in this regard. The 2020 Summer Games (which were ultimately held in 2021 due to the COVID-19 pandemic) integrated a national vision for Japan with localized metropolitan themes of sustainable city design, green transportation, and smart architecture.

Going back to 1964, the first time the Olympics were hosted in Tokyo, the Games have served as a venue for Japan's international diplomacy and storytelling. For example, the arrival of Yoshinori Sakai at Tokyo's National Stadium to commence the 1964 Tokyo Olympics not only represented a feat of logistics and athletics, it also symbolized the emergence of a new Japan. Sakai, who was known as "Atomic Bomb Boy" because he was born in Hiroshima on the same day an atomic bomb was dropped on his city, was able to convey to the world Japan's desire for nuclear disarmament and world peace less than two decades after the conclusion of World War II.

That symbolism of creating a better world carried though at the more recent Tokyo Games with an emphasis on green design. Olympics architecture provided an opportunity to offer national and metropolitan metaphors of Japan's aspirations of global peace and planetary protection, including the showcasing of high-rise office and residential buildings. Tokyo's Torch Tower, located at what was formerly Tokiwabashi Gate near Tokyo Station, is one such example. According to developer Mitsubishi Estate, the tower should be perceived as an Olympic torch lighting up the world. Then there is the Olympic Stadium itself. Designed by world-renowned architect Kengo Kuma, a unique aspect of the stadium is its emphasis and use of wood, which points to Japan's architectural traditions as well as to trends in the sustainability of building construction materials.

Ryoko Morita, a commercial manager for the Tokyo 2020 Summer Games, and Hirokazu Shibata, a sustainability executive with Dow Olympic & Sports Solutions (2020), maintain that the Olympics' built environment helped integrate sporting competition with science and the environment. Furthermore, sustainability gains are now an expected legacy of any Olympic Games. The Tokyo experience has also set the stage for international and professional teams to consider their high-profile infrastructure and venues as aspirational metaphors for what happens ecologically beyond the sporting field.

← **Tweet**

Global Climate Action Summit   ···
@GCAS2018

Will the 2020 Tokyo Olympics get the gold medal when it comes to
#sustainability? Find out the city's plans for meeting UN Sustainable
Development Goals via @innovatorsmag bit.ly/2Kij1gd #GCAS2018
#StepUp2018

12:33 PM · Jun 25, 2018

7 Retweets   **9** Likes

*Figure 13.2.   The Tokyo 2020 Summer Olympics, which actually took place during
2021 due to the COVID-19 pandemic, served as a model for sustainable city-building
and the hosting of a global sporting event. (@GCAS2018/Twitter.)*

The Summer Olympics, as a spectacle that simultaneously communicates
the story of individual athletes as well as the narrative of the host nation and
its global relationships, provides an important example of how the ecology of
sport is transmitted and consumed. This helps explain in part why the Olympics has captured the attention of nations, cities, and other civic jurisdictions,
which look to the Games as a means to promoting new ideas, establishing
diplomatic ties, enhancing foreign investment and tourism, and projecting
an image of "modernity" (Rivenburgh, 2009). For Tokyo, the Olympics provided an opportunity to situate the urban environment as a platform both for

international sport and global diplomacy and for the sustainability opportunities inherent in city-building design, infrastructure, and aesthetics.

DISCUSSION QUESTIONS

1. How are sustainability and climate issues embedded into global and national sporting events like the Super Bowl and World Cup?
2. How can professional sporting franchises in leagues such as the NHL, NBA, and WNBA infuse their athletic brands with pro-environmental appeals?
3. How does the Olympics work to create a greener games in terms of not only athletic competition but also sporting venues, transportation, and stadium architecture?

KEYWORDS

Built environment
Carbon footprint
Carbon neutrality
"Greenest Games"
LEED certification
Net zero
Sustainability report

KEY EVENTS, LOCATIONS, AND ORGANIZATIONS

2010 Vancouver Winter Olympics
2020 Tokyo Summer Olympics
2022 World Cup of Football in Qatar
Climate Pledge Arena (Seattle)
GreenSlam
Green Sports Alliance
International Olympic Committee (IOC)
U.N. Framework Convention on Climate Change

REFERENCES

Belson, K. (2021). An arena where the goal is "net zero" carbon emissions, even from fans. *New York Times.* Retrieved from: https://www.nytimes.com/2021/10/29/sports/climate-pledge-arena-seattle.html.

Cotsonika, N. (2020). Seattle Kraken reveal nickname for NHL expansion team. National Hockey League. Retrieved from: https://www.nhl.com/news/seattle-kraken-nickname-for-nhl-expansion-team/c-317588092.

McCullough, B. P., Pfahl, M. E., and Nguyen, S. N. (2016). The green waves of environmental sustainability in sport. *Sport in Society,* 19(7): 1040–65.

Morita, R., and Shibata, H. (2020). Materials science shapes Olympic Games venues in Tokyo. *Construction Specifier.* Retrieved from: https://www.constructionspecifier.com/materials-science-shapes-olympic-games-tokyo-2020-venues/.

Rivenburgh, N. K. (2009). Media events as political communication. In *Media Events in a Global Age.* London: Routledge, 187.

Rizzardini, J. (2021). Why does changing a team's name take so long? *FiveThirty Eight.* Retrieved from: https://fivethirtyeight.com/features/why-does-changing-a-teams-name-take-so-long/.

Trendafilova, S., McCullough, B., Pfahl, M., Nguyen, S. N., Casper, J., and Picariello, M. (2014). Environmental sustainability in sport: Current state and future trends. *Global Journal on Advances in Pure and Applied Sciences,* 3.

Chapter Fourteen

Grassroots Populism

This chapter focuses on the role of populism as a mode of environmental and political communication. Learning objectives of this chapter include the contextualizing of environmental populism through historical milestones and contemporary cases; and the understanding of populism concepts that energize, or undermine, environmental ideas or campaigns. The examples provided in this chapter demonstrate the growing role of populism as a force in U.S. and global environmental politics, and the use of populism as a means to citizen-centric democratic engagement.

THE PEOPLE VS. THE ESTABLISHMENT

On the eve of the United Nations Climate Change Summit in Glasgow, Scotland, in 2021, the eyes of the global media turned to the friendly skies. Host nation Britain, in a draft document published by *Reuters*, asked countries to reduce their aviation emissions to a standard compatible with the historic Paris Agreement. Furthermore, Britain urged countries to join a coalition of International Aviation Climate Ambition, which would encourage the U.N. to set long-term goals for global air travel. This was, according to the climate document, an "ambitious long-term aspirational goal . . . compatible with net-zero global emissions by 2050."

Yet the developments from the summit also known as COP26 revealed a paradox of messaging for global audiences. Only a couple of months before, U.S. climate envoy John Kerry had made headlines in conservative-leaning publications such as the *New York Post* for his personal carbon footprint by way of his family's private jet. Using flight-tracking data, the *Post* reported that the "gas-guzzling private jet owned by climate czar John Kerry's family has already taken 16 flights this year alone." While the White House downplayed the reports from the *Post* and other publications, the damage was done as headlines spread across digital and social media. The *New York Post*, and other news outlets, had situated John Kerry as the wealthy elitist crafting climate policy that ultimately did not apply to him as he commandeered his private jet around the country, thus contributing to carbon emissions in the process.

This is a trap that politicians and business leaders fall into often, and in many cases they only have themselves to blame for the emergent narratives of ecological irresponsibility or hypocrisy. The general public demands that its elected officials, government leaders, and CEOs—even when they are private citizens—live up to their public proclamations about the environment and, more importantly, the policies they create. Otherwise, events like the Climate Change Summit are vulnerable to accusations of elitism or, worse, being out of touch with the experiences of ordinary citizens.

Figure 14.1. Global leaders and dignitaries gathered at the United Nations Climate Change Conference in Glasgow, Scotland in 2021. Host nation Britain urged countries to join a coalition of "International Aviation Climate Ambition" that would encourage the U.N. to set long-term goals for global air travel. Political and business leaders have come under growing scrutiny for their own carbon footprints as a result of global air travel. (U.S. Embassy in U.K./Wikimedia Commons.)

This is not only an issue for high-profile politicians like Kerry, however. It also applies to those who engage in environmentalism and corporate social responsibility from the ranks of NGOs, international agencies, and Fortune 500 companies. The narrative of "us versus them" or "the people versus the elites" is one that can easily find its way into an issue like climate change and the environment when individuals can't or won't live in accordance with the values of their political or organizational mission statements. This is a challenge of great concern for environmental communicators who must reach across divides of class, occupation, age, and ethnicity to ensure that their message resonates across the political and demographic spectrums.

One of the great tensions playing out in the global arena of contemporary environmental politics is that of citizens rising up against global or national structures such as governments, NGOs, and corporations. One of the drivers of this rift between people and existing social processes is that of populism. *Populism* is a term that describes a political communication process that exists outside established political parties or societal conventions. It is a historical vehicle for protest, but also a medium for the construction of new ideas, policies, and engagement.

Populism is often seen as a means of increasing democratic engagement, because it provides citizens who feel alienated by the political or economic establishment with the opportunity to have their voice heard and also to affect real change. At the same time, populism can channel resentment, fear, or alienation. Reports of populism in the press often point to these latter attributes as driving this process, especially when referring to the marriage between populism and the political leaders who benefit from it.

FROM THE GRASSROOTS

At the heart of environmental advocacy is people, and it is everyday people that drive populism forward. In particular, such advocacy recognizes that people must coexist with the natural world in order to sustain their individual selves, their families, and their communities. In the context of green communication and public advocacy, it is not uncommon to hear organizations or news media using the term *grassroots* to define a movement of people, whether organized or not. This is a vital concept for the environmental communicator or persuader, because it recognizes the vitality of environmentalism that is directly connected to the earth's natural processes.

Given its connotation of human action being literally or metaphorically ground and connected to the soil, the term grassroots has a special place in environmental history and contemporary green advocacy. It communicates the idea that a belief or movement comes from the ground up and is supported by ordinary people. But where does the term originally come from? It turns out there is a strong linkage to the American West, and specifically the Great Plains.

In 1903, veterans of the American Civil War wanted to place General Eli Torrance, a former commander-in-chief of the Grand Army of the Republic who had fought in the Pennsylvania regiment, on the 1904 presidential ticket as a vice presidential candidate with Theodore Roosevelt. In an exchange with the *Kansas City Journal* at the time, one supporter indicated that to get Torrance on the ticket, organizing would have to happen at every locality and community. "We will begin *at the grass roots*," he said (*Salt Lake Herald*, 1903).

Later, in 1912, Indiana senator Albert Jeremiah Beveridge, another supporter of Roosevelt's candidacy, quipped that the former president's new Progressive Party had "come from the grass roots. It has grown from the soil of people's hard necessities." For over a century, then, the term grassroots has defined a movement or cause championed by those individuals in the places where societal elites typically are not.

NAOMI KLEIN TACKLES CARBON CREDITS
AND THE GREEN ECONOMY

Fast-forward to a century later. The publication of Naomi Klein's 2014 book *This Changes Everything* represents an interesting turning point in eco-activism, and an excellent example of environmental populism. In what has to be one of the most comprehensive accounts of the underpinnings and consequences of global climate change, Klein combined a populist style of narrative—appealing to mainstream American values—with a direct and quite scathing critique of the global economy.

At the same time, her book represents a potential new direction for how the mainstream media conceive of, and report about, the environment. That's because—far from proposing popular market-driven solutions to climate concerns and other environmental challenges facing the planet—Klein advances a rethink of the predominant economic system that is responsible for runaway carbon emissions and industrial pollution.

She implores her readers to embrace not incremental changes, but wholesale and dramatic shifts away from the political and economic status quo: "Sweeping bans on polluting activities, deep subsidies for green alternatives, pricey penalties for violations, new taxes, new public works programs, reversals of privatizations." If these changes sound like the once-in-a-generation governmental and societal efforts reserved for the monumental global wars and natural disasters of the past century, that's because they are positioned as exactly that.

Montreal-born Naomi Klein is no stranger to either contentious politics or dueling with ideologues—in her home country of Canada and particularly in the United States. Over a decade ago, she authored the best-selling book *No Logo*, which introduced the notion of culture jamming as a means to resisting rampant global consumerism. A follow-up effort, *The Shock Doctrine*, tackled the rise of free market and neoliberal policies in the wake of global wars and natural disasters. Not surprisingly, *This Changes Everything* has received criticism from pro-market media outlets. The libertarian website Reason.com, which champions "free minds and free markets," argued in a headline that "Naomi Klein Changes Nothing" with her publication. To her credit, Klein uses a deft touch in critiquing capitalism, and mostly holds up poor government policy and irresponsible corporate activity since the 1980s as the climate change culprit. This takes the focus away from her own political inclinations and puts it squarely on the climate conundrum itself.

Klein's counterintuitive argument is that the political right has a better grip on modern environmental debates—even if she disagrees with their motives—than political progressives, who are sometimes more intent on transforming green consumerism and environmental market schemes into social status or lucrative profits. Other green modernists have come under fire for carbon offset programs that allow jurisdictions such as British Columbia and California to play what amounts to shell games with their $CO2$ emissions. Even many environmentalists find themselves asking aloud whether such offsets amount to real change or are about making companies and governments look better on paper—a public relations ruse that happens to make the proprietors of offset exchange programs incredibly wealthy.

Mark Jaccard, an environmental economics professor at Simon Fraser University in Vancouver, provides another counter-perspective. Jaccard, a proponent of market-based environmental solutions including carbon offsets, reverts to the arguments that Klein's book had effectively challenged. He wrote, "'Changing everything' about global capitalism in just a few decades is a tall order. Fortunately, this is unnecessary for addressing climate change, as individual jurisdictions are already showing." Additional good news, as Paul Krugman noted in the *New York Times*, is that greenhouse gas reductions have proven to be not nearly as costly as science deniers on the right and anti-growth activists on the left would have us believe" (*Literary Review of Canada*, 2014).

In contemplating Klein's position, readers might be reminded of Franklin Delano Roosevelt's presidential policies both in the wake of the Great

Depression and during World War II. Indeed, Klein cites FDR and his policies at different intervals—making the case both for government intervention to mitigate climate change, but also to provide central government planning for a greener economy. In *This Changes Everything*, Klein uses her populist rhetorical style to introduce alternative political and economic ideas. While some journalists and opinion makers have tried to write her ideas off as foolish or inconsequential, Klein's arguments have gained traction with some members of the public.

Perhaps that's because her argument goes beyond one-off fixes for specific environmental problems, and ultimately gnaws away at the root causes of modern ecological issues—including those green opinion leaders who have effectively framed ecological debates in a way that extends the interests of specific groups, classes, and corporations. Klein's ecological populism has therefore served as a vehicle not only for deploying specific green appeals but also for ensuring that media debates will contend with the need for greening the economy.

If anything, Jaccard's association of climate change deniers with no-growth activists reinforced Klein's most controversial argument—that the solutions to date provided for ecological problems hardly go far enough and are rooted in the system that has created the untenable situation in the first place. That helps to explain why Klein has openly criticized schemes such as carbon offsets.

With a few exceptions, the emerging trade of carbon offsets has enjoyed remarkably good press from leading mainstream publications during the past decade. A *New York Times* headline from 2014 provided a good example, declaring a price tag on carbon—a solution increasingly deployed by governments globally, and subscribed to by corporations—as a "climate rescue plan." When British Columbia's auditor general went off script and blew the whistle on discrepancies in the Canadian province's Pacific Carbon Trust in 2013, his colleagues quickly turned on the whistleblower, accusing him of not understanding the mechanisms of the carbon-offsetting trade. The media narrative naturally followed the government's public relations talking points. However, the Pacific Carbon Trust quietly closed its doors shortly after, and was replaced by the government's Climate Investment Branch, sponsored by the government's climate action secretariat.

Klein's assessment, not surprisingly, predicted such disappointments—even abuses—in market-driven environmental schemes. In a 2013 article for *The Nation*, she took on both the practice and the mainstream environmental movements backing it. "Some of the most powerful and wealthiest environmental organizations have long behaved as if they had a stake in the oil and gas industry. They led the climate movement down various dead ends: carbon trading, carbon offsets, natural gas as a 'bridge fuel'—what these policies all held in common is that they created the illusion of progress while allowing the fossil fuel companies to keep mining, drilling and fracking with abandon. We always knew that the groups pushing hardest for these false solutions took donations from, and formed corporate partnerships with, the big emitters."

When it comes to writers like Klein, environmental sociologists John Bellamy Foster and Brett Clark have tried to make sense of the shifting political grounds within the media landscape. They point to Noam Chomsky's explanation of the role of liberal opinion as a crucial gatekeeper for the system by helping define the acceptable outer boundaries of contrarian political and social perspectives. According to Foster and Clark, the penalty for going "off script" from conventional liberal thought is "excommunication from the mainstream, to be enforced by the corporate media" (*Monthly Review*, 8).

Klein antagonized so-called liberal media gatekeepers by her admission that the "right is right"—insofar as the ability of conservatives to see the crystal-clear linkage between climate and capitalism that is missing from most discussions on the left. As Foster and Clark put it, "Liberal ideologues—caught in the selfsame trap of capitalism vs. the climate—tend to waffle, accepting most of the science, while turning around and contradicting themselves by downplaying the logistical implications for society."

CASE STUDY: BREWING COLLABORATION
SEEKS TO SAVE THE SNAKE RIVER

Over a decade ago, the Northwest advocacy organization Washington Wild decided that the best way to engage publics on issues of environmentalism and wildlife protection was to meet them where they live and play. The Brewshed Alliance was founded with a view to bringing environmental issues directly to the region's craft beer drinkers. After ten years of championing the protection of wildlife areas, celebrating Earth Days, and fundraising for environmental causes, the alliance claimed nearly ninety industry partners across the state. One of the overarching strengths of the partnership between Washington Wild and the Brewshed Alliance is the ability to reach people across the political spectrum by organizing community events. Washington Wild was able to get the word out about its mission through special events such as trivia nights, pub crawls, tap takeovers, and film screenings.

The alliance annually puts on a Brewshed Beer Fest, where enthusiasts of hops and barley can sample many of the special editions of craft beers that have been produced to raise funds and awareness for regional ecologies. Some of the popular offerings have included the Wild & Scenic Hazy IPA from Counterbalance + Peddler Brewing, the Brewshed IPA by Balebreaker,

Figure 14.2. Stoup Brewing's Save the Snake River Lager was brewed in conjunction with the Brewshed Alliance, a coalition of brewing companies in the Northwest focused on environmental conservation. The special edition beer called on politicians to remove the four dams of the Lower Snake River in order to restore habitat for salmon and steelhead trout.

and the Public Lands Pilsner from Lucky Envelope. Washington Wild notes that its biggest beer collaboration to date was the Save the Snake River Lager, which included fifty industry partners.

This latter effort is focused on the Snake River, a tributary of the Columbia River, which rises at Yellowstone National Park and traverses 1,078 miles across the West before emptying into the Pacific Ocean. Four dams on the Lower Snake River have been a long-running point of contention for advocates of the watershed on account of their devastating impacts for salmon and steelhead, and by extension the concerns raised by local communities and tribes. Washington Wild pointed to a government report determining that removing the dams was a key component to salmon recovery in the West. The Brewshed Alliance collaboration was the inevitable follow-up to that report, according to the organization: "This beer is a message to our Northwest elected officials: Now is the time to support salmon and steelhead recovery with a comprehensive plan to remove the four Lower Snake River dams."

DISCUSSION QUESTIONS

1. What are the advantages and disadvantages of populism as a mode of persuasion?
2. Why are publics increasingly wary of so-called "elites" from government, business, and media in debates about the climate and the environment?
3. How do green thinkers like Naomi Klein conceptualize people power in the context of environmental movements? What other contemporary writers are leading the charge in this arena?

KEYWORDS

Carbon offsetting
Eco-activism
Economic greening
Environmental populism
Grassroots
Green consumerism
Media gatekeepers
Populist appeals

KEY EVENTS, LOCATIONS, AND ORGANIZATIONS

Brewshed Alliance
International Aviation Climate Ambition
Paris Agreement
Progressive Party
United Nations Climate Change Summit (COP26)

REFERENCES

Foster, J. B., and Clark, B. (2015). Crossing the river of fire: The liberal attack on Naomi Klein and This Changes Everything. *Monthly Review* 66(9): 1.

Jaccard, M. (2014). I wished this changed everything. *Literary Review of Canada*. Retrieved from: https://reviewcanada.ca/magazine/2014/11/i-wish-this-changed-everything/.

Klein, N. (2013). Time for big green to go fossil free. *The Nation*, May 1. Retrieved from: http://www.thenation.com/article/174143/time-big-green-go-fossil-free.

Salt Lake Herald. (1903). Boom for Gen. Torrance. September 25. Retrieved from: https://chroniclingamerica.loc.gov/lccn/sn85058130/1903-09-25/ed-1/seq-6/.

References

Adams, R. B., Licht, A. N., and Sagiv, L. (2011). Shareholders and stakeholders: How do directors decide? *Strategic Management Journal*, 32(12): 1331–55.

Alagappa, H. (2023). The mystery of the world's oldest billboard. *Atlas Obscura*.

Alia, V. (2022). *The New Media Nation: Indigenous Peoples and Global Communication*. New York: Berghahn Books.

Arctic-Council.org. (2023). About the Arctic Council. Retrieved from: https://arctic-council.org/about/.

Arréllaga, M. M., Londoño, E., and Casado, L. (2020). Brazil fires burn world's largest tropical wetlands at "unprecedented" scale. *New York Times*. Retrieved from: https://www.nytimes.com/2020/09/04/world/americas/brazil-wetlands-fires-pantanal.html.

Auter, P. J. (1992). Psychometric: TV that talks back: An experimental validation of a parasocial interaction scale. *Journal of Broadcasting & Electronic Media*, 36(2): 173–81.

Bachand, T. (2023). Keystone Mapping Project. Retrieved online from: https://keystone.steamingmules.com/about/.

Barnett, C., and Svendsen, N. V. (2002). Making the environment news: Reporting industrial pollution in Durban. *Rhodes Journalism Review*, (21): 54–55.

Bavelas, A., Hastorf, A. H., Gross, A. E., and Kite, W. R. (1965). Experiments on the alteration of group structure. *Journal of Experimental Social Psychology*.

Beck, E. C. (1979). The Love Canal tragedy. *EPA J.* 5: 17.

Belson, K. (2021). An arena where the goal is "net zero" carbon emissions, even from fans. *New York Times*. Retrieved from: https://www.nytimes.com/2021/10/29/sports/climate-pledge-arena-seattle.html.

Benford, R. D., and Snow, D. A. (2000). Framing processes and social movements: An overview and assessment. *Annual Review of Sociology*, 611–39.

Blum, E. D. (2008). *Love Canal Revisited: Race, Class, and Gender in Environmental Activism*. Lawrence: University Press of Kansas.

Bob, C. (2005). *The Marketing of Rebellion: Insurgents, Media, and International Activism.* Cambridge, UK: Cambridge University Press.

Bogost, I. (2010). *Persuasive Games: The Expressive Power of Videogames.* Cambridge, MA: MIT Press.

Boyer, P. (1995b). Exotic resonances: Hiroshima in American memory. *Diplomatic History*, 19(2): 297–318. Retrieved from: http://doi.org/10.1111/j.1467-7709.1995.tb00659.x.

Boykoff, M. T. (2011). *Who Speaks for the Climate?: Making Sense of Media Reporting on Climate Change.* Cambridge, UK: Cambridge University Press.

Breum, M. (2012). When the Arctic Council speaks: How to move the Council's communication into the future. In *The Arctic Council: Its Place in the Future of Arctic Governance.* Gordon Foundation. Retrieved from: https://gordonfoundation.ca/wp-content/uploads/2017/03/2012_ArcticCouncilGovernance_WEB.pdf.

Breum, M. (2019). For the first time ever, an Arctic Council ministerial meeting has ended without a joint declaration. *Arctic Today*. Retrieved from: https://www.arctictoday.com/for-the-first-time-ever-an-arctic-council-ministerial-meeting-has-ended-without-a-joint-declaration/.

Bronfenbrenner, U. (2005). *Making Human Beings Human: Bioecological Perspectives on Human Development.* Thousand Oaks, CA: Sage.

Brox, E., Fernandez-Luque, L., and Tøllefsen, T. (2011). Healthy gaming—video game design to promote health. *Applied Clinical Informatics*, 2(02): 128–42.

Bullard, R. (2017). African Americans need a strong and independent EPA. *Op-Ed News*. Retrieved from: https://www.opednews.com/articles/African-Americans-Need-a-S-by-Robert-Bullard-African-Americans_Black-History-Month_Civil-Rights-Violations_Climate-170221-71.html.

Byun, S. K., and Oh, J. M. (2018). Local corporate social responsibility, media coverage, and shareholder value. *Journal of Banking & Finance*, 87: 68–86.

Cancel, A. E., Cameron, G. T., Sallot, L. M., and Mitrook, M. A. (1997). It depends: A contingency theory of accommodation in public relations. *Journal of Public Relations Research*, 9(1): 31–63.

Cancel, A. E., Mitrook, M. A., and Cameron, G. T. (1999). Testing the contingency theory of accommodation in public relations. *Public Relations Review*, 25(2): 171–97.

Carr, D. (2012). Hashtag activism, and its limits. *New York Times*, March 25.

Carroll, A. B. (2016). Carroll's pyramid of CSR: Taking another look. *International Journal of Corporate Social Responsibility*, 1(1): 1–8.

Centeno, Dave De Guzman. (2015). Constructing celebrities as political endorsers: Parasocial acts, cultural power, and cultural capital. *Philippine Political Science Journal*, 36(2): 209–32.

Chater, A., and Landriault, M. (2016). Understanding media perceptions of the Arctic council. *Arctic Yearbook*, 5, 60–72.

Chen, T., Dong, H., and Lin, C. (2020). Institutional shareholders and corporate social responsibility. *Journal of Financial Economics*, 135(2): 483–504.

Cho, C. H., Martens, M. L., Kim, H., and Rodrigue, M. (2011). Astroturfing global warming: It isn't always greener on the other side of the fence. *Journal of Business Ethics*, 104: 571–87.

Clancey, G., and Chhem, R. (2015). Hiroshima, Nagasaki, and Fukushima. *The Lancet*, 386(9992), 405–6. Retrieved from: http://doi.org/10.1016/S0140-6736(15)61414 -3.

Climate Justice Alliance (2022). Climate Justice Alliance applauds senators who voted with communities. Retrieved from: https://climatejusticealliance.org/how -we-work/#3.

Colpitts, G. (2013). Review. *Canadians and the Natural Environment to the Twenty- First Century*, by Neil S Forkey. *Environmental History*, 18(4): 805–7.

Contino, K. (2022). Jason Momoa shaves off his signature long hair. *Page Six*. Retrieved from: https://pagesix.com/2022/09/06/jason-momoa-shaves-off-his-long -hair-see-his-new-look/.

Cotsonika, N. (2020). Seattle Kraken reveal nickname for NHL expansion team. *National Hockey League*. Retrieved from: https://www.nhl.com/news/seattle -kraken-nickname-for-nhl-expansion-team/c-317588092

Cox, R. (2013). *Environmental Communication and the Public Sphere*. Thousand Oaks, CA: Sage.

Dahlsrud, A. (2006). How corporate social responsibility is defined: An analysis of 37 definitions. *Corporate Social Responsibility and Environmental Management*, 15(1): 1–13.

Dale, S. (1996). *McLuhan's Children: The Greenpeace Message and the Media*. Toronto: Between the Lines.

Dalrymple, K. E., Shaw B. R., and Brossard, D. (2013). "Following the leader: Using opinion leaders in environmental strategic communication." *Society & Natural Resources* 26(12): 1438–53.

Darian-Smith, E. (2022). *Global Burning: Rising Antidemocracy and the Climate Crisis*. Stanford University Press.

DeLaure, M., and Fink, M. (2017). *Culture Jamming: Activism and the Art of Cultural Resistance*. New York: New York University Press.

DeLuca, K. M. (2005). *Image Politics: The New Rhetoric of Environmental Activism*. London: Psychology Press.

Derville, T. (2005). Radical activist tactics: Overturning public relations conceptualizations. *Public Relations Review*, 31(4): 527–33.

Deshpande, P. (2013). 5 tips every content curator needs to write better calls to action. *Content Marketing Institute*. Retrieved from: https://contentmarketinginstitute .com/articles/tips-content-curator-write-better-calls-to-action/.

Dietrich, G. (2014). *Spin Sucks: Communication and Reputation Management in the Digital Age*. Indianapolis: Que Publishing.

EarthDay.org. (2022). History of Earth Day. Retrieved from: https://www.earthday .org/history/

Edelman (2021). Trust Barometer Global Report. Online Fieldwork in 28 Countries between October 19 to November 18, 2020. Retrieved from: https://www.edelman .com/trust/2021-trust-barometer.

Evenden, M. (1998). Harold Innis, the Arctic Survey, and the politics of social science during the Second World War. *Canadian Historical Review*, 79(1): 36–67.

Fischer, F. (2017). *Climate Crisis and the Democratic Prospect: Participatory Governance in Sustainable Communities*. Oxford, UK: Oxford University Press.

Fisher, D. R., and Freudenburg, W. R. (2001). Ecological modernization and its critics: Assessing the past and looking toward the future. *Society & Natural Resources*, 14(8): 701–9.

Forsyth, D. R. (1980). A taxonomy of ethical ideologies. *Journal of Personality and Social Psychology*, 39(1): 175.

Foster, J. B. (2012). The planetary rift and the new human exemptionalism: A political-economic critique of ecological modernization theory. *Organization & Environment*, 25(3): 211–37.

Foster, J. B., and Clark, B. (2015). Crossing the river of fire. The liberal attack on Naomi Klein and This Changes Everything. *Monthly Review* 66(9): 1.

Foster, J. B., Clark, B., and York, R. (2011). *The Ecological Rift: Capitalism's War on the Earth*. New York: NYU Press.

Fraisl, D., Hager, G., Bedessem, B., et al. (2022). Citizen science in environmental and ecological sciences. *Nature Reviews Methods Primers*, 2(1): 64.

Gandiwa, E., Zisadza-Gandiwa, P., Muboko, N., Libombo, E., Mashapa, C., and Gwazani, R. (2014). Local people's knowledge and perceptions of wildlife conservation in southeastern Zimbabwe. *Journal of Environmental Protection* 5(6): 475–81.

Ganesh, S., and Zoller, H. M. (2012). Dialogue, activism, and democratic social change. *Communication Theory*, 22(1): 66–91.

Gardiner, B. (2020). Unequal impact: The deep links between racism and climate change. *Yale Environment 360*. Retrieved from: https://e360.yale.edu/features/unequal-impact-the-deep-links-between-inequality-and-climate-change.

Giles, D. C. (2002). Parasocial interaction: A review of the literature and a model for future research. *Media Psychology*, 4(3): 279–305.

Gilliam, F. D., and Bales, S. N. (2001). Strategic frame analysis: Reframing America's youth. UCLA Center for Communications and Community.

Gilliam, F. D., and Bales, S. N. (2004). Strategic frame analysis and youth development. *Handbook of Applied Developmental Science: Promoting Positive Child, Adolescent, and Family Development Through Research, Policies and Programs*, 1: 421–36.

Glover, P. (2009). Celebrity endorsement in tourism advertising: Effects on destination image. *Journal of Hospitality and Tourism Management*, 16(1): 16–23.

Greenberg, J., and Knight, G. (2004). Framing sweatshops: Nike, global production, and the American news media. *Communication and Critical/Cultural Studies*, 1(2): 151–75.

Gretzel, U., and Hardy, A. (2019). #VanLife: Materiality, makeovers and mobility amongst digital nomads. *E-Review of Tourism Research*, 16(2/3).

Grunig, J. E. (1989). A situational theory of environmental issues, publics, and activists. In Grunig, L. A. (ed.), *Environmental Activism Revisited: The Changing*

Nature of Communication through Public Relations, Special Interest Groups, and the Mass Media, 50–82.

Grunig, J. E. (2005). Situational theory of publics. *Encyclopedia of Public Relations.* Thousand Oaks, CA: Sage, 778–80.

Grunig, J. E., and Grunig, L. A. (2013). Models of public relations and communication. *Excellence in Public Relations and Communication Management*, 285–325.

Grunig, J. E., and Kim, J. N. (2021). 15 The four models of public relations and their research legacy. In Valentini, C. (ed.), *Public Relations*, Vol. 27, 277.

Grunig, L. A. (1989). Environmental activism revisited: The changing nature of communication through organizational public relations, special interest groups and the mass media. *Monographs in Environmental Education and Environmental Studies*, Vol. V.

Guillory, S. (2015). How's your press release call to action? *Cision*. Retrieved from: https://web.archive.org/web/20150803072457/http://www.cision.com/us/2015/05/hows-your-press-release-call-to-action/.

Gunnarsson, E. (2020). Together towards a sustainable Arctic: One year into the 2019–2021 Icelandic chairmanship. Arctic-Council.org. Retrieved from: https://arctic-council.org/ru/news/one-year-into-the-2019-2021-icelandic-chairmanship/.

Habermas, J. (1990). Discourse ethics: Notes on a program of philosophical justification. In J. Habermas (ed.), *Moral Consciousness and Communicative Action.* Cambridge, MA: MIT Press, 43–115.

Habermas, J. (1993). *Justification and Application: Remarks on Discourse Ethics.* Cambridge, MA: MIT Press.

Hallahan, K. (2000). Inactive publics: The forgotten publics in public relations. *Public Relations Review* 26(4): 499–515.

Hallahan, K. (2002). Ivy Lee and the Rockefellers' response to the 1913–1914 Colorado coal strike. *Journal of Public Relations Research*, 14(4): 265–315.

Hansen, A. (2018). *Environment, Media and Communication.* London and New York: Routledge.

Hayter, R., and Barnes, T. (1990). Innis' staple theory, exports, and recession: British Columbia, 1981–86. *Economic Geography*, 66(2): 156–73.

Hernandez, K. (2023). Three reasons your messaging isn't pulling through. INK Communications: Brand Strategy. Retrieved from: https://ink-co.com/insights/three-reasons-messaging-isnt-pulling-through/.

Hertsgaard, M. (2019). "We're losing the race": UN secretary general calls climate change an "emergency." *The Guardian*.

Hessekiel, D. (2020). Changemaker interview: Kevin Martinez, VP, Corporate Citizenship, ESPN. Retrieved from: https://www.forbes.com/sites/davidhessekiel/2020/11/14/changemaker-interview-kevin-martinez-vp-corporate-citizenship-espn/?sh=7676f395441a.

Hochman, N., and Manovich, L. (2013). Zooming into an Instagram City: Reading the local through social media. *First Monday*, 18(7).

Holmes, S. J. (1999). *The Young John Muir: An Environmental Biography.* Madison: University of Wisconsin Press.

Huskey, L., and Southcott, C. (2016). "That's where my money goes": Resource production and financial flows in the Yukon economy. *Polar Journal*, 6(1): 11–29.

Ingenhoff, D., and Marschlich, S. (2019). Corporate diplomacy and political CSR: Similarities, differences and theoretical implications. *Public Relations Review*, 45(2): 348–71.

Jaccard, M. (2014). I wished this changed everything. *Literary Review of Canada*. Retrieved from: https://reviewcanada.ca/magazine/2014/11/i-wish-this-changed-everything/.

Joireman, J., and Liu, R. L. (2014). Future-oriented women will pay to reduce global warming: Mediation via political orientation, environmental values, and belief in global warming. *Journal of Environmental Psychology* 40: 391–400.

Kahne, J., Middaugh, E., and Evans, C. (2009). *The Civic Potential of Video Games*. Cambridge, MA: MIT Press, 111.

Karlberg, M. (1996). Remembering the public in public relations research: From theoretical to operational symmetry. *Journal of Public Relations Research*, 8(4): 263–78.

Katz, E. (1957). The two-step flow of communication: An up-to-date report on an hypothesis. *Public Opinion Quarterly*, 21(1): 61–78.

Kellert, S. R. (1980). *Knowledge, Affection, and Basic Attitudes toward Animals in American Society: Phase III*. U.S. Department of the Interior, Fish and Wildlife Service.

Kellert, S. R. (1994). Public attitudes toward bears and their conservation. In *Bears: Their Biology and Management*, Vol. 9, International Association for Bear Research and Management, 43–50.

Kilanowski, J. F. (2017). Breadth of the socio-ecological model. *Journal of Agromedicine*, 22(4): 295–97.

Kim, Y., and Ramos, M. L. Z. (2018). Stakeholder responses toward fast food chains' CSR. *Corporate Communications: An International Journal*.

King, C. W., and Summers, J. O. (1970). Overlap of opinion leadership across consumer product categories. *Journal of Marketing Research*, 7(1): 43–50.

Klein, N. (2013.) Time for big green to go fossil free. *The Nation*, May 1. Retrieved from: http://www.thenation.com/article/174143/time-big-green-go-fossil-free.

Kruckeberg, D. (1993). Universal ethics code: Both possible and feasible. *Public Relations Review*, 19(1): 21–31.

Lakoff, G. (2010). Why it matters how we frame the environment. *Environmental Communication*, 4(1): 70–81.

Lakoff, G. (2014). *The All New Don't Think of an Elephant!: Know Your Values and Frame the Debate*. White River Junction, VT: Chelsea Green Publishing.

Le Bon, G. (1897). *The Crowd: A Study of the Popular Mind*. London: T. Fisher Unwin.

Lee, C., and Chavez Jr, B. F. (1987). *Toxic Wastes and Race in the United States: A National Report on the Racial and Socio-Economic Characteristics of Communities with Hazardous Waste Sites*. New York: Commission for Racial Justice, United Church of Christ.

Lee, E., Lee, J. A., Moon, J. H., and Sung, Y. (2015). Pictures speak louder than words: Motivations for using Instagram. *Cyberpsychology, Behavior, and Social Networking*, 18(9): 552–56.

Leonard-Barton, D. (1985). Experts as negative opinion leaders in the diffusion of a technological innovation. *Journal of Consumer Research*, 11(4): 914–26.

Leppert, M. (2023). East Palestine's battle is a lesson for all Americans. *Indiana Capital Chronicle*. Retrieved from: https://indianacapitalchronicle.com/2023/03/07/east-palestines-battle-is-a-lesson-for-all-americans/.

Lesage, F., and Hackett, R. A. (2014). Between objectivity and openness—The mediality of data for journalism. *Media and Communication*, 2(2): 42–54.

Lester, M. (1980). Generating newsworthiness: The interpretive construction of public events. *American Sociological Review*, 984–94.

Levy, M. R. (1979). Watching TV news as para-social interaction." *Journal of Broadcasting & Electronic Media*, 23(1): 69–80.

Lifton, R. J., and Mitchell, G. (1995). *Hiroshima in America: Fifty Years of Denial.* New York: Harper Perennial.

Lopatta, K., Bassen, A., Kaspereit, T., Tideman, S. A., and Buchholz, D. (2020). The effect of institutional dual holdings on CSR performance. *Journal of Sustainable Finance & Investment*, 1–20.

Luttrell, R. M., and Capizzo, L. W. (2021). *Public Relations Campaigns: An Integrated Approach.* Thousand Oaks, CA: Sage.

Mangold, F., and Bachl, M. (2018). New news media, new opinion leaders? How political opinion leaders navigate the modern high-choice media environment. *Journal of Communication*, 68(5): 896–919.

Mann, C. R., and Twiss, G. R. (1910). *Physics.* Chicago and New York: Scott, Foresman and Company.

Manning, R. E. (2011). *Studies in Outdoor Recreation: Search and Research for Satisfaction.* Corvallis: Oregon State University Press.

McCright, A. M. (2010). The effects of gender on climate change knowledge and concern in the American public. *Population and Environment*, 32(1): 66–87.

McCullough, B. P., Pfahl, M. E., and Nguyen, S. N. (2016). The green waves of environmental sustainability in sport. *Sport in Society*, 19(7): 1040–65.

Meyer, D. S. (1995). The challenge of cultural elites: Celebrities and social movements. *Sociological Inquiry*, 65(2): 181–206.

Meyer, J. M. (1997). Gifford Pinchot, John Muir, and the boundaries of politics in American thought. *Polity*, 30(2): 267–84.

Michelon, G., Rodrigue, M., and Trevisan, E. (2020). The marketization of a social movement: Activists, shareholders and CSR disclosure. *Accounting, Organizations and Society*, 80: 101074.

Mintel.com. (2018). "The eco gender gap." Retrieved from: https://www.mintel.com/press-centre/social-and-lifestyle/the-eco-gender-gap-71-of-women-try-to-live-more-ethically-compared-to-59-of-men.

Morita, R., and Shiba, M. (2020). Materials science shapes Olympic Games venues in Tokyo. *Construction Specifier*. Retrieved from: https://www.constructionspecifier.com/materials-science-shapes-olympic-games-tokyo-2020-venues/.

Morse, K. T. (2010). *The Nature of Gold: An Environmental History of the Klondike Gold Rush*. Seattle: University of Washington Press.

Mundy, D. E. (2013). The spiral of advocacy: How state-based LGBT advocacy organizations use ground-up public communication strategies in their campaigns for the "Equality Agenda." *Public Relations Review*, 39(4): 387–90.

Murphy, P., and Dee, J. (1992). Du Pont and Greenpeace: The dynamics of conflict between corporations and activist groups. *Journal of Public Relations Research*, 4(1): 3–20.

Nelson, J. S. (2017). *Cowboy Politics: Myths and Discourses in Popular Westerns from The Virginian to Unforgiven and Deadwood*. Lanham, MD: Lexington Books.

Nerlich, B., and Koteyko, N. (2010). Carbon gold rush and carbon cowboys: A new chapter in green mythology? *Environmental Communication*, 4(1): 37–53.

Nilsson, S., and Enander, A. (2020). "Damned if you do, damned if you don't": Media frames of responsibility and accountability in handling a wildfire. *Journal of Contingencies and Crisis Management*, 28(1): 69–82.

Nisbet, M. C., and Kotcher, J. E. (2009). A two-step flow of influence? Opinion-leader campaigns on climate change. *Science Communication*, 30(3): 328–54.

Ohanian, R. (1991). The impact of celebrity spokespersons' perceived image on consumers' intention to purchase. *Journal of advertising Research*.

Olen, S. M. (2022). Citizen science tackles plastics in Ghana. *Nature Sustainability*, 5(10): 814–15.

Oravec, C. (1981). John Muir, Yosemite, and the sublime response: A study in the rhetoric of preservationism. *Quarterly Journal of Speech*, 67(3): 245–58.

Orr, J. J. (2001). *The Victim as Hero: Ideologies of Peace and National Identity in Postwar Japan*. Honolulu: University of Hawaii Press.

Perez, M. (2011, May 17). White papers: What you need to know. PR Newswire.

Pitchbook. (2021). The key differences between SRI, ESG and impact investing. Retrieved from: https://pitchbook.com/blog/what-are-the-differences-between-sri -esg-and-impact-investing.

Powell, L., Richmond, V. P., and Cantrell-Williams, G. (2012). The "Drinking-Buddy" scale as a measure of para-social behavior. *Psychological Reports* 110(3): 1029–37.

Rawlins, B. L. (2006). Prioritizing stakeholders for public relations. *Institute for Public Relations*, 1: 14.

REI.com. (2017). About REI. Retrieved from: http://newsroom.rei.com/company -information/about-rei/.

Reilley, M. (2017). Bring the world to the classroom with Google Earth tools. Mediashift. Retrieved from: http://mediashift.org/2017/08/bring-the-world-to-the -classroom-with-google-earth-tools/.

Rivenburgh, N. K. (2009). Media events as political communication. In *Media Events in a Global Age*. London: Routledge, 187.

Rizzardini, J. (2021). Why does changing a team's name take so long? *FiveThirty Eight*. Retrieved from: https://fivethirtyeight.com/features/why-does-changing -a-teams-name-take-so-long/.

Rome, A. (2021). The genius of Earth Day. *Environmental History*.

Ryan, C., Carragee, K. M., and Meinhofer, W. (2001). Theory into practice: Framing, the news media, and collective action. *Journal of Broadcasting & Electronic Media*, 45(1): 175–82.

Salt Lake Herald. (1903). Boom for Gen. Torrance. September 25. Retrieved from: https://chroniclingamerica.loc.gov/lccn/sn85058130/1903-09-25/ed-1/seq-6/.

Salvioni, D. M., and Gennari, F. (2017). CSR, sustainable value creation and shareholder relations. *Symphonya: Emerging Issues in Management*, 1: 36–49.

Seguin, C., Pelletier, L. G., and Hunsley, J. (1998). Toward a model of environmental activism. *Environment and Behavior*, 30(5), 628–52.

Seitel, F. P. (2013). *The Practice of Public Relations*. New York: Pearson Higher Ed.

Selin, H., and VanDeveer, S. D. (2011). Climate change regionalism in North America. *Review of Policy Research*, 28(3): 295–304.

Sheehan, K. B. (2015). The many shades of greenwashing: Using consumer input for policy decisions regarding green advertisements. *Communicating Sustainability for the Green Economy*, 53–65.

Shore-Goss, B. (2016). *God is Green: An Eco-Spirituality of Incarnate Compassion*. Eugene, OR: Wipf and Stock Publishers.

Shrum, L. J., McCarty, J. A., and Lowrey, T. M. (1995). Buyer characteristics of the green consumer and their implications for advertising strategy. *Journal of advertising*, 24(2): 71–82.

Sierra Club. (2020). A history of environmental justice in the United States. Sierra Club.org. Retrieved from: https://www.sierraclub.org/environmental-justice/history-environmental-justice.

Simmons, T. A. (1974). The Damnation of a Dam: The High Ross Dam Controversy. MA thesis, University of California.

Skelton, R. and Miller, V. (2016). The environmental justice movement. Natural Resources Defense Council. Retrieved from: https://www.nrdc.org/stories/environmental-justice-movement.

Slocombe, D. S. (1984). Environmentalism: a modern synthesis. *The Environmentalist*, 4(4): 281–85.

Smith, H. J. (2003). The shareholders vs. stakeholders debate. *MIT Sloan Management Review*, 44(4): 85–90.

Smith, M. B. (1998). "The value of a tree: Public debates of John Muir and Gifford Pinchot." *The Historian*, 60(4): 757–78.

Snow, D. A., Rochford Jr., E. B., Worden, S. K., and Benford, R. D. (1986). Frame alignment processes, micromobilization, and movement participation. *American Sociological Review*, 464–81.

Spurgin, E. W. (2001). Do shareholders have obligations to stakeholders? *Journal of Business Ethics*, 33(4): 287–97.

Sriramesh, K. (2008). Globalization and public relations. In *Public Relations Research: European and International Perspectives and Innovations*. Wiesbaden: VS Verlag fur Sozialwissenschaften, 409–25.

Stokes, A. Q. (2017). A rising tide lifts all boats? The constitutive reality of CSR in public relations. In B. Brunner (ed.), *The Moral Compass of Public Relations*. New York: Routledge, 62–76.

Takahashi, B., Pinto, J., Chavez, M., and Vigón, M. (2018). *News Media Coverage of Environmental Challenges in Latin America and the Caribbean*. London: Palgrave Macmillan.

Takaki, R. T. (1996). *Hiroshima: Why America Dropped the Atomic Bomb*. New York: Back Bay Books.

Tietjen, J. S. (2022). "Infrastructure Pioneers." In *Women in Infrastructure*. Edinburgh: Springer, Cham, 23–71.

Toncar, M., Reid, J. S., and Anderson, C. E. (2007). Effective spokespersons in a public service announcement: National celebrities, local celebrities and victims. *Journal of Communication Management*.

Trendafilova, S., McCullough, B., Pfahl, M., Nguyen, S. N., Casper, J., and Picariello, M. (2014). Environmental sustainability in sport: Current state and future trends. *Global Journal on Advances in Pure and Applied Sciences*, 3.

UN Environment Programme. (2020). Yes, climate change is driving wildfires. UNEnvironment.org. Retrieved from: https://www.unenvironment.org/news-and -stories/story/yes-climate-change-driving-wildfires.

Venkatraman, M. P. (1989). Opinion leaders, adopters, and communicative adopters: A role analysis. *Psychology & Marketing*, 6(1): 51–68.

Vittal, P. (2021). It's time for the federal government to address environmental racism. Greenpeace. Retrieved from: https://www.greenpeace.org/canada/en/story/46929/ its-time-for-the-federal-government-to-address-environmental-racism/.

Waldman, S. (2023). Meet the climate scientist taking on Joe Rogan and QAnon. *E&E News: Climatewire*. Retrieved from: https://www.eenews.net/articles/meet -the-climate-scientist-taking-on-joe-rogan-and-qanon/.

Watts, D. J., and Dodds, P. S. (2007). Influentials, networks, and public opinion formation. *Journal of Consumer Research*, 34(4): 441–58.

Weimann, G., Tustin, D. H., Van Vuuren, D., and Joubert, J. P. R. (2007). Looking for opinion leaders: Traditional vs. modern measures in traditional societies. *International Journal of Public Opinion Research*, 19(2): 173–90.

Welbeck, E. E. S., Owusu, G. M. Y., Simpson, S. N. Y., and Bekoe, R. A. (2020). CSR in the telecom industry of a developing country: Employees' perspective. *Journal of Accounting in Emerging Economies*.

Williams, B. A., and Carpini, M. X. D. (2020). The eroding boundaries between news and entertainment and what they mean for democratic politics. In L. Wilkins and C. G. Christians (eds.), *The Routledge Handbook of Mass Media Ethics*. New York: Routledge, 252–63.

Zamith, R., Pinto, J., and Villar, M. E. (2013). Constructing climate change in the Americas: An analysis of news coverage in US and South American newspapers. *Science Communication*, 35(3): 334–57.

Zelezny, L. C., and Schultz, P. W. (2000). Psychology of promoting environmentalism: Promoting environmentalism. *Journal of Social Issues*, 56(3): 365–71.

Zito, S. (2023). After two centuries, a dairy farm family near East Palestine worries for the future. *Pittsburgh Post-Gazette*. Retrieved from: https://www.post-gazette .com/opinion/insight/2023/03/19/salena-zito-east-palestine-derailment-norfolk -southern-enon-valley-farmer/stories/202303190049.

Index

About the Author

Derek Moscato is a professor of journalism and public relations at Western Washington University in Bellingham, Washington, where he teaches classes in environmental communication, public relations, and global media. He is also a research fellow with the WWU Center for Canadian-American Studies, and faculty affiliate with the Border Policy Research Institute and the Salish Sea Institute. His research, which focuses on the intersection of environmental communication, persuasion, and global media, has recently examined topics such as climate change discourses in global media, ecological diplomacy in the Arctic, and rural environmentalism. Moscato is the author of *Dirt Persuasion: Civic Environmental Populism and the Heartland's Pipeline Fight*. He received his doctorate from the University of Oregon's School of Journalism and Communication.